RUSSIA
AND THE
RESTORED
GOSPEL

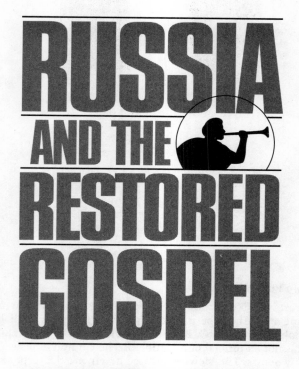

RUSSIA
AND THE
RESTORED
GOSPEL

GARY BROWNING

Deseret Book Company
Salt Lake City, Utah

Library of Congress Cataloging-in-Publication Data

Browning, Gary.
  Russia and the restored gospel / by Gary Browning.
    p.   cm.
  Includes bibliographical references and index.
  ISBN 1-57345-202-5 (hardback)
  1. Church of Jesus Christ of Latter-day Saints—Russia—History.
2. Russia—Church history—1801–1917. 3. Soviet Union—Church
history. 4. Russia—Church history—20th century. I. Title.
BX8617.R8B76   1997
289.3'47—dc21   96-37332
                                                                 CIP

Printed in the United States of America

10 9   8   7   6   5   4   3   2   1   18961

*For Wayne, Ole, Lula, Ray, Thelma, Hank
and hosts of other angels deceased and living
who were round about us and bore us up*

CONTENTS

THE RUSSIA MOSCOW MISSION, 1992 TO 1993

PREFACE

When our family prepared to leave Russia at the conclusion of our mission, some members spoke of presenting gifts to us. We then communicated to all the branches that, for reasons of principle and practicality, we could not accept gifts, but we would be grateful for letters from members telling how they learned of and joined The Church of Jesus Christ of Latter-day Saints and grew in testimony. These letters are precious to me and convey warm expressions of testimony. Those that contain unique information are included in this book, which begins with a survey of 147 years of Latter-day Saint Church history connected with Russia. The subsequent chapters focus on the three years my family and I served alongside many others in Russia and Estonia. From my journal; letters written by my wife, Joan, illustrating mission families' typical concerns and experiences; the conversion stories from members; and personal statements from missionaries, I have selected significant and distinctive examples for each month of our mission. To help preserve this period of Church history in Russia and to facilitate future research, I have included a generous number of names and dates.

Excerpts from letters are placed where the chapter narrative refers to a person or event further described in a letter. Otherwise, members' letters appear at the end of the month during which a member was baptized. Because members' letters were received at or after the completion of our mission, some converts refer to temple excursions or other experiences that occurred a year or more after their baptism.

As a rule I have included conversion stories and testimonies from those who, for at least a year, have been active Church members. A few letters are from early members who may not currently be active. I am hopeful that under more ideal circumstances, even if beyond this life, most will return to full communion with the Saints who, like them, struggle along toward perfection.

As I have tried to illustrate, a great many people contributed to the foundation of an emerging Russian Zion. Faithful men and women trying, failing, attempting again, achieving a part, in the aggregate accomplished a significant good work. Their challenging but appealing task parallels that of the newly arrived Saints in Jackson County, Missouri, who gathered to redeem their Zion. As they were told in Doctrine and Covenants 58:

> Ye cannot behold with your natural eyes, for the present time, the design of your God concerning those things which shall come hereafter, and the glory which shall follow after much tribulation. . . .
> For this cause have I sent you—that you might be obedient, and that your hearts might be prepared to bear testimony of the things which are to come;
> And also that you might be honored in laying the foundation, and in bearing record of the land upon which the Zion of God shall stand. (Vv. 3, 6–7)

Many have felt honored and grateful to have laid a portion of the foundation for a Russian Zion. This book is an attempt to bear record of that land, of her people, history, spirit, spirituality, and Saints. Together with Sister Klavdiia Bocharova, that dear *babushka* and Mother Russia figure whose words conclude this book, we pray, May God continue to help the Russians!

Reflecting on the message so many Church members over the decades have shared in Russia, I have been impressed again by the compatibility of Latter-day Saint ideals with those developed by Russians through the ages. These values were not brought into Russian life by a single religious, ideological, or political group in any one century, but all who succeed in engaging the Russian heart and soul have done so in large part because their message resonates with Russian ideals.

In a recent book by Tim McDaniel (*The Agony of the Russian Idea*, Princeton: Princeton University Press, 1996) several ideals of the Russian people are elaborated and analyzed, including the need for "a set of ultimate values to orient their lives. The routines of daily life are not enough to satisfy their larger spiritual cravings" (33). The Russians highly value a feeling of community, "a shared culture" and "economic interdependence" that create "a strong sense of belonging together" (43). Russians tend to believe that "material conditions in society should not vary too greatly among individuals" (47). And finally, they want leaders characterized by the highest ideals of "truth" and "pure spiritual values" (51).

I believe that The Church of Jesus Christ of Latter-day Saints embodies values Russians consider preeminent. My testimony is rooted in the fullest expression of those ideals found in the Sermon on the Mount as recorded in the Bible and, in several places, clarified and expanded in the Book of Mormon. My Russian brothers and sisters have been preeminent among those who have exemplified in their lives these most essential values.

Several important assumptions underlie this book. The Russian mission appears prominent largely because of the prominence and mystique of the country, but in reality LDS missions around the world are more similar than unique. Far more people than are apparent contribute to any significant accomplishment. The Church as a whole can further be strengthened by learning of the struggles, failures, and successes of members; the nearer one can approximate true accounts, the more inspiring they will be because, for all of us, experiences are complex and contradictory. Church members and leaders at all levels generally perform the best they can, considering capacity, circumstance, and opportunity, but individuals and leaders learn by trial and error, and, when the Lord deems fitting, through inspiration. The Lord's work can be hindered because of individual inadequacy, but it cannot be prevented from fulfillment. As we labor to proclaim the gospel (and perfect the Saints and redeem the dead), seeming coincidences rarely are. And finally, a mission's most recurrent miracles arise as divine powers bring together those prepared to convey truth with those who are prepared to accept it.

ACKNOWLEDGMENTS

To the many who have helped in the preparation of this book, I owe an appreciation impossible to adequately express. Among those who have generously sustained me are my colleagues and leaders in the Department of Germanic and Slavic Languages and Literatures and in the College of Humanities at Brigham Young University. Their moral and monetary support provided example, incentive, and means. The department, college, and Religious Studies Center generously funded student research assistants and supplies.

My capable assistants include Jennifer Warren Lloyd, Adam Sears West, Robert Brinton Couch, and David Brandon Wilsted. David's assistance covered the longest period of time and was especially extensive, perceptive, and esteemed.

Many read full drafts of this manuscript and provided valuable suggestions, among them my research assistants; my wife, Joan, and daughter Debi Dixon; LaRayne Hart, a close friend whose letters brought so much brightness into our mission; my colleague Don E. Norton; *BYU Studies* managing editor Nancy R. Lund; Deseret Book senior editor Suzanne Brady; and Christine Graham.

A special thanks is due to my remarkable wife, excerpts of whose letters add enlivening detail; to missionaries who served with us, performed masterfully, and continue to inspire our family, and whose letters provide a glimpse into their achievements; and, particularly, to those who accepted the gospel and baptism into the Restored Church. Quotations from their conversion stories give breath to this book.

Royalties will be donated to charities in support of those living in the former Russian Empire and Soviet Union.

CHRONOLOGY

988	Prince Vladimir of Kiev is baptized and takes Eastern Orthodox Christianity to Russia.
1453	The fall of Constantinople, the second Rome, gives rise to the claim of a Russian "third Rome" and a messianic destiny.
June 1843	Elder Orson Hyde of the Quorum of the Twelve Apostles and George J. Adams are called to go to that "vast empire of Russia" as missionaries of The Church of Jesus Christ of Latter-day Saints.
June 1895	Johan and Alma Lindelof are baptized in the Neva River at St. Petersburg, Russia.
6 Aug. 1903	Elder Francis M. Lyman of the Quorum of the Twelve Apostles offers a prayer of dedication in the St. Petersburg Summer Gardens.
9 Aug. 1903	Elder Lyman offers a prayer of dedication in the Aleksandr Gardens of the Kremlin in Moscow, Russia.
23 Sept. 1903	Letter from the First Presidency instructs Elder Lyman to postpone sending missionaries to Russia.
9 Oct.–5 Nov. 1903	Elder Mischa Markow visits Riga, Latvia.
late Feb. 1904	Tsar Nicholas II issues a proclamation on freedom of conscience.
Dec. 1904	A second decree on freedom of conscience is issued.
Apr. 1905	A third decree on freedom of conscience is issued.
Nov. 1917	The Bolsheviks triumph in the Russian Revolution.
1918	The Lindelof home is ravaged, and the Lindelof parents and their seven children are sentenced to imprisonment and hard labor.

1925–1980	Andrei Anastasion translates the Book of Mormon into Russian.
Sept.–Oct. 1959	Ezra Taft Benson, United States secretary of agriculture and member of the Quorum of the Twelve Apostles, visits Russia and speaks to Baptist congregation in Moscow.
1975	President Spencer W. Kimball asks Church members to fast and pray that LDS missionaries might be permitted to serve in all nations.
1978	The Brigham Young University Young Ambassadors perform in Russia.
April 1979	President Kimball exhorts the members of the Church to prepare to take the gospel beyond the Iron and Bamboo Curtains.
March 1985	Mikhail Gorbachev assumes leadership of the Communist Party and the USSR.
June 1987	Elder Russell M. Nelson of the Quorum of the Twelve Apostles and Elder Hans B. Ringger of the Seventy visit Russia to explore ways to establish the LDS Church in that land.
1988	Celebrations mark a millennium of Christianity in Russia.
24 July 1988	Muscovite Igor Mikailiusenko is baptized in the United States.
2d half 1988	Four Finland Helsinki missionaries, Sisters Leena Riihimäki and Carina Mahoney and Elders Bruce Bunderson and Clarence Dillon, begin missionary work among Russians in Finland.
1 July 1989	The Terebenin family is baptized in Hungary.
16 July 1989	Estonian Valttari Rödsä is baptized in Finland.
2d half 1989	Matti Ojala is called to fellowship the Terebenin family in Leningrad.
14–20 Sept. 1989	Dennis B. Neuenschwander, president of the Austria Vienna East Mission, and David P. Farnsworth, Church attorney, visit Leningrad to strengthen members and assess conditions.
16 Sept. 1989	Brother Terebenin is ordained a priest, becoming the

first Russian to receive the priesthood in the USSR after the Revolution.

23 Sept. 1989	Muscovite Olga Smolianova is baptized in Italy.
19 Oct. 1989	Elder Russell M. Nelson of the Quorum of the Twelve Apostles informs Steven R. Mecham, president of the Finland Helsinki Mission, and Dennis B. Neuenschwander, president of the Austria Vienna East Mission, that the First Presidency and the Quorum of the Twelve have decided the time has come to take the gospel to the peoples of Russia and Estonia.
9 Nov. 1989	The Berlin Wall is opened and then torn down.
3 Dec. 1989	President Steven Mecham and Sister Donna Mecham visit the Soviet Union for the first time and meet with the Saints in Leningrad.
8 Dec. 1989	President and Sister Mecham, accompanied by Elders Kevin Dexter and David Reagan, visit Estonia for the first time.
Jan. 1990	Jussi Kemppainen is called as president of the new Baltic District.
28 Jan. 1990	The Tallinn, Estonia, branch is organized, becoming the first LDS branch in the Soviet Union. Finnish missionary Elder Harri Aho is called as branch president.
Jan.–June 1990	Six Finnish couples serve as fellowshippers and missionaries in Leningrad and Vyborg, Russia, and in Tallinn, Estonia.
3 Feb. 1990	Anton E. Skripko from Leningrad is baptized in the pool of the Pribaltiiskaia Hotel, becoming the first member baptized in Russia since the Revolution.
11 Feb. 1990	In the Terebenins' Leningrad apartment, President Mecham organizes the first branch in Russia.
25 Feb. 1990	Andrei Semionov becomes the first Vyborg resident to join the Church.
25 Mar. 1990	The Vyborg branch is organized. Andrei Semionov is called as the first branch president.
Apr. 1990	Elder Russell M. Nelson of the Quorum of the

	Twelve Apostles, Elder Hans B. Ringger of the Seventy, President Steven R. Mecham of the Finland Helsinki Mission, and President Jussi Kemppainen of the Baltic District visit Tallinn, Estonia, and Leningrad, Russia.
25 Apr. 1990	In Tallinn, Elder Nelson dedicates Estonia for the preaching of the restored gospel.
26 Apr. 1990	In Leningrad, Elder Nelson offers a prayer of gratitude in the spirit of rededication of Russia for the preaching of the restored gospel.
10 June 1990	Galina Goncharova is baptized by Church member Dohn Thorton. She is likely the first Russian baptized into the LDS Church in Moscow.
26 June 1990	The Church is recognized by the Leningrad City Council and Council on Religious Affairs.
29 June 1990	Official recognition is granted the Church in Estonia.
July 1990	The Finland Helsinki East Mission is organized with four cities: Leningrad, Vyborg, and Moscow, Russia; and Tallinn, Estonia. Gary Browning serves as president.
13 Sept. 1990	The registration of the Church in Leningrad is approved by the Russian Republic and the USSR Councils of Religious Affairs.
9 Oct. 1990	Liberal legislation on freedom of conscience and religious organizations becomes law in the USSR.
24–26 Oct. 1990	The first six full-time LDS missionaries arrive in Moscow.
15 Nov. 1990	Mikhail Poniukhov is baptized in a swimming pool in Moscow. He is the first convert in Moscow taught by full-time missionaries.
16 Nov. 1990	Estonian Jaanus Silla becomes the first missionary called from the area of the Finland Helsinki East Mission; the letter is received 17 December.
Jan. 1991	The Leningrad branch is divided.
23 Feb. 1991	Sister Marta Guttierez is killed in Leningrad.
Feb. 1991	The first all-mission Finland Helsinki East Mission leadership conference is held.

Feb. 1991	Eighteen hundred humanitarian food boxes are delivered to Tallinn, Estonia, and to Vyborg, Leningrad, and Moscow, Russia.
23 Mar. 1991	The LDS Russian Religious Association is formed in Moscow. Andrei Petrov serves as president.
24 Mar. 1991	The Moscow group becomes a branch. Andrei Petrov is sustained as branch president.
Mar. 1991	Favorable article about Mormonism appears in the respected Moscow *Literary Gazette*.
Apr. 1991	Estonian missionaries receive the first congregational invitations and visas for their entire missions rather than for a few weeks at a time.
Apr.–May 1991	The BYU Young Ambassadors perform in the Finland Helsinki East Mission.
early May 1991	BYU President Rex and Sister Janet Lee speak in Leningrad and Moscow.
18–19 May 1991	The first all-mission youth conference is held near Leningrad.
28 May 1991	The LDS Russian Religious Association is registered and legally recognized by the Russian Republic Ministry of Justice.
12 June 1991	Russian president Boris Yeltsin and vice-president Aleksandr Rutskoi are elected in a landslide.
24 June 1991	The Mormon Tabernacle Choir performs in Moscow's renowned Bolshoi Theater. Aleksandr Rutskoi announces the legal recognition of the Church in Russia.
25 June 1991	Elders Russell M. Nelson and Dallin H. Oaks of the Quorum of the Twelve Apostles and Elder Hans B. Ringger of the Seventy visit Patriarch Aleksii II, leader of the estimated eighty million members of the Russian Orthodox Church.
25 June 1991	Elder Nelson offers a prayer of gratitude in the Kremlin near the Water Tower, the tower closest to the Moscow River.
19 July 1991	Russian Central TV telecasts the Tabernacle Choir concert to millions of viewers.

July 1991	Anton Skripko becomes the first full-time missionary from Russia, serving in the Utah Ogden Mission.
Aug. 1991	Elder Richard G. Scott of the Quorum of the Twelve Apostles and his wife, Sister Jeanene Scott, visit Moscow.
19–21 Aug. 1991	The hard-line State of Emergency Committee attempts a political coup.
20 Aug. 1991	Estonia and Latvia declare independence; Lithuania reaffirms its earlier declaration of independence.
6 Sept. 1991	Leningrad is officially renamed St. Petersburg.
Sept. 1991	The first Russian-speaking branch in Estonia is organized with Anatolii Diachkovskii as president.
Sept. 1991	Valerii Mariev, Aleksei Akimov, and others produce the first issue of the mission journal *Liahona*.
Sept. 1991	Tartu, Estonia, is opened to missionary work.
10 Nov. 1991	The English-speaking Moscow international branch is created; missionary Elder Joseph Pace is called as branch president.
Nov. 1991	An all-mission and member leadership conference is held with Elder M. Russell Ballard of the Quorum of the Twelve Apostles and Elder Hans B. Ringger of the Seventy.
Dec. 1991	Elder Dennis B. Neuenschwander of the Seventy and his wife, Sister LeAnn Neuenschwander, tour the Finland Helsinki East Mission.
20–22 Dec. 1991	The second Finland Helsinki East Mission youth and young adult conference is held near St. Petersburg.
25 Dec. 1991	Mikhail Gorbachev resigns as president of the Soviet Union, and the USSR ceases to exist.
Jan. 1992	All LDS missionaries in Russia receive Russian Religious Association invitation visas.
Jan. 1992	Two new branches of the Church are officially formed in Russia, one in Vyborg and another in Zelenograd.
3 Feb. 1992	The Finland Helsinki East Mission becomes the

	Russia St. Petersburg Mission and the Russia Moscow Mission.
29 Mar. 1992	The Moscow branch is divided.
10 Apr. 1992	The Russia Moscow Mission office is moved to Moscow from Helsinki, Finland.
21 July 1992	The city of Nizhnii Novgorod, Russia, is opened to missionary work.
22 Sept. 1992	The city of Samara, Russia, is opened to missionary work.
20 Oct. 1992	The city of Saratov, Russia, is opened to missionary work.
6 Dec. 1992	Andrei Petrov and Albert Walling are set apart as presidents of the first two Moscow districts.
16 Jan. 1993	The city of Voronezh, Russia, is opened to missionary work.
Feb. 1993	Full-time Church translators begin work in Moscow.
21 Feb. 1993	Nine new branches are established in Moscow; the total number of branches is now fifteen.
Mar. 1993	Elder Dennis Neuenschwander and Sister LeAnn Neuenschwander tour the Moscow mission.
Apr. 1993	The first LDS branch along the Volga River is formed in Saratov, Russia. Sergei Leliukhin is branch president.
Apr. 1993	Elder Frank Hirschi and Sister Carol Hirschi introduce the seminary and institute of religion programs to a group of local Church leaders in Moscow.
9–26 May 1993	The BYU Young Ambassadors tour Moscow, Nizhnii Novgorod, Samara, and Saratov, Russia.
24 May 1993	Elder Neal A. Maxwell of the Quorum of the Twelve Apostles and his wife, Sister Colleen Maxwell, visit Moscow.
July 1993	The cities of Samara and Saratov form the new Russia Samara Mission.
Sept. 1993	The first group of thirty-one Russian Latter-day Saints from Moscow attends the Stockholm Sweden Temple.

PART I

PROCLAIMING THE GOSPEL IN RUSSIA, 1843 TO 1989

1

"THAT VAST EMPIRE OF RUSSIA"

In 1843 the Prophet Joseph Smith called Orson Hyde and George J. Adams to serve as missionaries of The Church of Jesus Christ of Latter-day Saints to St. Petersburg, Russia's capital city. Ordained an apostle in 1835, Orson Hyde had acquired a rich store of missionary experience. He had served as a missionary in Ohio, the eastern states, and Missouri and participated in the first mission to Great Britain in 1837 and 1838. Later, on his way to and from Jerusalem in 1841 and 1842, Elder Hyde taught briefly in the Netherlands, in Turkey, in Egypt, and then extensively in Germany.[1] While in Palestine, Elder Hyde dedicated that land for the gathering of Israel. Then in June 1843, Elder Hyde was called to "that vast empire of Russia,"[2] which then encompassed, in addition to Russians, Belorussian, Ukrainian, Moldavian, Caucasian, Central Asian, and Baltic (including Finnish) peoples.

Elder Hyde's designated companion was George J. Adams. Brother Adams, born in New Jersey but a long-time resident of New York City, was descended from the prominent Adams family of American history. Before joining the LDS Church, Adams was a Methodist preacher and acted in amateur theater. Adams "preached with finesse" and was "a genius at recall of appropriate Scripture."[3]

Adams was baptized in February 1840, eight days after first hearing Heber C. Kimball speak in Boston. Within a year he accompanied Elder Hyde to England and preached there with considerable success, remaining to continue his mission in England when Elder Hyde went on to Palestine. Elder Adams served from 1841 to April 1842 as a missionary in Great Britain, mainly in Bedford. During that period he baptized "some hundreds" of people, traveled over fifteen thousand miles, gave more than five hundred public sermons, and held fifteen major public "discussions" with opponents of Mormonism.[4]

3

*Elder Orson Hyde
of the Quorum of the
Twelve Apostles, who
was called in mid-1843
as a missionary to
St. Petersburg, Russia*

Although Elder Adams had expected to leave with Elder Hyde for Russia in July 1843,[5] financial considerations, among others, prevented their departure. In October 1843 an announcement finally appeared in the *Times and Seasons* of George J. Adams' appointment to accompany Orson Hyde to Russia. Because the Russian mission would be "attended with much expense," any who could contribute to this venture were enjoined to do so. Contributors were promised that the blessings "of Israel's God, and tenfold shall be added unto them."[6]

Months passed, and Elders Hyde and Adams remained in the United States. After the martyrdom of Joseph and Hyrum Smith on 27 June 1844, Elder Adams was appointed to convey news of the tragedy to Brigham Young, who was on a mission in the eastern states. Later accounts censure Adams for not completing this important assignment.[7]

As candidates vied for succession to Church leadership following the Martyrdom, the apostle Orson Hyde remained in Nauvoo to support Brigham Young and the Quorum of the Twelve.

George J. Adams in time cast his lot with James J. Strang and eventually became a member of Strang's first presidency.[8]

What could have become, after Canada and Great Britain, a significant Latter-day Saint missionary thrust beyond the borders of the United States and one of the first foreign-language missions of the Church[9] was to remain a prophet's vision.

What would Elders Hyde and Adams have faced in the Russian empire during the mid-1840s? The Russian Orthodox Church was immensely powerful, possessing massive momentum from centuries of growth in Russia, great wealth, and status as Russia's state religion. In 1846 an evangelical alliance reported official Russian Orthodox statistics that more than 36,000 had converted from Catholicism and Protestantism to Russian Orthodoxy but none in the other direction. "Yet that cases of this kind do occur, and that not infrequently, is well known to all in any degree familiar with the private annals of Russian families." The alliance concluded that those leaving the Orthodox Church commonly fled the country, were exiled to Siberia, or were incarcerated in an Orthodox monastery for "better instruction."[10]

Despite harsh persecution of religious nonconformity during this period, groups disaffected from the Orthodox Church did survive and grow. Among them were the Old Believers and Khlysty, or Khristovovery, which had originated in the seventeenth century, and adherents of the Dukhobors, Molokans, and Skoptsy from the eighteenth century. Other religious groups entirely separate from Russian Orthodoxy also struggled, including nearly three million Roman Catholics and two million Lutherans. Subsequently, denominations new to Russia arrived and, despite persecution, persisted, beginning as early as the 1860s, including first the Baptists and later the Methodists, Seventh-Day Adventists, Pentecostals, and Jehovah's Witnesses.[11]

In 1843 in connection with the calling of Elders Hyde and Adams as missionaries to Russia, the Prophet Joseph declared that with the Russian Empire are connected "some of the most important things concerning the advancement and building up of the Kingdom of God in the last days, which cannot be explained at this time."[12] To my knowledge, neither Joseph Smith nor other Church leaders clarified these words.

If the Latter-day Saint faith had been preached with discretion and perseverance, perhaps at first among non-Orthodox ethnic groups, and if patterns of conversion and emigration had followed those of Great Britain, Scandinavia, and Germany, what might that have meant to the Church then and today? How might Russian converts have proven helpful in the "advancement and building up" of the kingdom and Church? One can only speculate. Considerable numbers of Russians would have journeyed to the United States to join with the Saints in the Great Basin. The sheer numbers of Russian immigrants might have resulted in substantial cultural influence.

Russians' contributions to the Church could have been prominent in areas such as architecture, music, and literature. Ceremonial and holiday observance among the Latter-day Saints might have developed differently. For example, Easter would likely be commemorated with at least as much joyful and elaborate tradition as Christmas.

Centuries of experience in agrarian communitarian societies—the *mir* social structures—might have helped preserve and extend principles of the united order, so seemingly contrary to American individualism and competitive spirit and apparently so integral to Zion.

What roles might members of Russian ancestry have played in public service and Church leadership during periods of difficult superpower relations and in current Latter-day Saint missionary initiatives?

Quite possibly, peoples from what was then that "vast empire of Russia" will yet take a prominent role in the "advancement and building up of the Kingdom of God in the last days." Joining with other members from around the world, peoples of the former Russian Empire will offer their uniquely significant sacrifice to the Lord in righteousness.

After the Church settled in Utah, missionary work again expanded. The principal thrust and greatest success were in Great Britain and Scandinavia, and modest attempts were made to proselytize in many other parts of the world. But missionary work was not attempted again in Russia until the twentieth century.

2

MISSIONARY EFFORTS BEFORE THE BOLSHEVIK REVOLUTION

An earnest attempt to establish a mission in Russia occurred in 1903. From 1901, Elder Francis M. Lyman, a member of the Quorum of the Twelve Apostles, had served as president of the European Mission. Church president Lorenzo Snow and his counselors in the First Presidency had encouraged Elder Lyman to extend the blessings of the restored gospel to all Europeans, including Russians. Consequently, for July and August of 1903, Elder Lyman scheduled another of many journeys to the Continent. This one would include his only visit to Russia. As recorded in the *Millennial Star* before his departure, "No Apostle of modern times has visited Finland and Russia, we believe, and President Lyman's going there may be preparatory to the opening of that vast field to missionary labors."[1]

Elder Lyman and his younger traveling companion, Elder Joseph J. Cannon, visited several countries, including Finland, then a semiautonomous Russian grand duchy, and Russia. On 6 August (24 July, according to the Russian Julian calendar) 1903, Elders Lyman and Cannon sought out an appropriate location in the peaceful downtown Summer Garden of St. Petersburg near the Winter Palace, currently the renowned Hermitage Art Museum. There, in a fervent and extended dedicatory prayer, Elder Lyman pleaded for religious liberty and tolerance and for the well-being of those "in whose veins the blood of Israel flows generously," as well as for the Gentiles, "that they might be grafted into the true olive tree, that their branches might become fruitful." Further, as Elder Cannon reported, President Lyman "called upon the Lord to bless this great empire, in many respects the greatest in the world, and endow its rulers with wisdom and virtue, that there may be peace and progress here, that darkness may flee and the voices of His

*Elder Francis M. Lyman
of the Quorum of the
Twelve Apostles, who
dedicated Russia
in August 1903 for
Latter-day Saint
missionary work*

servants may sound the glad tidings to the uttermost parts of this great land."[2]

Three days later, on 9 August 1903, the same two men stood in the tranquil Moscow Aleksandr Gardens bordering the Kremlin walls and renewed their supplication to the Lord in behalf of the Russian peoples. Elder Lyman entreated the Lord to send "servants full of wisdom and faith to declare the Gospel to the Russians in their own language."[3] He prayed for the tsar and his family, and "in connection with the recent prayer in St. Petersburg, President Lyman dedicated the land and turned the key for the preaching of the Gospel in the empire of Russia."[4]

The year 1903 and the period immediately following were particularly propitious for establishing the Church in Russia. In late February (Julian calendar) Tsar Nicholas II issued a proclamation of freedom of conscience, which the *New York Times* called "perhaps the most significant act of state since the emancipation of the serfs."[5] This 1903 order was buttressed by additional decrees in December 1904 and in April 1905. Indeed, heaven appeared to be endowing Russia's rulers with "wisdom and virtue." As a result, new denominations sprang up in Russia. As Elder Cannon optimistically observed regarding forces within Russian Orthodoxy: "Dissent in Russia is growing, and new sects of almost every description are arising and gaining strength."[6]

Although the tsar's decrees could not establish freedom of religion overnight, their effect was substantial. From 1905 to 1911 the Baptists embraced 25,000 new members, mostly from the Russian Orthodox and the Molokans. A Baptist leader explained, "In Russia this large movement of Baptists began with 1905, when God granted us religious freedom. Before this time we Baptists were suppressed." LDS Church archivist Kahlile Mehr concluded, "While dissent from Russian Orthodoxy was dealt with harshly by civil and religious authorities, the Baptist success demonstrated that it was not impossible to oppose this obstacle."[7] Seventh-Day Adventists grew from 356 members at the end of the 1880s to 2,200 by 1906 and 5,500 by 1912. Of the converts, 64 percent were from the Russian Orthodox Church and 36 percent from the Baptist and Lutheran Churches.[8] The membership of other non-Orthodox faiths also grew rapidly.

Having returned to mission headquarters in England, Elder Lyman found an experienced, enthusiastic missionary named Mischa Markow. Elder Markow, nearly fifty years old, had already completed his first mission two years previously. The Hungarian-born Markow had labored in Serbia, Hungary, Romania, Bulgaria, Belgium, and Germany. With the exception of Rumanian, Elder Markow is said to have known the languages spoken in all those lands.

President Lyman instructed Elder Markow to go to Russia and discreetly explore possibilities for Latter-day Saint proselytizing. Traveling alone, Elder Markow arrived in Riga, Latvia, then part of the Russian Empire, on 9 October 1903 and remained until 5 November. He received a warm reception from the German-speaking people there and, perhaps exceeding President Lyman's preferred pace,[9] prepared three families for baptism. He soon experienced antagonism, however. This hostility prompted Elder Markow to heed President Lyman's counsel to return to England immediately were any problems to arise that might endanger him or compromise the Church.

While Elder Markow was still in Riga, Elder Lyman received a letter dated 23 September 1903 from the First Presidency advising him, "We consider the appointment of missionaries to Russia a matter requiring more careful consideration than we have yet been able to give it, and will therefore defer speaking definitely in relation thereto until we again write to you."[10] A First Presidency letter dated two weeks later (8 October) informed President Lyman that he was to return to Salt Lake City, as he had just been sustained as president of the Quorum of the Twelve Apostles, and that Elder Heber J. Grant would serve as European Mission president. No mention was made of an imminent mission to Russia.

Mehr conjectured that the Brethren might have hesitated out of a desire for more convincing evidence that the Russian government and church would not arrest or otherwise persecute Latter-day Saint missionaries and members. Church leaders were also occupied with extensive preparations for the very important United States Senate hearings beginning in January 1904 on whether to seat Reed Smoot, the recently elected United States Senator from Utah and a member of the LDS Church's Quorum of the Twelve Apostles. Though these proceedings concluded successfully—Elder Smoot served in the United States Senate for thirty years and was able to communicate Church positions with persuasive clarity and depth—the Russian Mission again was delayed.

EARLY LATTER-DAY SAINTS IN RUSSIA

At least one family was baptized in Russia before the 1917 Bolshevik revolution made joining or establishing the Church impossible. In June 1895 Johan and Alma Lindelof were baptized in the Neva River in St. Petersburg. Years earlier Brother Johan Lindelof had heard of the gospel in his native Finland. A Swedish Latter-day Saint missionary taught and baptized Johan's mother, for which the missionary was imprisoned in Finland. Later Johan, a skilled goldsmith, and his wife, Alma, moved to Russia. After sixteen years in St. Petersburg, the Lindelofs welcomed Elder

August Hoglund, who had been dispatched to Russia by the Scandinavian Mission president in response to their letters. The Lindelofs met Elder Hoglund at the dock and invited him to dinner. He recounted that "after supper we commenced to talk about the Gospel, and so interested were we in the things forming the topic of our conversation that it was daylight before we thought of retiring to rest. We continued our conversation on the Monday, and they requested that they might receive baptism the next day; it was with longing they looked forward to the Tuesday."[11]

On Tuesday they rowed along the banks of the Neva searching for a secluded site. People seemed to be everywhere, and the Lindelofs began to despair of finding a suitable location. Finally they rowed to shore, walked behind some trees, and prayed for assistance: "Then we waited a few moments to see if the people would not leave the place; as if by a sudden command the boats sailed away and the people left us alone. The baptisms were performed and the new members confirmed."[12]

In a report to European Mission president Anthon H. Lund, Elder Hoglund expressed his opinion that "there is more religious liberty in Russia than is generally supposed." He noted a variety of denominations active in St. Petersburg and suggested a model that could be used by the Latter-day Saints: "The Baptists are holding their meetings at the homes of the members belonging to their religion. Nobody disturbs these meetings." Elder Hoglund recommended future missionary activity focus on non-Orthodox ethnic groups: Germans, French, and especially bilingual Swedish- and Russian-speaking Finns, such as the Lindelofs.[13]

After becoming members of the LDS Church, the Lindelofs were visited on occasion by missionaries and mission presidents, principally from Sweden. By 1903, two of the Lindelof children had been baptized.[14] Many felt that the Lindelof family could play a prominent role in support of the Church when missionaries arrived in St. Petersburg. But in 1918, after the Bolshevik Revolution, the Lindelof home was ravaged, their property confiscated, and the now seven Lindelof children "sentenced to imprisonment and hard labor." The primary motivation for this Bolshevik ruthlessness appears to have been to dispossess the wealthy Lindelofs, rather than to persecute them for their religion, although the latter could have played a role as well. Of the seven Lindelof children, the oldest son, Johannes Lenard, and a younger daughter survived; two daughters are known to have died in exile. The fate of the other three children is unknown.[15]

A possible though tenuous link to the Lindelof family is provided by John Noble, an American arrested by Soviet intelligence officers in Germany immediately following the Second World War. In 1958 Noble was finally freed from Soviet prison camps. He mentioned seeing in his compound Latter-day Saints, among other believers. In the Vorkuta coal mining camp beyond the Volga River and the Ural Mountains near the Arctic Circle, Mr. Noble described a community of Christians:

> Its denominations are as diverse as the religious backgrounds of the slave workers in the mines, Russian and Greek Orthodox, Roman Catholic, Jewish, Lutheran, Baptist, Mennonite, Mormon, Adventist—denominational lines do not mean much. Sometimes, literally only "two or three" men would gather in His name, as was the case with the Mormons. . . .
>
> Assisting the bishop in the stockroom was another elderly man, a Mormon. The Mormons in Soviet Russia and its satellite countries are a very small group. They are also relentlessly persecuted, due to the fact that belief in the Book of Mormon originated in the United States among followers of Joseph Smith, and that the international headquarters of the Church of Jesus Christ of the Latter-day Saints is located in Salt Lake City, Utah. Therefore, in addition to persecution for their religious beliefs, they are further suspected of being actively pro-American. Conversion to the Mormon faith was tantamount to a life sentence at the hands of the Communists, yet I noticed that this small group preferred to surrender worldly freedom than to give up their belief in Christ and in what they considered Christ's latter-day revelations. There were only a handful of Mormons in our compound, but on their days off they would always meet for meditation and prayer.[16]

3

PREPARING TO ESTABLISH THE CHURCH IN SOVIET RUSSIA

During the time of Soviet Communism (1917–1991), many sought to provide the Soviets, essentially the same peoples as in the former Russian Empire, with information about the Church. The Book of Mormon and other Church materials were translated into Russian. Latter-day Saint General Authorities, Utah Genealogical Society officials, government representatives, scientists, lawyers, educators, businesspeople, industrialists, students (notably, Brigham Young University performing groups, beginning in 1978), and tourists, made favorable impressions and discreetly answered questions about their faith.

Preparing for future missionary work, in 1925 European Mission president James E. Talmage encouraged a Russian emigré, then living in London and serving as the president of the London District of the Church, to translate the Book of Mormon into Russian. André Anastasion, born in 1894 in Odessa, left his homeland two decades later and joined the LDS Church in England in 1917. He labored five years on the translation, working before and after his daily job and Church responsibilities. The translation came to 2,400 pages of handwritten text, which he painstakingly verified and typed. Often assisted by others also fluent in Russian, Brother Anastasion participated in six extensive edits between 1945 and 1980.

Brother Anastasion spent a lifetime preparing the way for the gospel to be taken to his Slavic brothers and sisters. In a 1970 letter to apostle Spencer W. Kimball, Anastasion recommended personal contacts with Moscow officials and added:

> I wish to say again in answer to your question, that I feel confident and have no doubt whatever that eventually a church mission will be established in that vast country among the Slav

13

Peoples. President Joseph F. Smith directed to establish a mission in Russia sixty-seven years ago (1903). Presidents Heber J. Grant, George Albert Smith and David O. McKay all stated that the gospel is going to Russia. The last two presidents said the same words to me personally.[1]

André Anastasion died in 1980. In that very year, as a result of more than five decades of loving effort, the first Russian edition of the Book of Mormon was published. The initial 2,500 copies became available in 1981, just in time for the Gorbachev reform.

A 1937 article lauding Brother Anastasion's contribution rightly proclaimed, "When the time comes to introduce the Gospel to Russia, its missionaries will take with them the record of the Nephites, and the Russian people will read it in their native tongue. This will have been made possible by a native of that country who heard and accepted the message of Mormonism."[2]

In September and October 1959 United States Secretary of Agriculture and Latter-day Saint apostle Ezra Taft Benson visited Moscow. He spoke at the principal Baptist church in Moscow. His encouragement for this congregation of more than a thousand and his ringing affirmation of God's love and power left most present in tears of gratitude and hope. One American reporter confessed: "This backslider who occasionally grumbles about having to go to church, stood crying unashamedly, throat lumped, and chills running from spine to toes. It was the most heartrending and most inspiring scene I've ever witnessed."[3] Elder Benson was also deeply moved by this occasion: "It has been my privilege to speak before many church bodies in all parts of the world, but the impact of that experience is almost indescribable. I shall never forget that evening as long as I live."[4]

Beginning in the mid-1970s, President Spencer W. Kimball called on Church members to pray that the hearts of government leaders would be softened, that missionaries might serve in all nations, including Russia. In 1976 he requested that fasting be combined with prayers. In 1978 he urged regional representatives of the Twelve to teach all to prepare themselves for every possible opportunity, for "I can see no good reason why the Lord would open doors that we are not prepared to enter. Why should he break down the Iron Curtain or the Bamboo Curtain or any other curtain if we are still unprepared to enter?"[5] And at the April general conference in 1979, the prophet spoke with particular gravity and prophetic power:

> We have established new missions covering almost all of the free world, and we are turning our attention more diligently now to one day sharing the gospel with our Father's children behind the so-called iron and bamboo curtains. We have need to prepare for that day. The urgency of that preparation weighs heavily upon us. That day may come with more swiftness than we realize.[6]

Only a decade later, Soviet political leaders opened the door to religious pluralism in their Communist society. By late 1989 the first Soviet citizens were baptized members of the LDS Church in the Union of Soviet Socialist Republics.

In 1978 the Brigham Young University Young Ambassadors had performed before appreciative audiences in Leningrad, Moscow, and Kiev and in several cities in Poland. This was the first of several crowd-pleasing groups to visit Russia, which soon included the Lamanite Generation, Folk Dancers, University Singers, Synthesis, and Ballroom Dancers. Brigham Young University president Dallin H. Oaks accompanied the first Young Ambassador group during part of the tour. At a group sacrament meeting in Kiev, President Oaks expressed his belief that these students and their leaders were opening doors that would allow the gospel to be shared in Russia in the near future.

While in Moscow, the Young Ambassadors recorded their sprightly musical and dance review for Central USSR Television. This opportunity came about through a series of miraculous "coincidences" that resulted in a letter of introduction and promotion from a United States TV personality to Russian TV executive Svetlana Starodomskaia.

That program was shown repeatedly over several years to combined TV audiences numbering in the hundreds of millions. It was telecast when government officials wished to convey good feelings for America, for instance, as a tribute to America on July Fourth or before summit meetings between Soviet and American governmental leaders.

BYU performing groups visiting later had increased opportunity to give interviews and show video material on the university and, in time, the Church. The limiting factor was not language—Soviet TV had the staff and facilities to translate quickly and well—but the availability of recorded material on the university and Church suitable for telecasting on Soviet TV. Nonetheless, the performing groups' concerts and the existing video material helped create an atmosphere of credibility and respect for the Latter-day Saints and the Church.

CHANGES LEADING TO FREEDOM OF RELIGION

Despite President Kimball's injunction to prepare for the gospel to be taken to Russia, most who studied Soviet politics and society were cautious about the likelihood of the opportunity arriving anytime soon. Elder David M. Kennedy, formerly United States Secretary of the Treasury and ambassador-at-large under Richard Nixon and a special representative of the First Presidency beginning in 1974, contributed greatly to the Church's International Mission. Among other things, he helped open the doors of countries then closed to Latter-day Saint missionaries. For example, recognition for the Church was gained in Poland and the German Democratic Republic. Still, Russia seemed only a remote possibility for missionaries. At a Salt Lake Institute of Religion devotional in 1984, Elder Kennedy said candidly:

> In Russia, we make little or no progress. If we had twenty members in an area, we could get them recognized as a community, but we haven't that kind of membership in Russia. There are scattered members, but not a community of members in a local area. It will be some time, in my judgment, before Russia invites or permits religions to be established on an open basis. . . . Right now, conditions are pretty tense, and the timing would not be good.[7]

Nonetheless, when Mikhail S. Gorbachev assumed leadership of the Communist Party and government of the USSR in March 1985, he set in motion forces that quickly transformed Soviet society and much of the world. Genuine religious liberty and freedom of conscience for every citizen were officially secured through federal and Russian Republic laws in October and November 1990. For the first time in Russia's history, freedom of religion became a legal reality, although old traditions and behavior did not disappear overnight. Gorbachev led the Soviet government for less than seven years, but many changes occurred to provide vastly greater freedom of conscience. Change began slowly, with little obvious progress until 1988.

The year 1988 was memorable in Russian history for many reasons but especially for the celebration of a millennium of Russian Christianity. In 988, as recorded in early Russian chronicles, Prince Vladimir of Kiev, then the capital of a *Rus* growing in political unity, military strength, and cultural refinement, introduced a momentous change into Russian society. According to legend, after considering Jewish, Muslim, and western Christian alternatives, Prince Vladimir accepted Byzantine Christianity and urged or compelled his subjects to follow suit.

Over the centuries, ancient traditions of pagan nature worship and shamanism yielded to the elaborate dogmas and ornate rites of Eastern Orthodox Christianity. In time, to be Russian and to be Christian meant to be Russian Orthodox, as the faith came to be known after the fall of Constantinople to the Turks in 1453. Meanwhile, in Russia the perception grew of a "third Rome," a center of Christianity such as Rome and Constantinople had been. Moscow assumed the burden of a messianic mission to defend and promulgate Christianity. This third and last Rome, Russian ecclesiastical leaders asserted, would never fall.

In 1988 Gorbachev permitted a comparatively unrestrained religious commemoration, with hundreds of worship services, scores of church publications, and media exposure on a scale unimaginable during seven decades of atheistic Communism. As the door to the Russian religious world slowly opened, church groups at home and from around the world hastened to enter. Many Russians turned again to Russian Orthodoxy, the religion of their ancestors, in search of spiritual nourishment.[8]

Others looked to the religions established before 1917 or to groups new to Russia, now energetically positioning themselves to attract members. Among such seekers were nominal nonbelievers and those estranged from the Russian Orthodox Church, who often felt that their church hierarchy had acquiesced to or collaborated with Communist rulers and the KGB (the Soviet secret police).

After the 1988 ceremonies celebrating a millennium of

Christianity in Russia, a second momentous event occurred. On 9 November 1989, the opening and then the rapid fall of the loathsome Berlin Wall facilitated communications between the West and the East. With the physical wall fell mental walls hindering consideration of foreign economic, political, cultural, and religious messages.

In any population a relatively thin, "golden" layer is spiritually prepared to receive religious truth. The people of this layer are impressionable. If they discover truths and build rapport with fellow believers in a church, they become reluctant to abandon their commitments to embrace another church, even one offering them restored truth. The challenge is to provide the gospel of Jesus Christ in its fulness while these people are still searching.

LAYING THE GROUNDWORK FOR MISSIONARY WORK IN RUSSIA

In June 1987, a year before the millennium of Christianity celebration and more than two years before the Berlin Wall came down, Elder Russell M. Nelson traveled in an official Church capacity to Russia. He was accompanied by Elder Hans B. Ringger, a member of the Seventy and of the Europe Area presidency, a man well experienced in matters of Church recognition in Eastern Europe. They arrived in Moscow on a fact-finding and bridge-building mission. They met with the chairman of the USSR Council on Religious Affairs, the man responsible for regulation of religious activity and accountable to the government's powerful Council of Ministers. They also consulted with leaders of the Russian Orthodox, Protestant, and Jewish faiths. On this occasion and others, they probed the most current requirements and procedures for introducing the Church into the Soviet Union.[9]

Elders Nelson and Ringger learned that laws at the time required a church seeking registration (legal recognition) to present documents describing the church's organization, teachings, and purposes together with an application for registration signed by at least twenty Soviet citizens living within a specific geographic area, such as a city or a district within a city. For a Soviet citizen to sign such an application at that time required more courage and deeper commitment than most non-Soviets can imagine. Petitions

*Elder Russell M. Nelson
of the Quorum of the
Twelve Apostles*

such as these had recently furnished names for KGB investigation and often reprisal. Imprisonment had become less common since the Stalin era, but subtle and intimidating administrative punishment, such as the silent loss of opportunity to advance professionally, acquire a better apartment, or provide higher educational opportunities for one's children, was routine.

Church representatives of unregistered groups were not allowed to proselytize to obtain the twenty members. Although conditions were difficult, through extraordinary faith, inspiration, and will, what appeared impossible became reality. By the end of April 1990, Elders Nelson and Ringger met with officials of the Leningrad City Council on Religious Affairs to complete arrangements for the submission of all paperwork for LDS Church recognition, including the twenty Soviet signatures. The Church of Jesus Christ of Latter-day Saints was legally recognized and registered in Leningrad on 13 September 1990. That all this could occur in less than three years was a modern miracle involving many people guided by the Lord's hand.

Elder Hans B. Ringger
of the Seventy and
a member of the
Europe Area presidency

THE BEGINNINGS OF THE LDS CHURCH
IN CONTEMPORARY RUSSIA

The first Russians to join the LDS Church after Gorbachev's rise to power had generally been taught and baptized abroad. From Leningrad, Iurii and Liudmila Terebenin, together with their fifteen-year-old daughter, Anna, visited Latter-day Saint friends in Hungary. While there they learned about the Church, met with missionaries, and were baptized on 1 July 1989. Muscovite Igor Mikhailiusenko was baptized on 24 July 1988 in the United States, and Olga Smolianova, also from Moscow, was baptized on 23 September 1989 in Italy. Vyborg's Andrei Semionov discovered the Church through the efforts of the Finnish Jäkkö family from Lappeenranta, a city near the Finno-Soviet border. Andrei was baptized on 24 February 1990. In all cases, these first Russian members found ways to share their new faith and contributed mightily to the Church's momentum.

After these Russian converts returned home, experienced Latter-day Saints were urgently needed to fellowship and support them and to teach their families and friends. Two years before, in

June 1987, Elder Russell M. Nelson had set apart Finland Helsinki Mission president Steven R. Mecham. President Mecham was told that he would serve not only his beloved Finns but also their neighbors to the east. Elder Nelson enjoined him to prepare well for this opportunity. On 29 January 1988, President Mecham submitted to the Europe Area presidency a detailed plan for beginning proselytizing work among Soviet tourists and expatriates in Finland. By late 1989 when Elders Nelson and Ringger authorized President Mecham to begin officially home teaching and limited missionary work in Estonia and Russia, the Finnish Saints and the Finland Helsinki missionaries had had opportunity to acquire the experience they needed.

During the second half of 1988, Sister Leena Riihimäki, a Finnish missionary serving in Helsinki who spoke Russian, sought out and began teaching Russian expatriates and emigrés visiting or living in Finland. When Sister Riihimäki completed her mission in November 1988, American elders, at first Elders Clarence Dillon and Bruce Bunderson, continued to visit the investigators she was teaching. They also sought new contacts through meeting the daily trains from Moscow and Leningrad. They offered to carry luggage of those whom they felt impressed to approach and provided the Russian *Joseph Smith Testimony* pamphlets or copies of the Book of Mormon. They then volunteered to share more information. Missionaries also met passenger boats and airplanes arriving from the Soviet Union. Soon other missionaries were given the opportunity to prepare for service in the Russian Proselyting Program, or Section R, as the missionaries called it.

Sister Stefanie Condie wrote of her first experience meeting the Leningrad train, in March 1990. She and her companion Sister Heidi Moffett had spent the previous weeks reviewing the beginning Russian they had studied at BYU. On the bus to the train station they agreed to speak only Russian, but every topic they began to discuss flagged for lack of vocabulary. With inner trepidation they walked resolutely to the Leningrad train. After a few moments of indecision they approached a distinguished-looking, middle-aged man and introduced themselves.

> We presented him with a Russian Book of Mormon and in broken Russian explained the history of its origin. This man,

whose name was Grigorii, not only willingly accepted the book but gave us a gift of his own—Russian chocolate. We talked with him for a little while (fortunately he spoke English fluently) and he gave us his business card. We left for home in rapture, assured that we had found a future stake president. Although we never heard of Grigorii again, this meeting gave us confidence and helped us to continue contacting passengers from trains. . . . We never heard of any positive results from these efforts at meeting the trains, but at least they provided us the opportunity to speak Russian and accustomed us to a new culture.[10]

Beginning early in 1989 President Mecham and missionaries visited the Finland-Soviet Center for Culture, the Finno-Soviet Trade Center, and the Soviet Union Chamber of Commerce in Helsinki, meeting administrators and learning of current Soviet affairs and conditions for religion in the Soviet Union.

For a period in 1989, missionaries also distributed copies of the Russian Book of Mormon to Soviet tourists as they paused briefly on the steps to the Great Lutheran Cathedral of Helsinki. The address of the Finland Helsinki Mission appeared in each book, along with an offer for further materials and the testimony of the family who had provided the gift copy of the book.

In mid-1989, Elder Ringger requested that President Mecham send fellowshipping home teachers to strengthen the Terebenin family in Leningrad. President Mecham asked Matti Ojala to begin visiting the Terebenins. This Finnish construction engineer and former branch president from Mikkeli, Finland, was often in Leningrad. Beginning in August and over the next few months, Brother Ojala, despite knowing little Russian, brought a spirit of inspiring assurance to the little meetings with the Terebenins and their acquaintances.

About the same time, President Mecham asked Leena Riihimäki, who was returning to Finland from postmission study at Moscow State University, to stop in Leningrad to bolster the Terebenins and answer questions from others who might be with them. Sister Riihimäki eagerly accepted this assignment. On this and subsequent trips she was able to present most of the missionary discussions to approximately fifteen nonmembers, mainly referrals from the Terebenins and their friends, who gathered most often in the Terebenins' tiny apartment.

In September 1989, President Mecham asked Matti Ojala to take twenty-five copies of the Book of Mormon to Leningrad. Brother Ojala understood that customs officials and border guards might confiscate the books and create difficulties for him then and on future trips. But knowing of the need for the books in Leningrad, he courageously accepted the assignment. Before departing for Russia, Brother Ojala arranged for a priesthood blessing that he might fulfill his commission.

At the border the customs official "behaved in an entirely unaccustomed manner. He merely counted my money and directed no attention whatsoever to my baggage." One can only imagine Brother's Ojala's relief. He declared that this protection from the Lord was a testimony to him that when one "does good works and trusts in the Lord, success will crown one's efforts."[11]

Also in September 1989, Elder Ringger directed Dennis B. Neuenschwander, then president of the Austria Vienna East Mission, and David P. Farnsworth, Europe Area legal counsel to the Church, to visit Leningrad and determine what steps could now be taken to serve members, respond to questions from nonmembers, and establish the Church in Leningrad.

President Neuenschwander was fluent in Russian and a veteran traveler to Russia and Eastern Europe. In 1977 he and his family had moved to Frankfurt to promote the microfilming of genealogical records through the Utah Genealogical Society. Because he had carefully followed changes in that area, he grasped their significance long before most others from the West. In July 1987 he was appointed the first president of the Austria Vienna East Mission, with missionaries in Poland, Yugoslavia, Hungary, and Greece. He was also the mission president responsible for the Soviet Union. On this 1989 trip to Leningrad he was accompanied by Brother Farnsworth, who had dealt with legal issues in Eastern and Central Europe since 1977 and was experienced in registering the Church in these countries. These two brethren were uniquely prepared to evaluate conditions and opportunities in Russia.

While in Leningrad, President Neuenschwander and Brother Farnsworth addressed Church members and their guests. On 16 September 1989, they conferred the Aaronic Priesthood on Iurii Terebenin. Brother Terebenin thus became the first Russian after the Revolution to receive the priesthood in Russia. Brothers Neuenschwander, Farnsworth, and Terebenin paid a courtesy call on officials of the Leningrad Council on Religious Affairs. The brethren were pleasantly surprised by the warm reception they received. Upon his return to Vienna, President Neuenschwander recommended to the Europe Area presidency that the Finland Helsinki Mission receive stewardship for the northwest part of the USSR because of its proximity to Finland and the availability of Russian-speaking missionaries there.

On 19 October 1989, at the mission presidents' training seminar in Budapest, Hungary, Elder Russell M. Nelson told Presidents Mecham and Neuenschwander that the First Presidency and Quorum of the Twelve Apostles had decided it was time to take the restored gospel to the peoples of Russia and the Baltic Republics. Elder Nelson assured them they could "go forward without fear. The Lord will direct your paths."[12] President Mecham was to concentrate on the northwest area of the USSR; President Neuenschwander would continue to support Church members in Moscow and monitor developments and opportunities in the southwestern area of the USSR.

In November 1989, Elder Ringger met in Helsinki with President Mecham and Presidents Seppo Forsman and Pekka Roto, the two Finnish stake presidents. Further plans were discussed for taking the gospel to the Soviet Union. A decision was made to call several Finnish couples as stake missionaries—the wives had studied Russian: Jussi and Raija Kemppainen, Aimo and Nellie Jäkkö, Antti and Leena Riihimäki Laitinen, Vesa-Pekka and Minna Kirsi, and Arto and Katri Lammintaus. Elder Kemppainen, genial, visionary, and enthusiastic, served as a counselor to President Mecham and later as president of the Church's Baltic District authorized in late January 1990.

For six months, drawing on their abundant leadership experience and undaunted by language barriers or the scarcity of Russian materials, the Finns provided expert leadership training and warm support for the new Russian members, who were invited to serve as leaders and teachers virtually upon changing from their baptismal clothing. While the Finns guided the Russian and Estonian leaders, the full-time Finland Helsinki missionaries[13] taught

Baltic District couple missionaries in Lappeenranta, summer of 1990 (left to right): Elder and Sister Laitinen, Kemppainen, Jäkkö, Kirsi, and Lammintaus

Russian investigators referred by Russian members and baptized those requesting the ordinance.

The Mechams and Kemppainens traveled to all the cities of the Baltic District—Leningrad, Vyborg, and Tallinn—to strengthen and inspire members and investigators. Complementing their husbands' efforts, Donna and Raija accomplished a marvelous work through public addresses, leadership lessons, personal counsel, and spiritual enthusiasm.

For years, the Jäkkös served with quiet dedication several weekends a month in Vyborg, lifting and enlightening the members with patience, love, and generosity. When they were home in Finland, it was a rare week without Russian guests. There the Russians learned about the Church and Latter-day Saint family values, visited Latter-day Saint meetings, and experienced life abroad.

Even before anyone in Vyborg had been baptized, Sister Nellie Jäkkö's renowned skill in table tennis proved important to missionary efforts. On her way to Vyborg to participate in a table tennis competition, she offered a Russian border guard a copy of the Book of Mormon. As is common, because he was acting in an official and public capacity, he refused to accept anything that might be construed as a bribe. When he learned that Sister Jäkkö was twice the Finnish senior national table tennis champion, he offered to arrange for the best of their officers to play her that evening upon her return from Vyborg. That night in the officers' recreation hall Sister Jäkkö defeated the very Russian officer who had earlier declined to accept the Book of Mormon. To show his respect, he gave her a gift, the Soviet emblem from his officer's hat. She reciprocated with a present most important to her, the copy of the Book of Mormon, which he now accepted with a smile and a bow.

Upon the recommendation of a Finnish friend, Sister Jäkkö had taken two copies of the Book of Mormon on the Vyborg trip. The other copy she presented to Liudmila Bezikova, her vanquished opponent in table tennis that day in Vyborg. Liudmila Bezikova was among the first from Vyborg to be taught and baptized. She introduced several friends to the Church.

In connection with her prowess in table tennis, Sister Jäkkö was awarded a three-year, multiple-entry visa to Russia, enabling her to visit Vyborg with little hindrance. She and other members of her family often traveled to Vyborg to support the small branch there. Irina Maksimova from Leningrad met Sister Jäkkö in Vyborg and became interested in the Church:

> I finished school in 1972 and entered the Leningrad Pedagogical Institute in the College of Foreign Languages. I studied English and German for five years at the institute. . . . I received my degree and began to work as an English teacher at a school in Leningrad. . . . I was also very active in youth groups, such as the Communist Youth League, or Komsomol. Because I was active in this group, I was later offered a position on the Komsomol Committee. . . .
>
> For a long time, we were not allowed to buy Bibles. . . . It was possible to "get" one, as we say in Russian, "under the table." . . . I didn't really have a desire to get a Bible. I had heard that such a book exists, but I associated it only with the Orthodox religion. I didn't even know that the Bible existed in contemporary language, in Russian with modern Russian letters. . . .
>
> My mother was never a believer; neither was my father. Consequently, there was never any talk about religion in our family. But at home I have the Great Soviet Encyclopedia in which there is a small section, maybe twenty lines in all, about

Mormons. Once, when Nellie Jäkkö from Finland gave me a Book of Mormon, I came home and read the article. . . . It was interesting.

Thanks to my husband, we met the Jäkkö family at a sports competition. At that time Russians began to have more contact with foreigners, and a group of Russian sportsmen needed an interpreter. I know English, and since my husband was to participate in the competition, I was invited to be an interpreter. I became acquainted with Nellie Jäkkö, another participant in the competition. When they welcomed her with champagne, she said she would not be able to drink it because her faith would not permit her. When the schedule of events called for Sunday competition, she informed us she would not be able to participate on Sundays because she attends church. So I told her she could go to church another day, that I would show her one of the churches she could visit. But she insisted, "No, my church meets only on Sundays." These issues intrigued me and I thought to myself, what kind of a church is this that only meets on Sundays? She returned home after the competition and, although we kept in contact, I was left alone with my questions. . . . Sometime later a Finnish team came to a competition in a town about two hours away from Leningrad. Since Nellie Jäkkö was in the hotel room next to ours, we would spend time together in the evenings. That is when she gave me the Book of Mormon. I did not begin to read it, however.

But now [this book] is my life. I must read it. If I have many questions and all the answers are in the book, how can I not read it? I can find any answer. During a time we stayed in a hotel in Leningrad, Nellie Jäkkö introduced me to two sister missionaries, Sister [Heidi] Moffett and Sister [Stefanie] Condie. . . . I must honestly admit at that time I was not interested in religion. I was simply interested in talking with Americans in their own language. . . . They began to teach the discussions to me. When they asked me the question, "When will you be baptized?" I was frightened because I didn't want to be baptized. I was a member of the Communist Party. I was very active in it, and I really believed the Party wanted to do "good." I believed that! . . . What was I to do? The missionaries were very strong though. They called and called and called, but I avoided meeting with them. . . .

In September I went to Finland and visited [the LDS] Church there. Some Finnish missionaries talked with me and asked me why I didn't want to be baptized. I think by then it was because of fear. I was afraid of the consequences, that I might be fired from my work. During those times, a position like I had at the institute was very prestigious. . . . If you had a job, you did every-thing you could to keep it. "If I join the Church, a foreign church as it was explained in those times, they'll fire me because I work with young people." I was afraid, but also felt by [joining the Church] I could gain much for myself. In Finland the missionar-ies spoke with me for three hours. . . . I didn't know how events would further unfold in my country. I didn't know communism would collapse. There was a lot I did not know, but the mis-sionaries simply said, "All right, you don't know the answer. Go to the forest, get on your knees and ask God whether you should be baptized."

Later, I went into the forest where Nellie lives. It was very sunny and beautiful. I fell to my knees and began to ask my question, "Answer me please, should I be bap . . ." I had not even finished the question when it was as if the entire forest was shouting to me, "Yes, yes, yes, yes, yes." I repeated the question three or four times, and the answer was the same each time. When I returned home I said "Yes." I think it was the next day [25 September 1990] that Nellie Jäkkö's son baptized me. It was wonderful. . . . It was like a birthday, but not even my birthdays had been so celebrated with so much attention as my baptism. . . .

[Speaking of the Relief Society of which she had been branch and district president:] For more than seventy years [in the Soviet Union] there was little understanding about charity and loving one another. Love just seemed to have evaporated. It was forgotten. Unfortunately, I think even today few people under-stand the meaning of charity. . . . What we need to do is help those people who have difficulties in life. I believe that charity in its fullest expression is the love of Christ. . . .

[At the temple:] This was for me an immense blessing, because I saw *our* Saints there, our Russian Saints. I saw them before they went to the temple and I saw them after. . . . When I looked at them there in that most meaningful celestial room, I simply could not restrain my tears. These people really are angels. . . . And I saw how they were growing, how they were changing and becoming stronger, more committed. They truly understand that through their strength, the Church will develop.[14]

Each of the other Finnish families traveled to Leningrad approximately once each month to answer questions about the gospel and Church organization, help members understand basic Church programs and procedures, and convey a spirit of enthusi-asm and assurance that sustained their fellow Saints through times of perplexity or insecurity. The Finnish couples were asked to leave for Russia after work on Friday and return to Finland late Sunday evening, but it was not uncommon for them to add a day to this from their vacation time to extend the effectiveness of their visits.

The five couples and other Finnish members of the Church served the Soviets whenever they found an opportunity, housing and caring for recent converts who traveled to Finland to visit Church meetings and see the gospel in action, hosting young Soviets visiting at youth conferences, and supplying food and clothing during times of particular duress.

The Estonians and Russians stayed for days or even weeks and months in the Mecham, Kemppainen, Jäkkö, Roto, Forsman, and other Latter-day Saint homes during those early months when the Church was just beginning in the Soviet Union. One cannot begin to measure the positive results of this uncommon generosity and warmth.

Facilitating official recognition of the LDS Church in Estonia on 29 June 1990 were the good relations between the Church and Chairman Ants Liimets of the Estonian Council on Religious Affairs. On one occasion Mr. Liimets had found himself stranded in Helsinki following a professional meeting. Soviet authorities closed the ports of the independence-minded Baltic republics for days. Mr. Liimets called President Mecham late at night and asked for advice. The Mechams immediately drove to the port and welcomed Mr. Liimets into their home, where he stayed until conditions improved and he could return to Estonia. While living in the mission home he observed family prayers, scripture reading, missionary visits, and the personal lives of the Mechams. When bidding them farewell he promised to facilitate the registration process for the LDS Church, a promise he faithfully kept.

Stake presidents Pekka Roto and Seppo Forsman often provided facilities for baptismal services and eagerly participated in these meetings. In Russia and Estonia they presented inspiring leadership training. A medical doctor, President Roto also gave firesides, seminars, and workshops on health issues and arranged for much appreciated medical contacts and humanitarian assistance.

The Finnish contribution to missionary work in Russia is especially touching when one recalls the centuries of troubled relations between Finland and Russia, including the devastating war years from November 1939 to September 1944. During that time nearly 100,000 Finns perished, and the nation was compelled to cede to the Soviet Union southern Karelia and other land along Finland's eastern border on which, before evacuation, had lived 420,000 people, 12 percent of the Finnish population. Many more Finns, and others along the European borders with the USSR, have taught by their generosity a deeper meaning of the gospel injunction to love one's enemies.

PART II

DEVELOPMENTS IN THE USSR, EARLY 1990

4

TALLINN, ESTONIA

When American missionaries in Finland introduced Estonian Valttari Rödsä to President Steven Mecham, he felt through the Spirit that Valttari "had been foreordained to assist in establishing the Church in Estonia." For his part, Valttari related that he had been prompted by the Spirit to approach Latter-day Saint missionaries in Hyvinkää and to listen to their message. When he returned to Estonia, Valttari gathered his family and friends to hear the missionary discussions and meet in worship services. He accepted the gospel and was baptized 16 July 1989 in Finland.

Like several of the other early Estonian Latter-day Saint converts, Enn Lembit, Valttari's son-in-law, had been a Baptist. Through LDS Church teachings, he found answers to important questions concerning temples, prophets, priesthood, and kingdom building. Finnish businessman Pekka Uusitupa, mission counselor Jussi Kemppainen, Finland Tampere Stake president Pekka Roto, and the missionaries[1] provided Church materials in Finnish and Russian and powerful living examples of gospel teachings.

Enn Lembit shared his faith with others of his former church, among them Jaanus Silla and Urmas Raavik, both of whom accepted baptism and in time served as Latter-day Saint missionaries, Jaanus in Utah and Urmas in Washington. Missionary Alan Johansen recalls that Jaanus and Urmas were effective as member missionaries in Tallinn:

> It seemed as though a day didn't pass that they weren't out on the street talking to people and telling them about the Church. Throughout the day we would receive phone calls from them about someone they had found who was interested in the gospel. They would bring these people to our hotel room and then help us teach them the discussions.[2]

Enn Lembit also convinced his brother Aivar to listen to the missionaries. In time, Aivar Lembit became the Tallinn branch president, traveling each Sunday by bus ninety-five miles from his home in eastern Estonia to Tallinn. Thus the spiritual tree grew from Valttari to Enn, to Jaanus and Urmas, and to Aivar and sent out branches in profusion. This blossoming from one to a multitude was seen frequently in the Soviet Union.

Aivar Lembit shared the story of significant changes in his life at this time:

> A very important event occurred in my life at the end of 1989. That was the time of my first meeting with the Mormons. The meeting was entirely different from what I had expected. I imagined I would listen to long and rhetorical speeches, and would meet peculiar, unimpressive people. Instead, I met young men who talked about simple truths, and it seemed they knew why they were living and which path they should follow.
>
> I remember I was visiting my brother when he told me about the "miracle" that had happened to his father-in-law [Valttari Rödsä] who, while visiting in Finland, was baptized into The Church of Jesus Christ of Latter-day Saints. The same evening, I met [Finnish businessman] Pekka Uusitupa, a member from Finland. His testimony of God and the Church was so strong that I decided to study the scriptures and other literature. I had never belonged to a church before. I had rarely been to Lutheran services in Estonia, only to satisfy my curiosity or at Christmas. I had thought about the existence of God only at times when I was alone, mostly during illnesses.
>
> "The Testimony of Joseph Smith," *The Gospel Principles*, and the first chapters of the Book of Mormon impressed me so much that I decided to join the Church. . . . I felt a divine witness and it seemed to me I had found the way, the support, and the security that I had sought my whole life. And feeling that, I said to myself, "This church is true and I have to become a member." It was not hard for me to quit coffee, tea, alcohol, and smoking. On 27 January 1990 I was baptized.[3]

Others joined the Church through the missionary efforts of President Mecham, who introduced the gospel to everyone he met from his first day on Estonian soil, 8 December 1989. On that occasion he arrived in Estonia with his wife, Donna, President Kemppainen, and Elders David Reagan and Kevin Dexter. The first taxi driver to whom he spoke, Peep Kivit, soon joined the Church and served as the first native Estonian branch president. The first branch leader, called when the Estonian branch was organized on 28 January 1990, was Finnish missionary Elder Harri Aho.[4]

The second taxi driver to transport President Mecham felt little interest himself, although he and his brother were later baptized, but he wondered whether his mother might want to learn of the LDS Church. President Mecham eagerly asked to meet his mother. The next morning the taxi driver took her to speak with the missionaries and President Mecham, who offered to teach her about the Restoration, promising eventual baptism and a calling as Estonia's first Relief Society president. Her response was, "I don't know what that is, but I'll be a good one."[5] Marina Saarik soon accepted baptism and became an astonishingly effective Relief Society president and member missionary. Her spirituality and grace helped many grow in faith and testimony.

Eve Reisalu, another of the early Estonian members,[6] examined her spiritual journey and her feelings as she contributed to the missionary effort:

> Why was I baptized into this Church? It is hard to say. I don't exactly remember my thoughts and feelings. The Church was so new in Estonia and in the whole Soviet Union. That's why it caught my attention. And I remember the elders told me about the importance of the family, and I liked that very much. I read in the Book of Mormon that if you don't know whether this is true, then pray and you will receive an answer. That's what I did. I had dreams twice that were about my decision, but afterwards I couldn't remember whether they were positive or negative.
>
> At the same time I was having a difficult time at my institute [an institution of higher learning]. I had to pass a very difficult exam and feared I might fail. I asked God to help me pass the exam and felt everything would be all right. I believed God would help me. I passed the exam, but not very well. I felt disappointed and could not find peace. I decided to attend church regularly and listen carefully to what was said because I had begun to doubt in the goodness and existence of God.
>
> Our Church grew, and I became acquainted with Marina Saarik, who asked to speak with me. This was very good because she was able to explain much to me. She strengthened my faith, saying that the exam was a trial for me while my faith was being

Tallinn Branch in early 1990. Among those pictured are (row 1, left to right) Jaanus Silla, Urmas Raavik, Finnish Tampere Stake president Pekka Roto; (row 3, left to right) Enn Lembit, Aivar Lembit; (row 4, the two at right) Mai Silla, Marina Saarik; (in back on couch) Finland Helsinki Mission president Steven Mecham and Sister Donna Mecham

tested. I began to understand that what she said was true and that I had chosen the right path.

When my friend and roommate Eve Pärimets was baptized, I felt very happy. She heard about the Church from me. And when you have helped even one person join the Church, you feel very happy, and it also helps to strengthen your own testimony.[7]

The June 1990 visit of Brother and Sister Hans Peets to Estonia was an important event for members and missionaries. Brother Peets is a native Estonian who resides in Canada. A faithful LDS Church member, he has served as a stake president and as a counselor in the Toronto Ontario Temple presidency. His perfect knowledge of Estonian and his deep love for his people, combined with his broad grasp of the gospel and Church, made his weeks in Estonia deeply significant. President Mecham explained that "He taught them the order of the Church and how to function, and gave them a lot of practical advice. He understood the thinking and the ways of those people. They just sat for hours working with him. He really made a profound difference in developing the spirit and attitude of our branch to move forward."[8]

In April 1990 Elders Russell M. Nelson and Hans B. Ringger visited Tallinn with Presidents Mecham and Kemppainen. While there they were interviewed before a national TV audience and spoke to a congregation of more than two hundred members and guests.

On 25 April 1990 Elder Nelson dedicated Estonia for missionary work. The dedicatory prayer was offered very early in the morning near the beautiful Laululava Amphitheater in Tallinn, where hundreds of thousands attend the nation's twice-each-decade festival of song. Elder Nelson included in his prayer this plea: "Wilt thou grant unto [the Estonians] the ability to take on the Light of Thy Son and be a citadel of strength to the Baltic states that surround this site made sacred by this dedicatory prayer."[9]

5

LENINGRAD, RUSSIA

On 3 December 1989, President Steven and Sister Donna Mecham and President Jussi and Sister Raija Kemppainen visited the Leningrad Saints for the first time. They met in the Mecham's hotel room with the Terebenin family and others interested in the Church. President Mecham wrote that this sacrament meeting, in which he and others taught and bore testimony to the eleven people present, was "one of the most spiritual experiences that I have had as a mission president."[1]

Beginning on 19 January 1990 full-time missionaries traveled to Leningrad. They remained from a weekend up to two weeks to strengthen the Leningrad Saints and teach their referrals. The missionaries lived in the Motel Olgino on the distant outskirts of Leningrad. From the motel building, the missionaries were assigned to austere A-frame cottages without plumbing and finally to nearby trailers. In June they gratefully moved into city center apartments arranged for them principally by the Terebenins.

When the Mechams next attended a Leningrad sacrament meeting in January, twenty-two people crowded into the Terebenin apartment. President Mecham invited all to come to Helsinki to be baptized and, in what he described as a monumental experience and a great outpouring of love, they accepted. Some may have been interested in a trip abroad, but many substantiated the president's conviction: "The spirit of this great work is certainly moving upon the land. The Lord is bringing forth his elect to establish his church in this part of his vineyard. . . . Words cannot express the miracles that we have seen as he prepares his people in Leningrad to receive the gospel."[2]

In the Terebenin's apartment on 11 February 1990, President Mecham organized the first branch of the LDS Church in Russia. The next Sunday, 18 February, Elder Hans B. Ringger attended LDS

Church services at a new location in a house of culture (recreation center) named "Maiak" ("Lighthouse") on Red Street, Building 33. Elder Ringger spoke on happiness as the purpose of life and on developing a relationship with the Savior.

A summary of the subjects President Mecham covered during his training time illustrates what must be explained to new members in a fledgling church. He taught the importance of arriving at meetings on time, bringing scriptures, and taking notes; elements of a prayer; procedures for blessing and passing the sacrament; appropriate music; leadership training suggestions; translations of materials into Russian; payment of tithing; rental of buildings; home teaching; family home evenings; the Church reporting system; and the need to locate a larger meeting facility—sixty-five attended that day.

Most of the twenty Soviet citizens required for registration of the Church in the USSR were baptized in Finland during February 1990. After that, converts generally were baptized in Leningrad, typically in a hotel swimming pool or sauna facility with a small pool. Cooperative officials from the Leningrad Council on Religious Affairs had assured President Mecham that he could hold religious meetings, teach, and answer questions from interested citizens. Those requesting baptism could now receive this ordinance in Leningrad.

On 3 February 1990, Anton E. Skripko, a man in his mid-twenties from Leningrad, became the first member baptized in Russia. Although understandably apprehensive about taking this momentous step in a society in which similar behavior had long incurred harsh penalties, Brother Skripko manifested uncommon courage and deep faith. He was soon called to be a counselor in the branch presidency and a year later became the first full-time Russian missionary. Elder Skripko served honorably from July 1991 to July 1993 in the Utah North Mission, returning to his home city—which had been renamed St. Petersburg in September 1991—to continue his impressive contributions there. At this writing he presides as a branch president in St. Petersburg.

A glimpse of the early days of the Church in Leningrad is provided in an account from Andrei Kotov, who, emboldened by Anton Skripko's example, was baptized later the same day. He described the first Leningrad gatherings of only a few members and friends:

> These first historic meetings, the sacrament and baptismal services, stand as a witness to the entire world that the gospel is true and that God blesses those who choose to follow Jesus Christ. At first we held our meetings both on Saturdays and Sundays. Each time I felt more strongly the spiritual warmth we enjoyed among us and which I could not find in other churches. And I decided this was what I had been searching for so long. . . . At this moment [the first baptismal service], I felt that something very unusual was happening inside of me. I was experiencing this feeling for the first time in my life. I will remember this beautiful day forever.[3]

Late in April 1990, Elder Russell M. Nelson, Elder Ringger, President Mecham, President Kemppainen, their wives, several missionaries, and others visited Leningrad. The Saints there were grateful for the wonderful opportunity to meet and learn from an apostle. Elder Nelson spoke to them on several of the Articles of Faith: the Latter-day Saint belief in the Godhead; the first principles and ordinances of the gospel; belief in the same organization that existed in the Church established by Christ; obedience to civil law and civil rulers; and belief in all that is virtuous, lovely, or of good report or praiseworthy. Many later spoke of feeling deeply grateful for his apostolic blessing.

On 26 April Elder Nelson offered a prayer of gratitude in the spirit of rededication of Russia for the preaching of the restored gospel. Nearly eighty-seven years previously, Elder Francis M. Lyman had dedicated the land of Russia in the Summer Garden in St. Petersburg, and Elder Nelson wished to offer his prayer in the same place. But when the Church leaders arrived at the garden, they discovered the gates closed to the public that day. President Mecham appealed to the guard, but he refused until, as President Mecham recounted, being touched by the Spirit he relented, explaining how the group could enter through a closed but unlocked gate on the other end of the park closer to the Neva River. This entrance was not far from the apparent site of Elder Lyman's dedicatory prayer.

Elder Nelson offered his prayer near the elaborate monument

to the beloved nineteenth-century Russian fable writer Ivan Krylov. Elder Nelson entreated the Lord to bless those who would consider the Church's application for recognition that their hearts would be touched and that they would approve the request, "that Thy work may flourish in this part of the world." He asked the Lord to help the people of Russia to find Him and learn the truths of the gospel. Elder Nelson importuned specifically, "Wilt Thou bless them with religious liberty and freedom so that they may be able to unite with their families, both in this life and in the life to come."[4]

An example of the Lord's helping Russians to discover gospel truths occurred in Helsinki. Sister Raija Kemppainen, who played an instrumental role, recorded the following account of a series of conversions:

> I met Svetlana Artiomova the first time in April of 1989 in a park in Helsinki. Our first conversation was short because she was going to Leningrad in one hour.
>
> A few months later I met an older Russian lady in the same park. After talking with her a short time I realized she was Svetlana's mother and I was able to make contact with Svetlana again. Her husband worked in Helsinki and she was visiting him. I tried to help her in getting to know stores, children's clinics, etc. We became good friends.
>
> The first weekend of December of 1989 we had our first visit to Leningrad with President and Sister Mecham, and we visited with Svetlana in Leningrad. She told us that night that she grew up without believing in God. But when she got older she thought there had to be a God. She wanted a Bible, but Bibles were hard to find in the Soviet Union. She thought she would buy a Bible on her next visit to Helsinki; however, she was unable to find a Russian Bible. Later she went into the forest to pick mushrooms and there under the leaves she found a Russian Bible. We told her that was not by chance, but the Lord was preparing her to receive the gospel.
>
> Svetlana came to Finland before Christmas and I was able to give her the Book of Mormon in Russian, and bore my testimony. Missionaries started teaching her, and Svetlana was baptized in February in Helsinki.
>
> Svetlana later gave me the address of a friend in Leningrad, which I forwarded to a Finnish missionary couple [Antti and Leena Laitinen] going to Leningrad that weekend. The couple

tried to reach Svetlana's friend, but she was not at home. However, the next-door neighbors heard the knock and went to see who it was. They asked if they were from the Mormon Church.

Then the neighbors [Mr. and Mrs. Aleksandr Taraskin] told the missionary couple that they had been discussing that same week how to get in touch with the Church. They had visited the Church in Warsaw, Poland, the summer before, and now wanted to be baptized. These people were baptized later that year, and thus in miraculous ways the work expanded.[5]

New Russian members, Finnish missionary couples, American full-time missionaries, mission and district leadership, General Authorities, and others labored to prepare the way for registration of the first congregation of the Church in Russia. Brother Iurii and Sister Liudmila Terebenin made countless visits to Leningrad city government representatives and offices of the Council on Religious Affairs to provide materials, comply with myriad requirements, answer frequent questions, and supply needed assurances. They and many others worked hard and consistently credited the Lord for helping them surmount inertia, suspicion, hostility, and an intricate bureaucracy. Elder Nelson's prayer was answered when the Church was legally recognized in Leningrad on 13 September 1990.

6

VYBORG, RUSSIA

Vyborg, Russia, a city of about 75,000, is located midway between Helsinki, Finland, and Leningrad, Russia. There, on Friday, 23 February 1990, President Jussi Kemppainen and his family, the Jäkkö family, and Elders John Webster and Don Leavitt held a meeting in the beautiful central library building. Approximately thirty-five people came, many having received an invitation and information about the Church through the Jäkkös. All the Church representatives spoke, answering questions about how the LDS Church differs from other Christian churches and teaching basic principles of their faith.[1]

As on numerous other occasions, the Kemppainen family created a powerful impression as they spoke about love within the family and as their children sang "I Am a Child of God." Many converts to the Church commented on the Kemppainen family as having influenced them to search for what these and other Finns and their Church represented.

Andrei Semionov, having been taught by the Jäkkö family since a 1989 canoe trip, had begun to study the gospel with missionaries. At first Andrei tried to make Marxists out of the missionaries, but he soon approached the discussions with an open heart and spiritual vigor. Still, troubling questions hindered him from being baptized. He asked the missionaries, Why does God not reveal himself to all people—Christians, Buddhists, and Muslims— and tell them plainly and directly which path to choose? Elders Webster and Ivan Stratov (a young medical doctor of Russian descent from Australia), having noticed the weights Andrei lifted, replied that spiritual strength increases through rigorous exercise as does physical strength. By exertion our spirits are strengthened and enabled to bear life's burdens.

Visiting the branch in Leningrad on 25 February 1990 with

At Andrei Semionov's baptism. Left to right: Brother Aimo and
Sister Nellie Jäkkö, Elder John Webster, Andrei Semionov

Andrei, President Kemppainen invited him to be baptized immediately. Andrei demurred, saying he must study much more.
President Kemppainen convinced him that we all continue to learn
following baptism and even more fully after receiving the gift of
the Holy Ghost. Later that day, Andrei Semionov became the first
resident of Vyborg to join the Church. Andrei's wife studied the
gospel with her husband and missionaries and was baptized some
five months later on 4 August 1990.

The first sacrament meeting in Vyborg was held on 11 March
in the Semionovs' apartment. When the Vyborg branch was organized two weeks later on 25 March, fifty people participated in the
meeting, which was open to the public. President Mecham called
as branch president the confident medical doctor, Andrei
Semionov.

Each week President Semionov welcomed new members of
all ages. He often referred with genuine warmth to a small but

rock-solid group of older women as the branch's "greatest trea-sure." Those familiar with Russia acknowledge a centrally impor-tant truth: the older women, affectionately called *babushki*, continue to play important roles in the country, preserving and transmitting the finest of Russia's rich spiritual heritage. One of these cherished Vyborg members, Lora Maltseva, told the story of her conversion:

> I am sixty-three years old. I am a person of broad experience and elderly. Having raised two children, I now have grandchil-dren. I used to live like everyone else. There were hardships, sometimes life was good, sometimes bad. Of course in our coun-try during former years no one knew much about God. We were embarrassed to speak of him. The common words "praise God" and "if God wills" even evoked scorn. In my soul I always believed in God, but I didn't pray formally or attend church ser-vices much, perhaps a couple of times a year.
>
> And then missionaries appeared in our town. When I learned that it was all right to attend their meetings and study the Holy Scriptures and learn of God, I went. I felt joy in my soul and inspiration as I arrived at the music school. When they began singing hymns, tears flowed from my eyes. I was impressed by the missionaries and immediately started to believe. All the missionaries felt like my close friends. The beliefs of The Church of Jesus Christ of Latter-day Saints became dear to me.
>
> Soon, in June [1990], I was baptized. During the baptismal service I felt wonderful. The Holy Ghost was conferred on me. From that time until now I have been happy and bear this spirit within me. I love to be at church, to meet with the missionar-ies, with the elders. I love to be with my brothers and sisters. They support me and are my family, without whom now I would have no life. With them is where I feel myself a real per-son. I put aside all my cares and hurry to meetings. For me, church is like a holy celebration. . . .
>
> I am very glad that we have been given these boys from dif-ferent continents to help us learn the Holy Scriptures. A couple of years ago we couldn't even dream of this. They are bringing light into our darkness. Over the former years we lost much. We lost our spirituality, our morality. [In Russia] we had much harsh-ness, falsehood. People became coarse. There was little love. But when you are with the boys in church, you feel like you want to become a better person. You want to strive for perfection.

7

MOSCOW, RUSSIA

For decades previous to Gorbachev's reforms, American Latter-day Saints serving in the United States embassy in Moscow and others on temporary assignment there met in the apartments of embassy employees. As a rule an embassy person coordinated Sunday meetings and other activities. Typically the worship services were modest, at times only a brief meeting to partake of the sacrament and discuss gospel principles, view a video of general conference, or listen to the greetings and testimony of a guest passing through Moscow. Often Church members enjoyed a dinner and informal discussion together after the meeting.

In February 1989 Dennis B. Neuenschwander, the mission president for Eastern Europe, including Russia, made one of several visits to the Saints in Moscow. This was an important occasion for many reasons. The Moscow group had tended to feel isolated from contact with Church leadership. President Neuenschwander communicated enthusiasm, devotion to gospel ideals, and an expansive, invigorating vision of the rise of the Church in Russia that lifted the members. On later visits he imbued the members with the missionary spirit. He urged them to live the gospel fully. He assured them Soviet authorities were aware of them and interested to see how their behavior corresponded to their words.

Student Glenn Worthey, businessman Carl Lambrecht, embassy employee and businessman Daniel Souders, and embassy employee Dohn Thornton, among others, were active in sharing the gospel. Brother Thornton was fluent in Russian, having studied in school and with a private tutor twenty hours a week at the American embassy. He participated in community outreach efforts and in the course of that work had introduced the gospel to Russian Galina Goncharova, the founder of the Moscow group of Alcoholics Anonymous, a badly needed support organization for those suffering from alcoholism. In the meantime, the LDS group was informed of the conversion of Olga Smolianova, an eighteen-year-old student at Moscow State University who was baptized in Italy in September 1989. She quickly became an integral and sustaining part of the group. As Brother Thornton recalled:

> It was like a breath of fresh air for us when she came to church. She told us her conversion story and we were all touched. She had been invited by a friend of the family to go to Italy for two weeks. One of her friends there was LDS and took her to church, where she met the missionaries. She was impressed with everything she saw and heard, but it wasn't until the last four days of her stay that she seriously began to investigate the gospel. The missionaries gave her a Book of Mormon and taught her all six discussions in three days. She received a strong testimony of the truthfulness of the gospel and wanted to be baptized. At first the mission president was reluctant to give her permission because he was afraid she would have no support system in Moscow. Finally, after fasting and praying, he gave her permission and she was baptized the day before she left Italy for Moscow.[1]

With Olga now a part of the group, Brother Thornton felt that it was the right time to invite Galina Goncharova to visit Church meetings. Galina gradually grew in testimony and commitment. Over time, more investigators attended, and Brother Thornton acknowledged that "ever since Russian investigators began coming to church, the Spirit seemed to increase in intensity. Having investigators at church helped us 'old timers' rediscover the beautiful first principles of the gospel."[2]

By January 1990, Russian members and investigators attending Sunday meetings outnumbered Americans. Late in March Brother Thornton started holding a Book of Mormon study group in his apartment, usually on Wednesday evenings. More Russians, including Galina's and Olga's friends, joined the group. By June 1990 eight investigators attended weekday and Sunday meetings regularly.

On 10 June 1990, Dohn Thornton baptized Galina Goncharova, almost surely the first Russian to join the LDS Church in Moscow.[3] He described the first two baptismal services in the Moscow group:

> Galia's [Galina's] husband, Sasha [familiar name for Aleksandr], found a beautiful place outside Moscow where he

had played as a child. On June 10 we gathered on the bank of a beautiful small lake surrounded by green hills. We had planned to have the baptism at 8 A.M., but we didn't arrive until after 9. By the time we got there, swimmers and fishermen were everywhere. I was very nervous about baptizing her, but Galia said, "Dohn, I'm not afraid." We marched down to the bank and got ready. Galia appeared clothed in her wedding dress and she looked radiant. We waded into the water and I baptized her. There were tears in everyone's eyes. We went back to the apartment for church, where I performed the confirmation. The Spirit was very strong and it had an effect on the investigators at church. . . .

Next week Nina [Leonteva, Galina's friend] and Kersti [Alabert, an Estonian employee of Carl Lambrecht] were baptized in the same spot. This time we had even more people in attendance at the baptism, including more than fifteen investigators. Galia's husband, Sasha, organized everything and even rented a big bus for all of us to drive to the lake. Before and after the baptism he gave out copies of the Book of Mormon and testified about the truthfulness of the gospel to the driver and to all those who wandered over to watch.[4]

In succeeding weeks and months more investigators joined the Church. When Moscow became part of the Finland Helsinki East mission in July 1990, the Moscow group had seven Soviet members, four baptized abroad (Igor Mikhailiusenko in the United States, Olga Smolianova in Italy, and Igor and Tatiana Kibiriov in Poland) and three in Moscow—Galina, Nina, and Kersti. Four more were baptized during July and August from Dohn Thornton's Book of Mormon study group, in which, beginning in late June, he and Olga Smolianova also taught the missionary discussions.

The Moscow group grew rapidly, particularly after the arrival of full-time missionaries in late October 1990. Dohn Thornton reflected that "although it was necessary for us to move on, none of us who experienced the feelings of family and true brotherhood will ever forget this time."

PART III

THE FINLAND HELSINKI EAST MISSION, 1990

8

FROM MISSION CALL TO DEPARTURE, EARLY 1990

On Thursday, 24 May 1990, President Thomas S. Monson called my office at Brigham Young University to notify me and my wife that our mission calls had been changed from the Finland Helsinki Mission to Finland Helsinki *East*, a new mission created that very day. The cities of the new mission were Leningrad (with sixty-two members), Tallinn (forty-one members), Vyborg (twelve members), and Moscow (two members). In addition to northwestern Russia and Estonia, the mission would encompass the two other Baltic republics, Latvia and Lithuania, with no members and no missionaries assigned. We would be living but not serving in Helsinki until conditions in the USSR were favorable and arrangements could be made for our move to Russia.

As I hurried home to tell Joan, I was filled with joy at the thought of laboring in Russia and Estonia but regretted that I could not serve with the Finns I had come to love thirty years earlier as a missionary. It was just before dinner, but I asked Joan to walk around the block with me. She quickly understood that I had some important reason. Once outside, I told her of the change in our calls. She expressed astonishment—and quickly began to consider what clothing, personal items, household articles, and books we should have sent in place of what we had already shipped to the long-established and well-appointed mission home in the Finland Helsinki Mission.

Four weeks remained before we were to enter the Missionary Training Center for three days of mission president instruction prior to our late-June departure. On 4 January 1990, when President Monson had extended our original call to serve in the Finland Helsinki Mission, the Church in the Soviet Union had scarcely begun to grow. There were then only five members in Leningrad, about a dozen in Tallinn, one in Moscow, and none in Vyborg.

President Monson emphasized that our call was to Finland, to the Finnish missionaries, members, and people, and that firm plans for the Soviet Union had not yet been formulated. But in less than five months the Church in Russia and Estonia had developed from fewer than twenty members to approximately one hundred and twenty!

In January, President Monson had counseled us to "use good judgment" in deciding whether to tell others that our call was to Helsinki; normally the announcement of specific mission assignments is made closer to the April general conference. We were soon cured of our inclination to divulge nothing more than the call to preside over a mission. When we informed the few we needed to speak with early—colleagues and family—we received the same response from most: "Probably you are not giving more information because your call is to the USSR."

In a vain attempt to forestall imaginative rumors about missionary work in the Soviet Union, we began stating our assignment as Finland Helsinki. Even before we received our call in January, we had begun hearing ever more fantastic speculation about a coming Russian mission. Among the rumors were the assertion that the Finland mission had been renamed the Finland and Baltic States mission. There were reports of large numbers, even whole villages, joining the Church in Russia. We heard that potential missionaries had received mission calls on which the space for the mission name was covered by a note asking the missionary to call the Church offices and ask for President Hinckley or President Monson, who then told the missionary that the country of service would be the USSR and that the missionary should not discuss the call with others. Stories were told of missionaries who received telephone calls from the Missionary Department stating they would be serving in the USSR but that this could not be given in writing yet—later they would receive their official letters of appointment. Finally, news circulated that missionaries were studying Russian at the MTC for six rather than two months and that their missions, consequently, would be two-and-a-half or even three years long, after which the missionaries were obligated to fill a two-year commitment to teach Russian at the Missionary Training Center. None of the rumors proved true.

Early in January Joan and I and the three of our five children who would accompany us to Finland—Jonathan (seven), Kathryn (ten), and Elizabeth (fourteen)—began to study the Finnish language and culture. Among the most enjoyable evenings of my life I spent reviewing the old Finnish missionary language lessons and my shoebox full of homemade language cards. Long dormant memories sprang to mind and heart of experiences, people, and culture from my mission in Finland.

But my love for Russia, Russian, and the Russians was also strong. Before my mission I had studied Russian at BYU for one year and wanted to visit Russia. In 1963 I joined a Finnish schoolteachers' one-week tour and traveled to Leningrad and Moscow—and fell in love with the people, language, and culture.

By 1990 I had made a dozen trips to the USSR, living there with my wife and two older children twice for six months each time, mainly in Leningrad, Moscow, and Kiev. To make both longer trips I had interrupted my graduate program in Slavic. The first trip was in 1969 to serve as a guide for a United States Information Agency exhibition on American education; the second, in 1973, was to do dissertation research on a twentieth-century Russian author, Boris Pilniak. I had also accompanied BYU performing groups, students, and tourist groups. During those years, religious discussions with Russians were few and always carried a risk, less for me than for the Russians with whom I conversed. These discussions were private, intermittent, and fleeting.

As my family and I prepared to serve in Finland, an incident showed us how much we all had to learn. Late in January I invited our children to write a short testimony, which I would translate into Finnish and then ask the native Finnish tutors at the MTC to correct and polish. Memorizing these would show our interest in the Finns and Finland, and we would become prepared to bear our testimonies in Finnish. Katie brought me her testimony with a blank space, explaining she was nearly finished but needed to know who the prophet was in Finland. We assured her that the prophet is the same person for every country and that this would be one of our main messages while serving our mission.

When we told the children that our mission had been changed to Finland Helsinki East, their responses varied. Jon seemed not to comprehend the implications; Katie immediately asked when she could begin telephoning friends; Betsy became uncharacteristically quiet. When we returned an hour later from telling my parents, Betsy was still crying. For the first time she mentioned her sadness at leaving her close friends and missing her remaining years at Timpview High School.

9

JULY 1990

Upon arriving in Finland, we were astonished that in just over one month a mission home and office had been located, rented, and prepared for us, the two office elders, and others.¹ The fourteen other missionaries, who, like our office elders, had been transferred from the Finland Helsinki Mission, were residing in Russia and Estonia.

The mission home was located in Kauniainen, a prestigious suburban community fifteen miles northwest of Helsinki. These were temporary quarters, the expectation being that we would move to Russia after about one year in Finland. (In actuality, our home remained in Finland for two years.) The mission home was a comfortable two-story apartment with a five-person sauna, an amenity common in Finnish houses. By retrieving foam mattresses stored under the regular beds and having the children sleep with us downstairs or occasionally in the sauna, we could accommodate groups of up to ten new missionaries upon their arrival in Helsinki. Joan set about adjusting to all the complications of a different culture and economy. Her letters home often dealt with those issues:

> Kauniainen is a Swedish suburb northwest of Helsinki and is supposed to be one of the loveliest. The vegetation reminds me of being at Coeur d'Alene Lake [Idaho]. There are bike paths, nature walks, narrow winding roads, yet the bus stop is right in front of our house and a small grocery store and shopping center are just two or three blocks away.
>
> Shopping for food has been a real shock. We heard from everyone that food was very expensive, but still it is hard to adjust. Lean hamburger is over $10 a pound, carrots are $1 a pound, cereal over $5 a box, and bread is about $4 a loaf. The stores contain a large variety of items, so I'm sure we will do just

Finland Helsinki East Mission Home in Kauniainen

fine when I learn what to look for. It is a slow process when you have to take a dictionary with you.[2]

The mission office was further north of Helsinki in the Martinlaakso suburb of Vantaa, within twenty minutes of the mission home and fifteen minutes of the Helsinki-Vantaa Airport. Located in a many-windowed half-basement of a high-rise apartment building, the suite had a large office for missionary staff, a large mission president's office, and living quarters and kitchen for four to six missionaries.

On our first five Sundays, Baltic District president Jussi Kemppainen, at times with his wife, Raija, and I, with my wife and family when possible, visited fellow missionaries and members at Church meetings in the four cities of the Finland Helsinki East Mission: Vyborg, Tallinn, Leningrad, and Moscow, and in our Helsinki area ward. On the first Sunday President Kemppainen and I made the three and one-half hour trip by car to Vyborg. Vyborg, a city of approximately 75,000, is east of Helsinki on the Bay of Finland in the area ceded to the Soviets at the end of the 1939–40 Winter War preceding World War II.

The Vyborg branch met in a small music school hall on Sukhov Street in the same apartment building in which our two missionaries, Elders John Webster and Ivan Stratov, lived. At the time, Vyborg had twenty-six baptized Latter-day Saints. On that July 8, twenty members were in town, and eighteen attended Church services, along with thirty-two investigators and ten non-Russian visiting members, including the loyal Finnish Jäkkö family. The elders were deeply concerned for those who had been baptized, visiting them frequently and resolving concerns, providing encouragement, and holding testimony-building discussions. We did not yet have the missionary or new-member discussions in Russian or Estonian, so missionaries translated from Finnish or English to the best of their abilities and with sympathetic prompting from investigators and the Spirit.

That first Sunday I was astonished at being in a meeting of the Church in Russia. Decades earlier, Vyborg was the first Russian city in which I had ever set foot. In February 1963 at the time of my release as a Finnish missionary, our train stopped for nearly an hour in Vyborg and I walked around town, never imagining I would return in a missionary capacity.

While sitting in this sacrament meeting in July 1990, I recalled arriving in Russia just five years earlier with eleven students from BYU and eighty-nine others from universities across the United States. In March 1985 Gorbachev had just begun his tenure as Soviet leader, but freedom of conscience was still restricted. At Vyborg, some of our suitcases were searched. All of us from BYU had brought our own copies of the scriptures. Customs officials confiscated what books they found and sternly reprimanded us, despite previous assurances to me from a Soviet Embassy official in Washington, D.C., that we could take scriptures into the country for our own use.

Now, in July 1990, I sat peacefully in a Latter-day Saint sacrament meeting in which a large number of the sixty people present held a copy of the Book of Mormon on their lap and spoke openly and with enthusiasm about the gospel of Jesus Christ!

I was thrilled as I listened to a group of six Russian girls aged approximately three to nine and looked into their radiant faces as they sang *in Russian*, "I Am a Child of God." The evidence of religious freedom was appearing before me, but I could not comprehend it fully during that short meeting. It represented too great a change from my twenty-seven years of experience with Russia.

I was amazed and humbled as I imagined how difficult it must have been for each of these Russians to alter his or her religious perceptions so drastically.

The amiable Andrei Semionov was conducting meetings, talking with priesthood bearers about the need for more faithful home teaching (Communism had conditioned Russians to resist admitting "strangers" into their apartments and to feel uneasy about visiting others who are not close friends). In fluent Russian, Elder Stratov taught a powerful Sunday School lesson for investigators and new members. Throughout the day I enjoyed observing Elder Webster's discreetly whispered counsel to President Semionov regarding what he should do next.

President Semionov's story is an inspiring example of a Russian who progressed from atheism to faithfulness, to loving leadership in the gospel:

> It all began with a canoe trip in the Karelian forest. Perhaps it was even earlier, with the death of my mother. No, actually it was even earlier than that—with a lecture on atheism at the Medical Institute where I was a student. I was a dedicated Komsomol member, and easily accepted the theory on the origin of man according to Darwin-Marx-Engels-Lenin. During student debates I crushed without qualms any eccentrics who attempted to find a grain of rationalism in religion.
>
> However, while working in a hospital I became acquainted with the patients whom I tried to help. As I watched several of them depart this life, I would ask myself: Why did these people live? Where do people's minds, their talents, and life experiences disappear to when that which bore them up turns into cold flesh, indifferent to the rest of the world? And if there were a God, how could he allow so much unjust suffering, pain, and unhappiness in the world? I carried these questions inside for many years, and would have completed my earthly existence with them had I not met some people who illuminated and sanctified my life, giving me answers to all of these questions.
>
> In 1988, upon graduating from the Medical Institute in Leningrad, I moved to Vyborg, the home of my wife, Marina, and her parents. . . . In the summer of 1989 Marina's sister invited me on a canoe outing. I eagerly accepted, and was even more delighted when I learned that a family from neighboring "capitalistic" Finland would also be coming on the outing. I anxiously awaited the opportunity to practice my English, of which

I had a fair command, having earlier completed a course of study for guides and interpreters. The family turned out to be very friendly, sociable, and charming. . . .

In the evening on the gulf around a campfire, we began to ask questions about their life, work, and traditions. We all ate out of the same pot, but when we offered them tea, they politely refused. "And what about coffee?" "No, thank you," answered Nellie [Jäkkö]. "We probably seem like a strange family to you, but we never drink tea, coffee, or alcohol, and we don't smoke. Why? Because of our beliefs. We are Mormons." We spent the remainder of the evening discussing whether or not there is a God, why we live, and how difficult it is to be a believer in this cruel world.

And so for the first time I learned the truth about the Mormons. That which we had previously heard about this faith, to put it mildly, alarmed us. I remembered in the stories of Sherlock Holmes, Conan Doyle had depicted the Mormons as a bloodthirsty sect of persecutors. My companions were even more erudite, and immediately wanted to find out if Mormons today practiced polygamy. It turned out, no. On that note, I believe, our philosophical discussion ended and we became completely caught up in tourist interests. As we parted, Nellie invited my family and me to visit them in Finland. When I accepted this invitation, I did not suspect in the least that this would be an invitation into a new life.

It took nearly three months to complete the paperwork for my visa, and in the fall of 1989 we visited Nellie in Lappeenranta, Finland. There for the first time I saw and spoke with Americans. Fortunately for me, they weren't just Americans. They were missionaries. One of them was My Missionary. His name was Elder Webster. . . .

One of the greatest shocks in Lappeenranta was the Mormon meetinghouse. I had never supposed that there would be no icons in the church, or that there would be a kitchen, showers, a gymnasium, a huge room with an organ, and many classrooms. In that particular church building I also met some other missionaries. One of them, Bert Dover, was not only a decent volleyball player, but pleasant company as well. My conversation with him, which had begun on the court, became more intense and serious, and finally, having separated ourselves from the others, we exchanged ideas for nearly two hours. I tried to hold to materialist positions as before, but my "eternal questions" continued to bother me and Elder Dover answered them all so well! This conversation turned out to be the first [missionary] discussion and I think it was right then that the seed, of which I later read in the book of Alma, fell into my soul. And so I took with me from Lappeenranta this "good seed" in my soul and a Book of Mormon in my travel bag.

I don't know how soon after I would have begun to read the Book of Mormon, but in the winter of that same year I again arrived in Lappeenranta, now on business, and that untiring Nellie put me up for a night at the house where the missionaries lived. One of them was John Webster and he did all he could to ensure that the good "seed" in my soul would take root and grow. I really liked John, his views on life, his confidence and zest for life; and as soon as I realized that John truly and sincerely believed in God, the last prejudices and reservations I had in my heart in relation to a foreign church disappeared without a trace. That same evening, I invited John to come to Vyborg and give preaching a try there.

After I returned, I mustered up my courage and began to read the Book of Mormon. I won't say it was easy. The ecclesiastical style forced me to really exert myself, but gradually the reading went more easily and more quickly. Halfway through I already realized a human mind did not have the power to create such a thing. I knew almost nothing about Joseph Smith himself, his education or intellectual qualities, but I didn't need to know anything about that at all. I knew these were the words not of a man but of God, and the fact that Joseph Smith was able to reveal these words to the world made him a true prophet in my eyes. It was right then that I even tried to pray, asking about the truthfulness of the writings. I chose not to share my thoughts and experiences with anyone.

In the fall of 1989 an event occurred that would be impossible to forget. Nellie and Aimo once told me that there was a family in Leningrad that had joined the LDS Church, and asked me to make contact with them. They were Iurii and Liudmila Terebenin and their daughter. They had been baptized during the summer of that year, and were also seeking to meet brothers of the same faith. I was able to set up a meeting for brothers and sisters of our faith at my brother Pavel's apartment in Leningrad. There we held the first meeting of the Church in the Soviet Union. As I accompanied the entire Jäkkö family to Leningrad for that meeting, I saw how worried they were, which in turn made me anxious as well.

Besides the Terebenins, Jäkkös, my brother and his wife Alla, and me, there was one more member of the Church at the meeting: a Finnish builder, Matti Ojala, who at that time was working under contract in Leningrad. I was the interpreter at that meeting and at times it was amusing to translate Church terms, but in a manner rather incomprehensible to me, I managed. It was there I saw for the first time a real sacrament service and heard the blessing on the bread and water, and although Nellie and Aimo's eldest son Timo read it in Finnish, I understood what was expressed in it. It was that same incomprehensible feeling and it was amazingly powerful. My lack of understanding and confusion even compelled me not to take the sacrament. Of course I was afraid of appearing impolite, but much more urgent than that, I wanted to remain sincere, and I could not do that which I did not believe in whole-heartedly. . . .

I would like to take a break from my narrative in order to say a little about the Finnish people. These northern people are characteristically reserved and unsociable; I myself saw evidence of this on more than one occasion. But the Finnish Latter-day Saints really countered this rule! They gave so much strength, heartfelt warmth, and time in order to help us, the Russians, find happiness and learn about the Church and the Kingdom of our Heavenly Father! Love made them genuine Saints in our eyes, and even yet I still don't know how to fully express my gratitude to our saviors from neighboring Finland, and above all to the Jäkkö family from Lappeenranta, the Roto family from Tampere, and the Kemppainen family from Helsinki. We will love and have faith in them for the rest of our lives.

And so, February 25, 1990, came and with it the beginning of my new life. On that day, Sunday, the first conference for the first Russian members of the Church was held in Leningrad. I accompanied Nellie and Aimo, and was pleasantly surprised when I saw so many, about fifteen, members of the Church from Leningrad in a room of one of the houses of culture where the meeting was held. The everpresent Elder Webster was also there. He arrived from Finland along with the president of the Helsinki mission, President Mecham, and his counselor Jussi Kemppainen.

Before the meeting began, Jussi smiled at me very sincerely, shook my hand and said, "You did the right thing in coming here. I have heard a lot about you and have been waiting to meet you." I don't remember much of what was said at the meeting. I kept thinking, could I go on with my life without these people, without the excitement in my heart and the chills that run down my spine when I pray and read the scriptures? All my doubts vanished when Jussi Kemppainen came up to me after the conference and said, "I think you are ready to be baptized; what do you think?" The words immediately and instantly escaped my lips—I didn't even have time to think—when I heard my response: "Yes, of course I am ready." With that Jussi turned and addressed the closest missionaries (of course one of them was John Webster), and said, "This young man by the name of Andrei should be baptized today. Do you understand me? Today!"

"That's interesting," I thought, "where will they find water in which to immerse me at six o'clock in the evening in the middle of winter?" The missionaries didn't think long about such a foolish question; they took action. On the way to Vyborg we stopped at the Olgino Motel. "There is a sauna here," they said, "and that means there should also be a pool." And there was. True, it took a good forty minutes to open the sauna and convince the workers that we were not planning to do anything immoral there. They dressed me in white clothing and asked who I would like to have baptize me. I requested Aimo Jäkkö. At that I saw how Nellie's eyes filled with tears of gratitude for her husband. Her eyes were not dry at all for the rest of the evening. Everything was festive, yet restrained and inspiring. I received the gift of the Holy Ghost from Kurt Wood, another wonderful and talented missionary. . . .

And so, on the evening of 25 February 1990, I lay down to sleep as a priest in The Church of Jesus Christ of Latter-day Saints. It wasn't long that I was the only member of the Church in the city of Vyborg. John Webster, who was transferred from Finland to Russia, set to work while simultaneously beginning his study of the Russian language. Even now I'm amazed how he managed to proselytize not knowing the language. True, he had help from his cohort: his companion, Ivan Stratov, was from Australia, and his grandpa had emigrated from Russia at the beginning of the century. Ivan spoke Russian beautifully. These two missionaries were a living legend. . . .

In March, President Kemppainen ordained me an elder and set me apart as the leader of the branch. This was unexpected for my wife, Marina, who had been trying up to that point to read the Book of Mormon. Now it became necessary for her to think more seriously about the future of our family and about God. Her pure and sincere soul could not be rushed. She went to meetings with me, prayed and supported me. I did not want to pressure her and knew that everything would happen in its own time. This time did come in August of 1990. I baptized Marina in the waters of the Gulf of Finland, five kilometers from our home. The water was very cold, but we paid no attention to that. John was a witness at the baptism, along with his companion.

*Marina, Roman, and Andrei Semionov with Stockholm Sweden
Temple president Reid H. Johnson and matron Donna Johnson*

Since that time our life has begun to flow in a new direction. The blessings could not be contained. In spring of 1991
I received an invitation to work as a doctor three days a week
at a Finnish polyclinic in Leningrad. This work demanded
continual improvement from me, but such had already become
my goal in life. . . .

A special joy in my life was made manifest to us after we
were sealed for eternity in the Stockholm temple in January
1992. During the course of the past two and a half years I've
been to this temple with every group from Russia and I try to
help my brothers and sisters prepare to enter into the eternal
world. I am happy for all who come to the temple and I know
that I will see them again in the Kingdom of our Father in
Heaven.

In September 1992 I received my patriarchal blessing in
Germany. . . . It is my greatest hope that I will be able to endure
to the end and that the "Lord Jesus Christ will meet my family
on the morning of the first resurrection with tears of joy in his
eyes."[3]

I noted in Vyborg and other mission cities that the members had few printed materials, only the *Joseph Smith Testimony* pamphlet, *Gospel Principles*, Articles of Faith cards, sacrament prayers, and Brother André Anastasion's translation of the Book of Mormon. Although *Gospel Principles* was understood without much diversity of interpretation, I was amazed at how Book of Mormon passages which I understand one way through years of gospel study were read very differently by others. If well-meaning but inexperienced Church teachers accepted astrology, reincarnation, extrasensory perception, and other mystical ideas, passages from the scriptures could appear to provide support. This meant the missionaries had to review correct doctrine and gospel principles frequently.

On 13 July, our family and President and Sister Kemppainen traveled by boat southeast from Helsinki across the Bay of Finland to Tallinn, Estonia. The capital of Estonia, Tallinn had approximately 480,000 inhabitants, half of whom were Estonian and half ethnic Russian.

At our hotel room we held a district meeting with the elders[4] who were struggling to make the difficult transition from speaking Finnish to speaking Estonian. Estonian is related to Finnish, but it requires great effort and considerable time to absorb the distinctions among beguilingly similar forms. Brad Woodworth, a former Finnish missionary and Brigham Young University graduate studying in Estonia, agreed to teach the missionaries Estonian grammar. Brad's Estonian language "school," which ran four hours each day, three days a week, for four weeks, was pivotal in the missionaries' transition.

Elder Christopher Gooch, one of these elders, described both his challenges in Tallinn and the Estonian family who strengthened his testimony:

> Upon arriving in Finland, I was assigned to the eastern portion of Helsinki where, for the next four months, I would slowly begin to grasp the basics of the Finnish language. At the end of my fourth month in Finland and my first month as a senior companion, I was called by President Steven Mecham to serve in Tallinn, Estonia.
>
> The early weeks of my new calling were unique. . . . Every Thursday we would take the ferry to Tallinn and remain until the following Monday. In Estonia we would speak either Finnish or English, depending on the person with whom we

were communicating. Estonian is a close cousin to Finnish in much the way Italian and Spanish are related. Fortunately, the residents of Tallinn were able to watch Finnish television stations and many of the younger people could understand Finnish quite readily.

Being four months "younger" than the other missionaries in Estonia, my Finnish was proportionally weaker. Whenever possible, I opted for English because my imperfect Finnish became more convoluted in translation. After several attempts at conversation were met with blank stares, I began to worry that I would spend the next eighteen months caught in a limbo of language—and a big smile would only get me so far.

Compounding my frustrations was my calling as Sunday School teacher. My first Sunday as teacher resulted in forty minutes of stammering rudimentary Finnish sentences to the encouraging nods of fifteen compassionate members. We all knew that my days with Finnish were numbered. For the next several months, English was the language of choice, but because far fewer people understood English than Finnish, we would take English-speaking members everywhere as interpreters. However, their time was tightly budgeted between school and work, so this method would prove to be merely a stopgap until another alternative was discovered.

That summer saw the arrival of President Gary Browning. After witnessing our methods of communication during an early visit, President Browning called the missionaries to his hotel room where he firmly insisted that we learn to speak Estonian. Although this was the inevitable option, I was frightened and took offense at such a suggestion. Nonetheless, we all knew it was the correct decision. During the next few days we scoured the city for language materials and found only two Estonian grammar books, one written in Russian, the other in highly technical Finnish. While these materials were far from ideal, we had a starting point for our study of Estonian.

In addition to this literature, we were fortunate enough to discover a language tutor living in Estonia. There happened to be two Americans in Tallinn at the time who were former students of President Browning. We had seen them at church occasionally, buried in stacks of dictionaries and scribbling notes during sacrament meeting. Now Harvard graduates, the Woodworths had been studying Estonian while working for a local newspaper. Brad had served his mission in Finland and was curious to understand Estonian's relation to Finnish. Before long, Brad Woodworth became our tutor. He would coach us through grammar principles, making references to the Finnish that we had learned in the MTC and translating the Russian from the basic grammar book we found in the stores. Brad's diligence in understanding the minute details of the language was an inspiration to me as I undertook the task of learning a new language.

After a very slow start, an outpouring of the Spirit, and a great deal of help from the Estonian members, we began to utter our first Estonian sentences. By late October we were teaching our first discussions in Estonian. One of our first Estonian teaching sessions was with the Kirisberg family. This mother and father of five listened patiently to the message we brought and eventually joined the Church.

Our ability to communicate in Estonian, although far from perfect, opened literally hundreds of doors for missionary work. The Estonian people were amazed that other Americans who had lived in their country there for years could not utter a complete Estonian sentence. During my final six months we were given the opportunity to participate in newspaper, radio, and television interviews as a result of our limited Estonian knowledge. . . .

The Kirisberg family became an important part of my mission experience. During my time in Estonia, Tallinn was the only city open for missionary activity. This meant I would spend nearly eighteen months in the same branch, having the opportunity to watch members grow in the gospel. In particular, I was able to watch the Kirisberg family move from curious investigators to steadfast members.

The economic strain placed on the Kirisberg family was enormous. As a family of seven, the oldest child only nine years old, they struggled to provide a basic standard of living amid conditions where even families of three were forced into one-bedroom apartments and double work shifts. Yet, their faithfulness under these conditions was remarkable.

During one of my last testimony meetings as a missionary, I was deeply touched by the Spirit as a normally shy and reserved Brother Kirisberg proceeded to the podium to bear his testimony. He quietly and proudly began to bear his testimony of tithing. During the previous month he had suffered a decrease in pay at his job as his company began to feel the effects of economic transition. This pay decrease meant that the family would fall short in its budget; some debts would not be able to be paid.

The Kirisbergs decided that regardless of the sacrifice, they would pay their monthly tithing on time. The meeting hall grew silent as we all contemplated the extreme sacrifices this family would have to make. With his children quietly sitting on the edge of their seats, the resolute father of five struggled to hold back the tears while describing how his supervisor had come to him last week to return his salary to its previous level. Lifting his head gratefully to look at the congregation, Brother Kirisberg stated firmly, "I believe in the law of tithing." Witnessing his powerful testimony proved to be one of the most spiritual moments of my mission experience. Then I learned of the incredible spiritual power contained within a simple testimony.[5]

I enjoyed becoming acquainted with branch leaders in a training meeting on principles of priesthood leadership. First counselor in the branch presidency Jaanus Silla, elders quorum president Enn Lembit, and Relief Society president Marina Saarik attended. Enn's brother Aivar, the branch president, lived in Kokhtla Yarve, 153 kilometers (95 miles) to the east and hours away by bus, and could come to Tallinn only for Sunday meetings.

The Estonian branch with forty-three members then met in a small but light-filled tennis clubhouse in the rolling, verdant hills of Kadriorg Park. In July 1990, the Estonian and Russian members met together, and one could hear during meetings the harmony and cacophony of Estonian, Russian, Finnish, and English.

I asked two branch leaders whether I should give my talk in Russian or Finnish and was advised to speak Russian because I was more fluent in Russian and more members understood Russian well than Finnish. On my next trip I spoke with a larger group of leaders and learned that English or Finnish would be better, although Estonian was best. I tried at least to bear my testimony in Estonian, used whatever Estonian phrases I could muster, and gave my talks in English with an interpreter.

Even before 1990, Estonian nationalist feelings were steadily rising. Virtually all Estonians spoke Russian, but it was more courteous to speak Estonian. Germans, Danes, Poles, and Swedes had each controlled parts or all of Estonia from the thirteenth century until 1710, when the Russians asserted sovereignty. Estonia declared independence two hundred years later in 1918 and resolutely maintained her right to remain free until 1940, when the country was involuntarily incorporated into the Soviet Union. Since the eighteenth century, Russians, even those able to trace their families back for generations in Estonia, generally were considered occupiers and aggressors.

The following week Joan and I flew with the Kemppainens to Leningrad, a city of more than five million. Baltic District President Kemppainen and I spoke at length with branch president Iurii Terebenin. His diligence and persistence had contributed to the Church's being approved in the Leningrad City Council and Council on Religious Affairs on 26 June 1990. The application was then sent to Moscow for the Russian Republic and the all-important Soviet Union approval. All this was essential for the Church's registration in Leningrad to become legal.

In a letter, President Iurii Terebenin recalled his spiritual growth and his part in the struggle to obtain registration for the Church in Russia:

> My father was a member of the Communist Party, but my grandmother was a true believer, and I was secretly baptized in my infancy. I did not become a good Christian, although I visited the Orthodox Church on major holidays because of the beautiful services and choir there. I did not know how and did not want to pray, nor did I fast; basically I was not a believer. At that time in our country militant atheism was propagated.
>
> In 1988 I had a very bad accident. The doctor in charge was astonished that I had even survived. According to him I should have died while still in the ambulance, or during the operation, or during the two weeks following the operation. But I was fortunate and God saved me. A year later my whole family went to visit my wife's friend Ilona Djord in Budapest, Hungary. At that time, Ilona and her son were already members of The Church of Jesus Christ of Latter-day Saints. On the day we arrived we immediately went to church.
>
> This was the first time I had been to a worship service in a church where there were no icons or professional priests—in other words, where there were no attributes of an Orthodox or Catholic service. We didn't understand a word of the service, but were filled with delight. As I now understand, we felt the presence of the Holy Ghost at that meeting. From that day the missionaries began to share the discussions with us. This is how it was done: the missionaries taught the lesson in Hungarian or English, and Ilona or her son, Miklosh Bekefi, translated into Russian for us. And so it was during all of the discussions. A

missionary from Germany, Rafael Meyer, with whom we still correspond to this day, often worked with us. . . .

Just before our departure for the USSR, on July 1, 1989, we were baptized. Miklosh Bekefi baptized my wife, Liudmila, and me, and a missionary from the U.S. baptized my daughter, Anna. After our return to the USSR we didn't advertise our baptism at first, as at that time it was not [politically] safe to do so. After the visits to Leningrad by Finnish Church members, the Ojala and Laitinen families, however, investigators began to meet on Sundays (and later on both Saturdays and Sundays) in our apartment at Sovetskaia Street 4, or sometimes at someone else's home. We took the lessons from Leena Laitinen, and everybody had many questions.

Oh, how many people passed through our apartment! Part of them remained and in time were baptized and became active members of the Church. . . . On September 16, 1989, President Dennis Neuenschwander and an attorney from the Church visited us in Leningrad and gave me the Aaronic Priesthood. On April 26, 1990, President Ringger and Apostle Nelson visited our city. During our visit, I told them that according to Soviet law, a petition of twenty members of the Church was needed for the registration of the Church in the USSR. . . . After this visit President Ringger came to Leningrad several times and on September 13, 1990, our Church in Leningrad was registered for the first time in Russian history. . . . The day we received the registration documents was an unforgettable day for all of us.

But even before the registration, much work here had already been done by missionaries from the U.S.: President and Sister Mecham and our first young missionaries, Kevin Dexter, David Reagan, Kurt Wood, and Sisters [Heidi] Moffett and [Stefanie] Condie. Now, sometime later, I see what a tremendous work we all accomplished, and how we did it relatively quickly. We had such enthusiasm and fervor. The Lord granted us this strength and joy in the work. I am convinced of it.[6]

The Church members in Leningrad soon began to hold their Sunday meetings at Novgorodskaia Street 9, in a house of culture at which films and videos were shown. President Terebenin had arranged for this facility on very favorable terms and developed cordial relations with the management. They allowed us to hold occasional meetings and conferences there on days other than Sunday, a rare privilege. The walls displayed Communist slogans, such as "We Will Implement the Decisions of the XXVII Party

Congress" and "Long Live Friendship among Fraternal Socialist States." The auditorium seemed oppressive with heavy drapes that could not be opened. Nonetheless, during the next two years, scores of warm and enlightening meetings were held there.

Vladimir Batianov, among the early leaders of the Church in Leningrad, recounted the events leading to his conversion and the concerns he and other early members felt:

> Before becoming acquainted with the Church, I had no religious convictions. At the time, the Soviet Union was still an atheistic country. We were raised in the spirit of Marxism and Leninism. I was a Pioneer and a member of the Komsomol, although I did not join the Communist Party. . . . Later, with the onset of "new times," we began to become acquainted with various religions. . . .
>
> I knew very little about the Mormons. Once when I was about sixteen, there was a television broadcast on the state of Utah and the Mormons that live there. The information was rather stereotyped—that polygamy was practiced and so on—the kind of information that will follow Mormons for some time. And I learned other things from the stories of Conan Doyle. That was all the information I had about Mormons.
>
> In 1989, my wife and I received permission to travel to Poland. There we met a couple by the name of Czeslaw and Janina Mazur in Warsaw. As we talked with them, it became evident that they were religious people, but they weren't Catholics, as are most Poles. They invited us to their church meeting. That first Sunday we went with them. It turned out to be the Mormon Church. . . . While in Poland we received both a Book of Mormon and a Bible in Russian. We were very happy to get these books. When we returned to Leningrad, I began to read them. . . .
>
> When I started reading the Book of Mormon, I understood it simply as the record of a people. For me it was appealing merely as a history. I was interested in a book that might tell about the origin of the American civilization. That is how I understood the book at that time.
>
> In 1990 we received a telephone call from Iurii Terebenin. He had been given our phone number and address. He invited us to a church service in Leningrad. At the time they were being held in apartments. On the 20th of January, a Saturday, we went to the meeting. . . .
>
> We began meeting regularly on Saturdays and Sundays. On Saturdays the meetings were more like lessons, and on Sundays

were sacrament services. We met many interesting people. We talked a great deal, often disputing, but had very many enlightening discussions. Some of these people did not remain in the Church, but our association with them was very beneficial. We began to accept the life of Jesus Christ. As we continually became acquainted with more people and missionaries, we saw that these people differed from us in that, well, they were people of light. It was very pleasant to associate with them. There were no conflicts. . . . This warm feeling amidst these people was perhaps our main confirmation. I had read Dostoyevsky and Tolstoy, and knew the Orthodox view that people suffer in life, and that for these sufferings they will inherit the kingdom of God. But from the [LDS] Church's point of view, we are here not only to suffer, but also to learn to be happy. Over time, this and the warm feeling we felt through our bodies as we began to pray, formed a major part of our testimony and the reason we were baptized. We were baptized in Finland. I was baptized first and then baptized my wife and several of my friends. . . .

Before joining the Church when my wife and I would reflect on life and why we were living, we'd say, "How can it be this way? We'll live and live, and then die and decay, and nothing will remain of us." Sure, from the perspective of Communist morality we'd heard "Our children, our deeds, memory of us remain." But, still, that wouldn't be for long. When one or two generations pass, we would be forgotten. Think of the millions who lived during the last century. Maybe only a thousand or so are still remembered. I constantly felt distress over this.

When we joined the Church, this distress vanished. First, we understood that our life ceases only in relation to our physical bodies. Second, we can learn to be happy during this life and continue that happiness in the next life with our Father in Heaven in his kingdom. An entirely different perception of life arose. Life is not arbitrary. Our path to God may be winding and hard, but we now see the goal. This helps us in many spheres, even in the upbringing of our children. Now there is a goal toward which we all are striving as a whole family, each individually and all together.[7]

Viacheslav Efimov, another early Leningrad member (who has served as branch, district, and, since July 1995, mission president in Ekaterinburg), portrayed his and his family's quest for spiritual truth:

I, Viacheslav Ivanovich Efimov, was born 27 April 1948 in Leningrad. My parents, Aleksandra and Ivan, met in a military

*Viacheslav and Galina
Efimov at the Stockholm
Sweden Temple*

hospital where my father was recovering from a serious injury at
the end of the war in 1945. After he was discharged from the
army they came to Leningrad, where they settled down. Within
five years my father passed away at the age of thirty-five due to
complications from the injury sustained in the war. My mother
and I were left alone. Religion was always present in our family,
as the only thing left for us was to rely on God.

I learned to pray from the time I was five years old. When I
wanted treats, candy or cookies, I would do as my mother told
me and whisper something. I would pray and ask God for food
as I stood next to a store window with its tasty treats. Mother
would use her money to buy me candy, and cry because she was

not able to do so more often. That was how I learned about prayer and my mother's love. I had a very difficult childhood and adolescence. I went to work early on—at the age of fifteen. I had to bring money home because my mother was exhausted from working at two jobs so that I would have food and clothing.

I worked in a factory and went to school in the evenings. We had received a copy of the New Testament from my grandmother. As I read, my thoughts were directed to understanding the word of God. But I was not successful. I read the magazine *Science and Religion* where there were passages from the Bible. As I had been baptized at the age of five into the Orthodox Church, I really wanted to have a knowledge of God.

And there in the journal where they attacked religion, I found out about its truth. I later served in the army and then was married in 1971 when I was 23. My wife, Galina Petrovna Efimova, was born 14 April 1947 in Uglich, an ancient Russian city. She was raised in a military family and moved from city to city. Upon completion of his service, her father stayed in Leningrad to live. She was an atheist. No one in her family ever talked about God because they were Communists. She lived in a family that was complete with parents, brothers and sisters, in contrast to me, an only child. . . .

Our daughter Tamara was born in 1972 and our son Piotr in 1978. When Tamara was five years old I had her baptized in the Orthodox Church together with my wife, Galina, who was thirty years old. We began to attend the Orthodox Church, light candles, pray to icons and to the Savior, but we always had the feeling that God did not hear us, that we were hardly noticeable among all the gold, icons, and beauty of the churches. We would go home disappointed, where we would sit down at the table and drink a glass of vodka, and start to feel warmer. . . . That's how it was for fifteen years. We would sin and repent, then sin again. . . .

In the spring of 1990, in March, while at her friend's house, my daughter became acquainted with missionaries from The Church of Jesus Christ of Latter-day Saints, Elders Kurt Wood and Bill McKane. I did not go into the room for the first discussion because I wondered what these young men could tell me about God . . . ; after all, God had always been a part of me. But that which I heard at the following discussions gave me the opportunity to receive answers to my own questions and, most important, to understand that God loves each of us—we are his children and he has given us a Savior, his Son Jesus Christ, and each of us will be resurrected.

From that moment our life changed. We became a family. Although we had lived in the same house, we were each involved in our own activities and spent little time together. The cares of everyday life drew us apart. Then for the first time in ten to twelve years we began to spend more time together; we began to read the Bible and the Book of Mormon, which the missionaries had given to us. For three months we waited for an answer to our prayers and then we made our decision to be baptized. On June 9, 1990, we were baptized into The Church of Jesus Christ of Latter-day Saints as a family. . . .

After our baptism, the relationships in our family greatly improved: we became more attentive to each other, more patient, and have tried to overcome anger and other negative qualities that were present in us before. We began to spend more time together. We would gather in the evenings and would read the Bible and the Book of Mormon and would then discuss what we had read. Sometime later, I received the Aaronic Priesthood from leaders of the Church, so that I could be the patriarch in my family. I was granted the right to bless family members, give encouragement when needed, conduct family home evenings, and act in the name of the Lord, bless the food, and also perform other ordinances in the name of Jesus Christ.

We attached great importance to holding family home evenings. We happily and enthusiastically prepared for them, since we could completely devote ourselves to God on these evenings. We would begin with a hymn, then I would ask someone to pray. As a rule our daughter Tamara would start the lesson, as she was our family teacher and she would prepare lessons from the New Testament or the Book of Mormon. Then I would read a chapter from the scriptures and we would discuss it. We would then sing a closing hymn and pray.

After we had finished the first hour of the evening, we would then proceed to dinner, setting the table and making it as festive as possible. My wife and daughter took charge here. On days when we set out for walks or went to our dacha [summer cottage] we would utilize our travel time so that each of us could share a favorite verse or chapter from the scriptures. That's how our summer went. In the fall, we were given callings in the branch. Since my son had turned twelve, he received the Aaronic Priesthood and became a deacon. I was called to be the second counselor in the branch presidency. My wife, Galina, became the branch librarian and my daughter, Tamara, [was called] to be a teacher in the Relief Society. Piotr helped during the sacrament: he passed the blessed bread and water. We began to serve our brothers and sisters. And so 1990 came to a close, having brought us the joy of our spiritual birth.

In conclusion, I would like to say that we all need to make efforts so that our home on earth will be a place where we can learn and prepare to meet our Heavenly Father, who wants us, his spirit children, having received a mortal body for our own perfection and having experienced this mortal life, to return to him not alone, but together with our families, our parents, children, and relatives, and to continue that joyful life in the home of our Father in Heaven.[8]

In Estonia, our children and Joan had borne their testimonies in Finnish, but on their first visit to Leningrad and other Russian cities they did so in Russian, receiving effusive appreciation from the members. Joan and I had long observed Russian adoration of children. Owing largely to the ravages of the Second World War and subsequent Stalinist terror, most of a generation of women had not married or raised families. Russians of all ages, but especially these women, lavish concern on others' children. They feel vicariously fulfilled when children appear healthy and aspire to do well. Largely because of economic pressures, even today, most Russian city families have only one child. Often Russian LDS members would call our family "prosperous," not because of material wealth, but because of our five children.

On this first trip to Leningrad I baptized Jon, our youngest child, in Lake Kavgolovo. Jon and I were somewhat concerned about the water being cold until we waded into the lake. The rocks on the lake's bottom were so jagged that we scarcely noticed the water temperature. Jon had the honor to be among five baptized that beautiful Saturday, 21 July. The missionaries had organized a fine baptismal and confirmation program and later a branch picnic nearby.

Considerable time was required to find wood and prepare coals for cooking, so we had the leisure to become acquainted with our fellow missionaries and several branch members. I also enjoyed meeting Pavel Alenichev, who had never joined the Church but had made a vital contribution to its establishment through his interpreting and translating skills and wise counsel. He continued to be an appreciated asset as he translated the missionary discussions into Russian. Joan provided a good perspective on this visit to the Leningrad Branch:

Leningrad branch picnic. Anton Skripko (with sunglasses on head) tends the fire

Leningrad has over eighty members, but the summer plays havoc with attendance. The missionaries don't know if members are inactive, working, or just away in the countryside. Every Sunday there are many new investigators who appear and the missionaries are always completely booked up with appointments. . . . It was wonderful to hear the church hymns sung in Russian, and the spirit in their meetings is strong. In Relief Society they sit in a circle and introduce each person every week because there is always such a turnover. Some people tell about their conversions and though the lesson time is short, they learn from each other. One lady visited in Washington, D.C., for a month and was taught the missionary lessons there. Another was from Tashkent and had four of the lessons so far in Leningrad. She was sure that her friends at home would be interested in the Church and wanted to take material back to them. She also invited the others to come and visit her there. The branch president and his wife joined the Church a year ago while visiting outside of the Soviet Union and are now hoping to make arrangements to go to Stockholm to the temple.[9]

What a contrast it was to attend meetings the last Sunday of July in Haaga, Espoo Ward, Helsinki Stake. The modest meeting house seemed opulent after our rented facilities. There was a tasteful chapel with a good supply of Finnish hymnals (in our mission we used photocopied booklets containing a few hymns), cultural hall, library with Church books in Finnish, baptismal font, family history facility, classroom space, and kitchen.

As a Finnish missionary I had visited the Saints in Haaga in 1962. The Haaga branch then appeared outwardly far less grand. They met in a rented school and had fewer amenities and materials. Yet the Spirit felt among them was the same then as today and the same one felt in the meetings of the new Soviet branches.

10

AUGUST 1990

In the first week of August, President Jussi Kemppainen and I flew to Moscow, the capital of the Soviet Union and city of more than nine million people. Through the considerable efforts of Olga Smolianova, we met with Leonid Kolesnikov, chairman of the Russian Republic Council on Religious Affairs, and his deputy Eduard Gatseptian, head of the section for Protestant churches, among which our church was included. We wanted to become acquainted with them and offer our assistance with the application for registration of the Church in Leningrad.

After exchanging perspectives and experiences from our common profession of university teaching, the chairman spoke of our application. He was noncommittal, requesting additional copies of printed Church material already provided from Leningrad and seeking a clarification of our purposes for Sunday Schools. He was concerned that instructing children openly in a Sunday School setting would confuse children taught atheism during the week in schools. Would Sunday Schools be better for adults only? I emphasized that the values we seek to develop in our members are most effectively taught from an early age. He agreed politely but without enthusiasm.

After the meeting, Mr. Gatseptian accompanied us down the stairs and said that he was pleased to have the assignment of processing our church's application. Ours was, he volunteered, the first application for a *"new* (post-1917) Protestant" church to have reached the final stages of consideration. He predicted the registration would be granted. Apparently, he had already recommended approval of the registration; however, it seemed obvious that the Russian Republic was hesitant to commit itself openly before receiving permission from the USSR Council on Religious Affairs through its chairman, Iurii Khristoradnov.

We tried several times to call on Chairman Khristoradnov. At that time, he was heavily involved in drafting and promoting a new law on freedom of conscience. I had wanted to verify with him that his office had all necessary materials to consider our church's application for registration in Leningrad. An assistant assured me that everything was in order.

At that time, Russian and American Latter-day Saints in Moscow were meeting in Dohn Thornton's apartment on Leninskii Prospekt 45. Daniel Souders, a U.S. Embassy employee who was now a manager at Aeromar, a firm catering international Aeroflot flights, had served faithfully as group leader. He was experiencing extreme job pressures. I released Brother Souders and extended a call to Albert Walling, manager of Huntsman Chemical in Moscow, to become the new group leader. He selected Dohn Thornton as his first assistant.

On Fast Sunday, 5 August, I first attended Sunday services at Dohn Thornton's. Approximately thirty people were crowded into his apartment living room. The meetings were well organized, but the warm spirit of Christlike love is what I particularly remember. Galina Goncharova was present that day and later wrote this account of her life and conversion:

> The circumstances of my birth were remarkable. On the day of my birth, my mother sent my older brother to the hospital for an ambulance because contractions were beginning. No one was at home, there were thundershowers outside, and my brother had been gone for a long time. My mother began to feel terrible. She started to cry and began praying, when suddenly the door opened and in walked my grandmother—my father's mother. She lived very far away, and she would rarely come for a visit. She helped Mother with the delivery, I was born, and everything necessary was done. The ambulance came and they took me and my mother away to the hospital only after I had been swaddled and my life and my mother's were no longer in danger. When I was younger, I used to wonder how it was that I survived such an experience, and now I know that God works through other people. . . .
>
> My father had a common education and worked in a factory. He had grown up in a large peasant family. . . . My mother was a simple working woman. She had two years of schooling in a parochial school. Her father was a Russian Orthodox priest, but

after the Revolution, they put him in jail and no one heard from him afterwards. As a result, my mother was always afraid of speaking about religion in the home. My parents were very good people, despite our poverty and unhappiness. Somewhat later, my father became an alcoholic, and as a result we suffered a great deal, both as a family and as individuals. But as I now know, God is merciful to all of his children. . . .

My relationship to faith [as a young woman] was, first, fear and uncertainty. Second, school and even all society taught that there is no God and that people are highly developed apes, and so on. But I often asked myself the same questions over and over. I don't know why, but I always wondered where I and others came from, why there is sorrow and happiness, why there are good people and bad people. My mother often said that God sees everything and that he knows each one of us. She would say such things very quietly, always worrying that someone might hear her. In school we were all, of course, Pioneers and Komsomol members. At all the parent-teacher meetings, our teachers would reprimand and criticize any parents who told their children about God. Thus, I found that my life had two sides to it—one at home and the other at school. But despite all this, my soul yearned for something.

I found myself wanting to leave home because things there were not always good. And thus, I met my future husband and got married. He is a very kind and good person, but after a little while following our sons' birth, I began to notice that my husband was starting to drink a lot more than before. And our family started to become more and more like the one I was in as a child. At first, I did all that I could to insure that our lives might be happy. I hadn't known, however, that alcoholism could be a terrifying and burdensome sickness for the whole family—spiritually, emotionally and physically.

Our family life had turned into a nightmare. Our two sons grew to adolescence, and our family relationships seemed to be getting only worse. My sons began to drink and smoke, and it seemed as though my sorrow would be endless. My teenage boys would spend all their free time out on the streets with others who would also smoke and drink. I continuously blamed my husband for all our problems and demanded that he do something about his drinking problem. It was all in vain.

In those years of despair I turned to both the hospital and the police for help. I even started going to church. I stood for two hours in a cathedral. I understood nothing and left the church in the same disconcerted state that I was in before, only to return to my nightmarish home. All I could think about was, "Why is God punishing me like this? What for?" I felt worse and worse. At the end of 1988, I found out about Alcoholics Anonymous, a program for alcoholics and their families. This wonderful program helped me to understand and accept God as a friend, and thus I began to grow spiritually.

A year later, I met an American [Dohn Thornton] who was working in Moscow and had started coming to AA meetings for the friends and relatives of alcoholics. After about a year, this friend began telling me about God and about his church. He felt as though I needed to find out more about God, so he brought me a Book of Mormon in September of 1989 and urged me to read it. . . . I now know that God brought me to the AA program and that he sent this good person to me. I now know that God loves every single one of his children and that he doesn't cause them suffering.

I began reading the Book of Mormon and I started receiving answers to my questions: "Where have I come from?," "Why am I here on earth?" and "Where am I going after I die?" As I read the Book of Mormon, I was filled with warmth and light. My fear of God began to be replaced with gratitude and love. In December of 1989, my friend Dohn invited me to my first LDS Church meeting. The meeting took place in his apartment. There were only about eight or ten people in attendance: one girl from Moscow, me, a woman from the Baltic states, and several Americans.

I was most amazed by how everyone at the meeting spoke about God. They spoke of him as a friend and savior, and said that he lives and helps each of us. And that meant he helps me. Two hours went by, and it seemed to me as though I had had a brief and yet marvelous dream. There was a unique, warm and friendly spirit in the room. Now I know it was the Holy Ghost who had been with us. Everyone there was so warm and kind to me that my heart was filled with wonderful feelings which I had never before experienced. It seemed almost as if I had grown wings and was able to fly home.

When I walked into my home, I began telling my family about the meeting, and my husband and children immediately noticed that something had happened to me. From that moment, I started going to these meetings every Sunday at ten o'clock. . . .

It was then that my friend said he felt I was ready to be baptized, but that first I would need to have an interview with the group leader—Daniel Souders. I was very worried that he

The Goncharov family: mother, Klavdiia Bocharova; daughter-in-law, Galina; Galina's husband, Aleksandr

wouldn't allow me to be baptized or that maybe I wouldn't know something I needed to know before being baptized. Dohn put my mind at ease, and the day of my baptism was set for the ninth of June, 1990. . . .

[On the day of my baptism] it was a cold morning and the sky was filled with storm clouds. My elder son, Sasha, cheered me up and came with me to the baptism. More people came to the baptism than I could have ever imagined. When we got to the river we took some time picking out just the right spot. As soon as we found the place and got everything set up, the sky cleared and the warm, bright sunlight shone down on us. God was showing his joy at my baptism into the true Church. Everything was wonderful. The water was cold, but I couldn't really feel the cold—God's love kept me warm inside. I wore my long white wedding dress for the baptism. God made me so beautiful and so happy. All of my friends stood close by and were also very happy about my baptism.

After being completely immersed in water, I stepped out of the river a thoroughly new person. My body felt free and my thoughts were joyful and enlightened. The fear and despair of my life left me completely. In its place was hope for a new and happy life on earth, and eternal life with my Father in Heaven. I knew then, as I know now, that there is still much to learn: kindness, honesty, and diligence. I also know I must be a worthy example for my sons and others I might chance to meet along my path. I am no longer alone. God is helping me, and I have an elder brother, Jesus Christ, who loves me and who shed his blood for me. I am very grateful to my Heavenly Father for the plan of salvation.

With time, my elder son and my husband started coming to our church meetings, and then the missionaries arrived. They were sent by our Heavenly Father. They have done a wonderful job helping my sons and my husband to better understand God and his Church. They are Elder [Heath] Thompson, Elder [Adam] West, Sister [Zdzislawa] Chudyba, Sister [Stefanie] Condie and many others. My elder son was baptized in February of 1991, and my husband was baptized in May of 1991. My younger son was baptized in July of 1992, and my older sister was baptized in August of that same year. My mother-in-law and my husband's nephew also became members of The Church of Jesus Christ of Latter-day Saints. It is the Lord's great blessing that we now gather together not only for important holidays three or four times a year as we once did, but also for Sunday scripture reading. We help each other, and in doing so, we have become happier and more loving. . . .

About twenty of my friends have been baptized into our Church and I am so happy to see how their lives are also changing, and to see how the Lord blesses all of his children.

After my baptism and confirmation, I served as Sunday School teacher. I started teaching on the Sunday after my baptism, June 17, 1990. I was very worried, but a priesthood blessing gave me strength and inspiration. I learned much by teaching others. After about a year, I began teaching the investigator class. This has strengthened my testimony and has helped me to be more patient and humble. In the beginning of 1992, I was called to serve as the Relief Society president in the North Branch, and later in the Timiriazevskii Branch. The Lord then blessed me with a new calling in the Timiriazevskii Branch: I am now the Primary president. I am so happy in my new calling, and I really love my young sisters and brothers.

My testimony grows with the baptism of every new member. I know that God lives, that Jesus Christ is my Savior and Redeemer, that Joseph Smith is a prophet of God and that he also suffered for the restoration of the Church. The Book of Mormon is true and contains the fulness of the gospel of Jesus Christ. I know that there is a living prophet who guides The Church of Jesus Christ of Latter-day Saints in our day. I express my gratitude to all those brothers and sisters in America and other countries who have prayed for Russia, that the Church of Jesus Christ might finally come to us.[1]

Elder Scott Dyer provided a glimpse into Sister Goncharova's wisdom and firm support of her fellow leaders:

> As young men and women we had the responsibility to teach adults how to live the gospel and essentially to run the Church. The difficulty, though, was that most of us actually had not been mature adults in the gospel. The story of the young stripling warriors in the Book of Mormon often came to my mind at this time. We had to remember the words of our mothers and fathers and especially their actions. We had instruction from our mission president and other Church leaders, but in "on the spot" practical Church questions, I found myself asking, What did my father do in such situations? . . .
>
> Working together in the branch council, we were all discussing the advice and instructions of the branch president. The branch president, excused, had left an outline of actions on a particular issue. Some of the branch leaders did not fully understand or agree with the branch president. Even I personally, but silently, did not fully agree with the proposed plan. Sister Goncharova spoke up and said that there was not anything improper about the plan, simply that it was not exactly what we would have done. She continued that he was our leader and a righteous man, and she would fully support him. We all learned a lesson about supporting our leaders that day. I grew by watching Sister Goncharova.[2]

In August I visited the Leningrad City Council on Religious Affairs chairman Igor Vyshchepan and deputy chairman Nikolai Kirov. They told me that copies of the Book of Mormon, *Gospel Principles,* and other materials were urgently needed in Moscow by the USSR Council on Religious Affairs before further study of our application could be undertaken. I telephoned Brother Walling in Moscow, who immediately delivered the materials.

I also learned that the man primarily responsible for our application at the USSR level was Evgenii Chernetsov, who administered the government section dealing with Protestant churches. He was the person I met on subsequent trips to Moscow. I developed great respect for Mr. Chernetsov and his deputy, Konstantin Blazhenov.

Mr. Vyshchepan apparently had been charged with finding

answers to several questions troubling the USSR Council: Is tithing voluntary or compulsory? Who pays for a missionary's expenses? Will returned missionaries serve in the armed forces where such service is required of all young men? Is it true that the Mormon Church has a disproportionately high number of United States senators and congressmen and considerable influence in the American government?

Several days later while jogging in Helsinki early on the morning of 16 August, I earnestly prayed the entire time for my family, for the missionaries and the members, for the Estonians and Russians in general, and for relief from other concerns. Only one and a half months into my mission, I already felt overwhelmed and, too often, discouraged. I was apprehensive that I might hinder more than advance the Lord's work in Russia and Estonia, and I poured my heart out to the Lord. Later as I drove to the mission office, I had what I can only term a vision. It must have lasted only a very few seconds for I continued to drive the car without accident.

It seemed to me that I glimpsed eternity behind the veil and perceived a large group of people in two or more long lines, all facing in my direction. I immediately recognized Wayne Olaveson, a favorite cousin who had been killed within the last year in a farm accident, my grandparents Ray and Thelma Browning and Ole and Lula Hansen, standing before the host of others, who, I sensed, were my departed ancestors, although I do not recall distinguishing other individuals.

Though not hearing distinct words, I understood clearly that these ancestors were concerned for me and us, would do all possible to bear me up, and would help me here and my family at home in ways I could not conceive of or accomplish myself.

As I contemplated this experience, Doctrine and Covenants 84:88 came to my mind: "I will be on your right hand and on your left, and my Spirit shall be in your hearts, and mine angels round about you, to bear you up." Suddenly this passage acquired far greater meaning. Until now I had either not thought at all about who these angels might be or had considered them faceless and impersonal. Suddenly it all seemed so reasonable. Who would desire more to help than those loving family members who feel an ancestor's empathy for a descendant? What comfort to know I was not alone with my inadequacy.

From that day I felt more confident and tranquil, fortified by this broader perspective and ardent reassurance. I am confident several within my family and the Church wrote profoundly encouraging notes and letters in response to heavenly inspiration. Often at times of tension or adversity a letter arrived from a friend or even a stranger assuring me that I was in their thoughts and prayers and providing me relief. One General Authority in particular wrote several heartening notes, each of which lessened my anxiety while lifting and reassuring me. I soon discovered that other missionaries and members were experiencing trials and distractions similar to my own and were comforted by hearing of my experience.

11

SEPTEMBER 1990

In September the Church was notified that the first registration (legal recognition) in Russia had been granted. President Hans B. Ringger, David Farnsworth, and I had gone to Moscow to meet with USSR Council on Religious Affairs officials and with Church members. During a dinner following a fireside at the Thornton apartment, I telephoned council offices to verify the schedule for the next day's meetings and spoke with Mr. Konstantin Blazhenov.

With evident pleasure, he told me that the Leningrad LDS Church registration had been approved and documents signed on 13 September, six days before. I was elated and thanked him for his assistance. Elder Ringger, who had just spoken about the purpose of the Church being to bring happiness, now shared with those gathered his immense joy and gratitude in seeing The Church of Jesus Christ of Latter-day Saints officially recognized in a major Russian city.

Approval in Leningrad meant that the Church itself had been rigorously examined and approved at the all-Russia and all-Union levels. Future applications from cities within the Soviet Union could be expeditiously approved. That of which so many had dreamed and for which they had unstintingly labored and prayed had finally become reality.

The next day, 20 September, President Ringger, David Farnsworth, Olga Smolianova, Andrei Kostin (a university friend of Olga's baptized in August), and I met in the offices of the USSR Council of Religious Affairs with Mr. Evgenii Chernetsov, Mr. Blazhenov, a *Moscow News* newspaper reporter, and a writer for the journal *Science and Religion.*

At the meeting Elder Ringger explored how the registration might affect acquiring meetinghouse facilities, printing Church materials, receiving and sending missionaries, and training leaders

*Early Leningrad
member and branch
president Iurii Terebenin
exhibiting Leningrad
LDS Church registration*

at meetings in Frankfurt. He skillfully answered reporters' questions about distinguishing features of the Church and its aspirations in the Soviet Union.

Finally, President Ringger and David Farnsworth presented Mr. Chernetsov with a detailed commentary on the draft version of the law on freedom of conscience and religious organizations being considered by the legislature. Mr. Chernetsov expressed appreciation for the suggestions. He regretted they were three weeks too late to be considered for adoption but assured us the suggestions would be helpful when the legislature considered the law for revision.

During the month, another very happy event occurred. On 25 September, Elder Dale and Sister Rene Warner from Ogden arrived in Helsinki to serve in the mission office. I quickly extended their spheres of responsibility to mission administration and Leningrad leadership training for our new members. Elder Warner had served as a stake president in Ogden. Over the next year and a half, they served with exemplary vigor, diligence, and good humor in support of every dimension of the mission.

Much of September was devoted to "work in the trenches." Joan began the very large monthly task of entering data into the computer for branch membership lists with telephone numbers, addresses, birth dates, baptismal dates, gender, and priesthood offices, where applicable.

Joan and I prepared Russian translations of the Young Women Values and Personal Progress program. I compiled and translated job descriptions of principal branch callings and typical agendas for Sunday meetings. I also reviewed and approved *Ensign* material being translated by a capable friend of the Church in Vyborg to provide teachers and speakers with current materials.

In addition, Konrad Nagele came from Frankfurt to meet with city architects and planning officials in Vyborg and Tallinn. His purpose was to explore possibilities for acquiring meetinghouse facilities. In Moscow, Al Walling arranged for me to meet with a group of very generous volunteers attempting to teach skills and provide work for the disabled, an especially disadvantaged class of people in Russia. They hoped to receive moral and modest financial support from the Church.

In Vyborg Sister Nadezhda Martaller played a helpful role in the growth of the Church. She recorded the following account of her spiritual strivings, conversion, and endurance:

> I was born and grew up in a village, far away from the nearest city. My parents were married after they each already had three children, and I was the only child they had together. . . .
>
> In this village I was baptized by Old Believers. The Orthodox Church was divided during the reign of the Tsarina Sofia, the sister of Peter I. The Old Believers were banished from their homes, and they burned themselves in churches as a sign of protest. Those who did not renounce their beliefs were forced to flee to the Urals and to Siberia. They lived in harmony; they did not drink or smoke, and had large families. They did not accept outsiders, however, as they feared for their faith. So I grew up in such a village, though my parents were not Old Believers. All that I had that was good came from there, from

these people, and from the nature that surrounded us. If you only knew how beautiful it is there! In this village no one worked on Sunday, my mother taught me prayers, and in the evening I always prayed, though I didn't understand why. In school they taught us that there was no God, but we wore both a crucifix and a red neckerchief [for Pioneer children sponsored by the Communist Party] around our necks. Of course, that's awful, but the Lord is merciful towards children.

When I left to go to school in the city at the age of fifteen, I entered an entirely different world, a cruel world. I got married when I was eighteen, and my son was born when I was twenty-one. . . . My husband became an alcoholic, and all my efforts led to nothing. After enduring thirteen years together we were divorced. During all these years I prayed to the Lord, but sporadically. That is, when things were difficult, I would pray and ask for help, but when things got better, it was as if they had taken care of themselves. I had my son baptized into the Orthodox Church, despite the fact that at the time there were few who were doing this, or even believed in God. And when my father died we had an Orthodox Church burial service for him.

After divorcing my husband, I often traveled throughout the country, and wherever I was, I searched for church buildings. Be it in Moscow, Leningrad, Kiev, or Tallinn, I would enjoy being there. I really didn't know the scriptures, as there was no place you could even get them. Do you know how I studied them? I would get political literature and fiction in which there was some mention of the Bible and I would read it; that is how I found out about the contents of the Bible. I would go to museums and look at pictures that were painted on biblical themes. Though it was a strange way to learn the scriptures, I had no other way and I really wanted to find out about them. The first books of the New Testament appeared in conjunction with the millennial anniversary of the baptism of Russia, and of course I bought a copy immediately.

The church in my city was located far away from where I lived. After all, there were hardly any churches, and where there was one it was usually on the city outskirts. So in order to get to a service I had to wake up at five in the morning just to make it there, but even this didn't stop me. At that time I was already searching for the Lord. Although not everyone could understand this, several people as a result actually turned to me for help. Nevertheless this was a very difficult period in my life, as I was still quite young at that time and it was impossible not to notice the world around me. With no knowledge of the Lord's commandments and without the support of the priesthood, I made many, many mistakes. I remember every one of these sins; and maybe this is strange, but I know all of my sins, and although I have been baptized and have repented, it is very humiliating and painful for me to remember them.

It was at that time that I suddenly decided to leave the city where my mother and brother lived, where I had a good job, an apartment, and friends. Nobody understood me at all; my mother and brother would not help me and would not speak to me. But I left anyway and went to Vyborg, where I didn't know one single person, where I didn't yet have a job, and where I had a very small apartment. I imagine that as you read this, you will think that I am somewhat of an adventuress. In reality I am not a decisive person and when I undertook this, I didn't understand how it would all work out. Now that my son and I are in the Church, I am beginning to understand that it was the Lord guiding me. He wanted my son to be with me and for us both to come into his church. Of course the Lord did not abandon me. I got a job and my son went to school, and I even began making friends. Now I know that the Lord "giveth no commandment . . . save he shall prepare a way" for us.

In Vyborg there was a church next to my apartment building, and of course I went to services there. At that time in Vyborg almost no one went to church; sometimes no more than five people came. But my soul sought counsel from the Lord, and although I did not know how to pray, he heard me, as he hears all people—good and bad—and loves us all.

Within a year, my mother died, and I felt guilty and suffered greatly because of this. I decided that I would go to church every week and light a candle in memory of her. Mother died in September. In December my friend Liudmila Bezikova went to Finland for a sports competition, and there her acquaintance Nellie Jäkkö presented her with a Book of Mormon. Liudmila gave this book to me, as she was far removed from religion at that time. But having read the Book of Mormon, I found nothing of interest in it, only wars and contentions. The Lord did not open my eyes. I recognized only the Bible.

But in February 1990 we were invited to a meeting with some American missionaries at the city library. Of course it was interesting for us to see Finns and Americans, and I was eager to find out who these Mormons were and what they wanted here in Russia when we had our own Orthodox Church. The Kemppainen and Jäkkö families and Elders Webster and Leavitt came to the meeting. Of course the size of their families and their love for each other surprised us all. We asked questions and they answered them. Everybody present felt a sense of joy. This meeting was on February 27, 1990, and on March 16 the first public service was held at Music School Number 2. Within a week the first pair of missionaries, Elder Stratov and Elder Webster, and the first mission president, President Mecham, came to Vyborg. And something compelled me to come every Sunday for the service.

I should tell you that since March 1990, I have missed church at most a few times, and then only because I have been on vacation. Even when I have been sick I have come to church and have felt only joy. I tried to bring my son and my friend Liudmila with me to every meeting. At first this was very difficult, but the missionaries worked very hard, and the Jäkkö family did not give up on us. Liudmila accepted their efforts with sincerity. Our first missionaries, Elder Stratov and Elder Webster—oh, how they worked! Although Elder Webster did not know Russian and sometimes even fell asleep (we'd laugh then, and he'd get very flustered), but with the help of the Holy Ghost he learned Russian very quickly, and I love him very much. I received so much attention, sympathy, and help from them. . . .

And so on April 15, Liudmila decided to be baptized; she was the first woman to be baptized in Vyborg. It was still very cold out, but she decided to get baptized in the Gulf of Finland. Everything went well and nobody fell ill. The Kemppainen and Jäkkö families, Elder Webster and Elder Stratov, myself and Andrei Semionov were at the baptism. It was also on that day that Andrei Semionov received the Melchizedek Priesthood and gave the gift of the Holy Ghost to Liudmila. And that is how we began.

I was not baptized then only because I was afraid of betraying my parents; after all they were Orthodox, and I had not yet understood the missionaries' teachings about baptism for the dead. All the same the missionaries continued the discussions with me, and I felt that this was my church and that I wanted to be a part of it. I went to every church meeting.

On April 26, 1990, Apostle Nelson came to Leningrad for a conference. Although I was not yet a member of the church, I experienced the Holy Ghost's great influence. I wanted to love and help everyone; it was such a bright moment. It was heartening that so many people wanted to come to the Lord. . . . I made the decision to be baptized. But inside I still doubted and it was only when I came out of the water that I felt such a lightness and a calmness that I had never felt before, and I knew that

I had made the right choice. There were many people at the baptism, and Andrei Semionov gave me the gift of the Holy Ghost.

Only one week later, President Semionov came over and asked if I would be a Sunday School teacher. He had prayed and had received the answer that I could be the teacher. Now you know that I didn't have much knowledge at all, though I had read both the New Testament and Book of Mormon. But what could I tell people who had not even read the scriptures? It was simply awful. But Andrei Semionov said that everything would be okay. And on May 27 I was called to be the Sunday School teacher. How I would worry! I started to prepare for every lesson on Monday. I was afraid that I wouldn't be able to speak in a manner that others would understand and believe that our Father in Heaven exists, that he lives and loves us. . . .

During all of this my son was with me, but he did not want to be baptized, and he had no faith in any of this. But I wanted so much for us to come to the Lord together. Unfortunately nothing came of it, and so I then turned to the missionaries and asked that they come not to me, but to Oleg. Oleg was baptized a year after me. What a blessing this was, and what happiness it brought. But that was not all; he was not fully active—he was afraid to give talks. He would go to the services, but everything else was terrifying for him. Sergei Krushinskii helped him greatly, though he has now left the church. After the branch was divided, Oleg was called to be the branch clerk, and then also to be the president of the elders quorum. And you know how the Lord helped him? Oleg studied the scriptures, he prepared lessons, and helped men who were more than twice his age. Do you know how both men and women, not only from our branch, love him! He who was not even nineteen years old became the elders quorum president, and, thanks to the Lord, he was able to understand the importance and responsibilities of his calling. Now he is also an institute teacher. This year we are studying the Book of Mormon. And all this thanks to the Lord's concern for us. He heard my prayers, and my son and I are together. The Lord helps him in his studies; he is now completing his fourth year at the university.

A year after my baptism I was called to be the Relief Society president. This calling taught me much. As I became involved in the problems of the sisters, my own problems seemed not so great. Of course, we did not have experience or materials. I remember how Sister Browning gave me a book of Relief Society lessons in English. I was so glad. We found some girls, members of the Church, who translated them for us, and our lessons

Sisters at the Stockholm Sweden Temple (left to right): Irina Maksimova, Liudmila Bezikova, Nadezhda Martaller, and Elena Smirnova

became interesting. This was a great help. In these lessons we learned how we should help the priesthood, how to improve our homes, how to study the scriptures, and how to raise our children. All this came from the scriptures and talks from our leaders.

In the beginning not everything was easy. Several people were not able to overcome their pasts. But gradually we became more patient with each other's weaknesses. We learned to listen to priesthood leaders and to love and help each other. Visiting teaching was organized, and this helped us to better know each other, though this didn't happen immediately. At first nobody wanted to waste time on visits, and only with time did we understand how essential it was for us. We had an evening for Relief Society once a month where we learned how to dress, sew, cook, do housework, raise our children, and help our husbands. We learned how to be women and mothers. We learned patience and humility, and how to pray and to keep the commandments of our Heavenly Father. If only I could express to you all of this, but unfortunately it is not possible to tell everything. I learned as I taught others, and if it were not for help from the Lord, our missionaries, and the Jäkkö family, I would not have been able to accomplish anything. I see how our sisters have changed, and my heart is filled with joy and thankfulness to our Lord. . . .

Two-and-a-half years ago I was unemployed. You understand that Oleg was a student and I wanted him to study, but I didn't have any money and there was no one to help me. It was very difficult to find work, the city is small, firms were closing, and no one but the Lord could help me. I had no work for almost a year, and tried to eat as little as possible so that there would be more for my son.

It's necessary to know the situation in our country in order to understand the position I was in. I was working for miserly wages washing floors as a cleaning woman, but I was glad even to have this. I knew that the Lord would remember me. I recalled the words "Whom the Lord loves, he also chastens," but in particularly difficult moments I wondered, was he chastening or punishing? I prayed and asked for help. All of this affected my health, I had a nervous breakdown, and it took half a year to recover. But I think that what helped me most was not the recovery, but the blessing that President [Charles] Creel gave me. Even during those difficult days, the days of my illness, I didn't miss church once and I was with my sisters.

The Lord of course heard me, and I found work. Although it's not in the field that I had worked for twenty years, I have a job and my son can study. My son and I survived and are grateful for the support which we received from the Lord and our brothers and sisters. . . .

In April 1993 I went to the temple in Sweden. Oh, how I did not want to return to the world; I wanted so much to remain in the temple, in the house of our Lord. And if I chance to suddenly get some money, then I will surely go again, even if it takes ten years to get the money together. I was also able to get the baptisms done for my parents and my sister. I felt very relieved that I could help them. How wonderful our Church is, the Church of our Lord. . . .

Do you know how Russian Mormons differ from an ordinary Russian person? We have learned to smile. And this is simply wonderful.[1]

12

OCTOBER 1990

Because of increasing numbers, the Moscow Saints began meeting in a veterans hall at Butyrskii Val 97 in October. The facility was larger than the Thornton apartment, and at one end of the hall stood a podium and lectern. The building was not well maintained; the Church members held a clean-up activity before the first Sunday gathering.

A heroic-size bust of Lenin gazed out sternly at the congregation. Some members wanted the bust covered; others good-naturedly responded that he also could benefit by exposure to spiritual discussions. In most of our meeting facilities, Communist banners, pictures, placards, and busts adorned the podium and walls. Russians generally paid scant attention to them; they were more likely to offend or amuse foreign guests.

Brother Albert Walling now selected Daryl Gibb as an assistant group leader. Brother Gibb taught computational linguistics and conversational English at the Moscow State Linguistics University. During the year that he and his energetic Finnish-born wife, Pirkko, and their two daughters spent in Moscow, significant maturing occurred in the Church. The Gibbs and the Wallings effectively taught and exemplified gospel ideals and Church administration.

Two new Russian members of the Church also began to serve in the group leadership: Andrei Petrov and Igor Kibiriov. Brother Petrov and his wife, Elena, were baptized in Vyborg in September 1990. Andrei learned of the Church while visiting his wife and daughter at the home of Elena's parents in Vyborg, where Elena retreated each summer from the Moscow air pollution and heat. Igor Kibiriov and his wife, Tatiana, had been baptized while visiting friends in Poland and later emigrated to the United States.

Brother Petrov became a pivotal Church leader in Moscow.

*Andrei and Elena Petrov
with daughters Ania
and Katia*

Soon after his baptism he wrote a letter telling of influences in his decision to be baptized:

I first learned of the Church from a friend, a local [Vyborg] musician and composer. He spoke with such enthusiasm about its members—how everything seemed beautiful, good, and pleasant at church; how everything is glorious and one feels oneself a real person there. My wife and I became interested and started attending meetings. At our first visit it was odd to look at grown people who, as we thought, were engaged in strange behavior [congregational singing]. But gradually this passed and we began feeling good when we were with the others and singing together.

Essentially this is what I thought: the [LDS] Church is more open and more directed to the individual person than are others. God is not used to frighten people, but rather people strive to become nearer to God in order to be better themselves.

Then, I observed very beautiful families of visiting Finns where the husband and wife treat each other respectfully and the family is the basis for everything. That's what appealed to me at first.

Next, I read *Gospel Principles* and encountered a perception of the world that was whole—what took place before, what its purpose is now, and how it will all end. After I left [to return to Moscow], I read many interesting books. Not all were religious in nature, but scientific and philosophical. But everything seemed to confirm the basic points that I had found in the Book of Mormon and in *Gospel Principles*.[1]

Early in the month the Europe Area presidency transferred two of our missionaries to the Austria Vienna East Mission under President Dennis B. Neuenschwander.[2] Later that month, from 24 to 26 October, the first six full-time missionaries arrived in Moscow.[3] Like most others in our mission, each was exemplary. Until apartments could be arranged, they lived in a moderately priced downtown tourist hotel. As had earlier missionaries, they traveled to Russia on tourist visas and stayed in the hotel on a pre-paid voucher.

Eventually all missionaries were able to move into Russian apartments. As a rule, missionary apartments were moderate-to-upper class by Russian standards. Often these apartments belonged to couples who had access to two apartments and found a welcome source of income in renting one. Other landlords were going abroad for an extended period and wanted to earn money while away. In 1990 we rented apartments for rubles at an equivalent rate of approximately forty dollars per month, but the rate steadily climbed to one hundred fifty dollars and more by the end of our mission three years later—with payment in dollars, not rubles.

Much time since July had been spent attempting to devise a way for missionaries to travel to Russia without the high costs of tourist visas and hotels. We saw only two practical alternatives: secure invitations from private individuals, or secure invitations from an organization with legal entity status in the USSR. When the Church was recognized in Leningrad, the international office of the USSR Council on Religious Affairs, the only office that could then approve requests from a congregation to invite a foreign guest, appeared cooperative. I was assured that the Leningrad branch could begin to submit invitations both for missionaries already in the country and for others to come.

On 9 October 1990, the much-heralded and really very liberal legislation on freedom of conscience and religious organizations became law in the USSR. It granted all citizens full religious liberty in worship, publication of religious materials, proselytizing, and much more. The spirit of that law would have permitted foreign missionaries. But, upon receiving our documents, the USSR Council on Religious Affairs arbitrarily ruled that the Leningrad branch could invite only two missionaries from abroad and that only two missionaries could serve in any one city. The law itself made no numerical restrictions. Apparently the council could have chosen to approve any number of invitations. With the council's approval, the Ministry of Foreign Affairs would have authorized visas. Mr. Evgenii Chernetsov and Mr. Konstantin Blazhenov attempted to persuade their colleagues in the international department to cooperate but to no avail and without explanation.

Securing private invitations through members was far less ideal. Individual members of the Church volunteered to stand in lines for hours to receive the proper forms, to submit the forms, to inquire about the progress of the applications, and finally to receive the approved invitations. Generally the resulting visa was valid only for a few months, after which an application for renewal or a new invitation was needed, requiring a repetition of the same lengthy procedure.

Each approved and stamped private invitation was hand carried by returning missionaries to Helsinki, where Sister Rene Warner would stand in lines outside the Soviet Embassy in downtown Helsinki to deliver the invitation and, later, to receive the visa. The system was very time consuming, wearisome, increasingly expensive as application fees continued to rise, and difficult to track and administer. If a member moved to another city while an application was in process, we had to begin again. Renewals and new invitations were not always approved by the time the earlier visas expired. Further, we often received required information about new missionaries coming to our mission too late to process the invitations and acquire visas before they arrived. Nonetheless, we had no reasonable alternatives but to ask local Church members and Sister Warner to assist us. And they responded with the generosity characteristic of devoted Saints.

In Leningrad the Terebenins introduced me to two men influential in city government who were willing to help the Church acquire meetinghouses: Georgii Chetchuev, responsible on the city council for freedom of conscience and religious organizations, and Mikhail Gubkin, a deputy mayor accountable for all issues related to building and architecture in the city. Eventually our association resulted in an offer of a desirable building site. The Terebenins, Frankfurt physical facilities representatives Konrad Nagele and Hanno Luschin, and I spent many hours here and in all mission cities in an effort to secure our own meetinghouses. In few areas did we feel more frustrated or did we expend more effort than in the futile attempt to obtain facilities so essential to our deserving members.

In the middle of the month Joan and I traveled to Potsdam, Germany, for our first fall mission presidents' leadership training seminar. Elders Russell M. Nelson and Hans B. Ringger, among others, provided valuable instruction and motivation. Joan described some of our experiences:

> The seminar schedule consisted of a four-hour morning session, lunch, followed by a short sight-seeing tour in the area in the afternoon, followed by another two-hour session, supper, and then an evening meeting. Elder Nelson spoke to us on Tuesday evening and again Wednesday morning. He gave us a synopsis of the conference addresses given by the First Presidency and the Twelve while Gary and I wrote frantically, since our missionaries are most anxious to know what went on at conference. . . . His second address was on convert retention and consisted entirely of selected portions of scriptures on a fourteen-page handout that he provided for us. It was very well done. The rest of the sessions were presented by Elder Ringger and assigned mission presidents.
>
> One morning session was for the women and included a session on feeding the multitudes, with each wife bringing two recipes that were quick, delicious, and economical. . . . We had a bus tour of Berlin before we left on Thursday.[4]

At the end of the month we held a one-day missionary conference in Leningrad. All twenty-six missionaries were there. This was the first time all became acquainted, obtained a common understanding of mission policies, shared inspiration and testimony, and built mission morale and spirit. Before the five-hour conference meeting, we toured the magnificent Russian Museum art gallery to help deepen our appreciation for Russian culture.

While in Leningrad I met with branch members and leaders, including a dozen young Saints who wanted to learn of requirements for filling a mission. I generally recommended two years of membership and active participation in the Church to allow for greater maturity and stability. I also asked missionaries to provide as much of the full cost required to serve as possible—at least enough to cover twelve months in Russia at current ruble costs. Generous Church donations covered the remaining amount. Most Russian missionaries completed honorable missions, but problems arose in convincing those who served abroad to return to live in Russia to share their rich experience with members at home. The interest in serving missions is reflected in these words from Karina Oganesian, St. Petersburg:

> I would like to become a missionary because I love to read the Holy Scriptures and explain them to my friends. But I'm only thirteen years old and still must wait for a long time and prepare for this. I am studying music and play the piano, organ, and synthesizer. My mother is teaching me piano. In Sunday School I help the missionaries by accompanying the choir. Now we are having a hard time in our country, but I hope that God will help us.[5]

Sister Mariia Frolova, also of St. Petersburg, is another young convert with a desire to share the gospel:

> I have never had any great friends until I met the missionaries. I had never seen such wonderful people. When I got to know Sister Madsen and Sister Gutierrez, I wanted to become like them. They have tremendous faith. . . . I am now fourteen years old, but I plead with you to allow me to serve a mission as soon as it is possible (before I turn twenty-one). This is my dream and my life's goal. I plead with you to make this one exception, in the name of Jesus Christ.[6]

Mariia's parents, influenced by their daughter's example, have accepted the restored gospel. Her father and mother have served in branch leadership positions in St. Petersburg, her father as a branch president.

Among other faithful Leningrad Saints serving in leadership positions was Svetlana Glukhikh. Her service as Relief Society president blessed sisters and their families alike. Sister Glukhikh had joined the Church in February 1990. Her story shows the series of miracles that brought her to the gospel:

My father was a Communist and worked as a laborer at the Kirovskii Factory. Mama is a believer and a housewife. After I was born, the question of whether I should be baptized in the Orthodox Church arose. My father was categorically against it. Mama gave up her desire to have me baptized. I also had an older brother, Oleg. Mama had him baptized, even though he was born in 1952, a very difficult time in our country. . . .

Time passed. I was happy and cheerful. But once I was asked to perform in front of a large group of people. I wasn't more than twelve years old, and I was afraid. But just before I was to go out on stage, I knelt down and began to pray. Nobody had taught me to do this. I simply asked God for help. And he helped me. My performance was a success. Did I believe in God? I don't know. It was a belief that someone existed who tests us. Can we be honest, kind, and as a child would say, "good"? Now I know that this is to live according to God's commandments. But at that time I was reading fairy tales and believed that good is always victorious over evil. And I was good, sincerely.

Everybody liked me and always shared all of their innermost feelings with me. I always listened, sympathized, and tried to help. By the time I was eighteen years old, I considered myself an adult and thought I knew everything. My youth returned to me about two years later, and since then I've not completely grown up again. I know now that I am a child of God and that I need to continue learning throughout my entire life. But at that time I didn't know that. And so I started to believe in God and began to desire baptism.

Eight years passed before I was baptized. I wore a crucifix around my neck and kept thinking that I really needed to be baptized. No one around me believed in God, but everyone knew that baptism was necessary. It was a national tradition for us. . . . In 1989 I was baptized in Estonia in a convent. It was a lengthy ordinance and no one attended my baptism. I felt overcome with my feelings. I was very afraid of baptism—there was something terrifying about it. There was a sense of emptiness

*Svetlana Glukhikh (right) with Leningrad members
Liliia Chuprova and her daughter Aleksandra*

after the baptism, and it was awful. As I descended the stairs of
the cathedral I thought that God was justly punishing me . . .
and that he did not love me and did not accept me, and would
not help me.

All my life I had thought that the Orthodox, Catholic, and
Lutheran Churches were the only ones that believed in Christ. I
also knew there were some other sects. I knew about the
Baptists; there were lots of terrible stories told about them here.
One day I saw on television a particular American church where
the priest was wearing an ordinary suit, like everyone else. And
people who went to the service for his sermon went as families
and they were very happy and cheerful. I really liked it. I wanted
to be able to attend such meetings. But in my city we had only
Orthodox churches, and I didn't like to go there. I felt sad and
depressed. . . .

Two months later, I was invited to attend a meeting with
missionaries from Finland: the mission president and his wife,
President and Sister Mecham; and a family from Finland, the

Laitinens. It was an amazing meeting. It was the first time I'd ever seen such wonderful, beautiful people who loved each other. I saw how they complemented each other, and how husbands helped their wives, and wives, their husbands. Curiosity had brought me to the meeting, or so I thought at that time. But now I know it was my loving Father in Heaven.

As I listened to Leena Laitinen and saw her eyes, I grew more and more astonished—it seemed impossible, it was a miracle. They told me about our Heavenly Father's plan and about his church on the earth. I had just one question for Leena, "What will happen to those children of our Heavenly Father who lived during the time of the apostasy?" And then Leena told me about redeeming the dead and about temple work. Everything I heard made a strong impression on me. Then when Leena showed me a photograph of the temple in Salt Lake City, I thought for a moment, and had a strong witness that it was literally God's house. A miracle had taken place. I realized that God is my Father in Heaven and he loves me very much. And so my friends and I who had gathered for the meeting all believed and planned to be baptized.

But at that time our laws were strict, and we had to go to Finland for baptism. I waited for the documents to be prepared. But again a miracle occurred, and we were able to be baptized in Leningrad. The first baptism occurred during the winter on 3 February 1990. It was held at a pool next to a sauna in the Pribaltiiskaia Hotel. It wasn't the most sacred place, so I decided to wait. In Finland the baptism would take place in a church. Within a week three of my friends were baptized. Galina Zhukova, who had invited me to the meeting with the missionaries, said, "You simply do not understand what you are refusing."

I now impatiently waited for February 17 when I would be baptized. And then the day came. Elder Ringger, the leader of the Church in the European Area, arrived in Leningrad at that time. I received a powerful witness from my baptism and from the gift of the Holy Ghost. As I listened to the words of Elder Ringger, I was convinced of the power of the priesthood in the Church. What he told me then has come to pass. All of the words spoken in my confirmation are also coming to pass.

In the Church I've had many different callings, which bring me happiness and blessings and provide me with spiritual growth. I feel that my soul needs spiritual nourishment and that I feed it as I read the scriptures, pray, fast and serve in my branch.

I visited the temple this year [1994] and it gave me an even more powerful witness of the truthfulness of the Church, as well as a greater knowledge about the Plan of Salvation. Every minute I sense that God is my loving Father, who always loves me and is teaching me everything that he himself knows.[7]

While in Vyborg on 21 October, I attended a very enjoyable sacrament meeting in which Elder John Webster presented his farewell speech and testimony before leaving for Tallinn to establish a new Russian branch there. Elder Webster had served in Vyborg for eight months. When he visited the first time, there were no members in the city. Together with other members and missionaries, he had played an important role in helping more than fifty people grow spiritually and accept the restored gospel.

Elder Webster spoke in his imperfect but greatly improved Russian to more than one hundred members and investigators squeezed into a music school auditorium near downtown Market Square on Lenin Street in Vyborg. I observed their rapt attention, glistening eyes, and gentle smiles during his entire talk. This was the first time I had experienced this abundant, reverent love for one of the missionaries.

As I spent the remainder of the day with Elder Webster in meetings, a dinner, and a baptismal service, I noted his constant interest in and even deep anxiety for the spiritual and temporal life of each individual. Like all Church members, Russians profoundly appreciated the fine missionaries who, as they said, "enthusiastically cheered us on." One of those grateful members was Natalia Turutina, who told of her joining the Church:

> In the spring of 1990, my older brother Andrei came home and suggested that we meet with two young Americans who were missionaries from The Church of Jesus Christ of Latter-day Saints. My parents had completely different reactions. My mother smiled and agreed. I think it was right then, from the very first moment, that she fell in love with the Church. Papa said that it didn't matter to him, as long as we didn't bother him. . . .
>
> The missionaries of the then-unknown church were supposed to come over to our home for the first time. I helped my mother prepare for our guests, but just before their arrival I suddenly decided to leave the house. I kept leaving the house like this for three months, but once my curiosity won out and I stayed home. By that time Andrei and my mother had already

been baptized. I listened to one of the missionary discussions. . . . Time passed and the missionaries came over more and more often. In my soul I had already perceived that this church meant more than simply a good association with people. After all, I saw how much better my brother and mother had become!

Sometime later at one Sunday meeting, the leader of the branch announced that one of the Apostles would be coming to Leningrad. I decided to go hear what this man wished to say to all of us. I thought, "He's an American. He doesn't know anything about our life in Russia. How can he give us advice on how to live?"

I remember that after the conference I could hardly hold back the tears. As I returned home to Vyborg on the *elektrichka* [train], I opened a book and tried to read but couldn't. I was looking at the page but thinking about the Apostle's words and recalled the feeling that had come over me then. I later understood that at that time I was feeling the very powerful influence of the Holy Ghost, which was present at the conference. . . . Within a week I was baptized. . . .

Looking back I remember the first time I spoke in sacrament meeting. I thought that I would not be able to say a single word, but as soon as I stood up and greeted everyone, I saw smiling faces in front of me, people who wished me well and who had already become like family. The words themselves flowed from me. I spoke about the importance of prayer. At the end of the talk I bore my testimony. When I finished my talk, I felt peace within and a desire to share my testimony more and more. One Sunday morning about a year ago, I heard on the radio a Georgian proverb: "If you want to keep that which is good, give it away to others." How wise! Here that which is good can be understood in two ways: things or kindness. But then the thought came to me that the more we share our testimony with others, the stronger it will become for us. And the other way around.[8]

13

NOVEMBER 1990

In November the solution to our visa woes began to emerge. Church attorney David Farnsworth and I met with Irina Saveleva, a representative of a Moscow law firm and a member of the law faculty at Moscow State University. She was a brilliant attorney with excellent connections in government circles. Mark Davis, a former Russian student at Brigham Young University, had met her through his Washington, D.C., law firm, which was developing a partnership with her firm in Moscow. She counseled the Church to register through the Russian Republic rather than through USSR channels. The USSR and Russian legislatures often approved conflicting legislation and essentially disregarded each other's laws. Many had observed that political power was shifting to the more powerful of the fifteen republics, especially to Russia.

The parliament of the Russian Federation had now approved legislation on freedom of conscience and religious organizations that provided new churches a less cumbersome registration procedure. Applications could be channeled through the Russian Ministry of Justice rather than through city councils and the often unresponsive city, republic, and national councils on religious affairs. Brother Farnsworth subsequently recommended to Europe Area leaders that the Church be registered in the Russian Republic. As a legal entity, the Russian-led Church corporation could, among other things, invite missionaries to serve throughout Russia.

Meanwhile, the Leningrad city council through Georgii Chetchuev offered the Church property on which to build a chapel. The site seemed ideal: an attractive neighborhood relatively close to a subway stop, but the Church did not approve. I believe a principal problem was the city's requirement that the Church, rather than paying the city cash for the right to use the land, construct an additional building for city use, such as a youth center, sports hall, or medical facility; furnish a hospital or educational institution with modern equipment; or develop a municipal genealogical research center.

At the time there was no private property. If the city could demonstrate that citizens would benefit significantly by allowing the construction, the Church and the city would be less vulnerable to attacks from competing interests. If the city had named a reasonable price for the land, the problems would have been fewer. But business in Russia was not conducted with the relative clarity of financial transfers. Russian practices rightly concerned our legal and real estate specialists and Area leaders, although several other churches had obtained property and built new facilities following procedures common in Russia.

Preparations had long been underway for the Tabernacle Choir to visit Russia in June 1991. Beginning in November 1990 we in the mission began directing more attention to this event. An early task was to identify influential friends and potential friends of the Church in Moscow and Leningrad who might be invited to concerts and dinners afterward. This was difficult because able government, professional, and civic leaders frequently changed positions, mainly moving to new opportunities with greater financial potential.

During her tenure at the USSR Ministry of Culture, Natalia Myshkova proved to be an exceptionally influential, gracious, and enduring friend of the Church. Introduced to Beverly Campbell (the public affairs and communications director for the Church in Washington, D.C.) by the Soviet ambassador to the United States, Ms. Myshkova arranged numerous important meetings with city, republic, and all-union governmental leaders. She energetically assisted with the Tabernacle Choir visit and introduced the Church to officials who were central to decisions affecting religions.

In Leningrad, branch leaders were reluctant to discuss dividing the branch. In President Hans B. Ringger's experience, branches with 120 members and an expanding group of investigators benefited from a division. The ten missionaries serving in the one Leningrad branch often stumbled over one another to meet visitors at meetings and provide support for new leaders. But a branch division still seemed frightening. The Russians, like everyone, feared losing dear friends. I emphasized that leaders young in the Church could better meet members' needs in a smaller organization, that branches in two parts of the city would provide meeting facilities more convenient to more people, and that two branches would allow more opportunity for members and missionaries to serve in leadership capacities, providing important experience for new branches and districts to follow.

The smaller Moscow branch offered another example of steady growth. At the time of my November visit, thirty-six of the sixty-three who attended sacrament meeting were nonmembers. After a fine Sunday School lesson on testimony, teacher Galina Goncharova invited class members to share their feelings. Two recently baptized members expressed their joy following baptism, two regularly attending nonmembers announced their intention to be baptized, and a man who had come to our meetings for the first time spoke at length, complimenting members on their choice and on the warm spirit he had felt during the meetings. We soon discovered, however, that this man was interested primarily in seeking financial contributions.

After the close of the services in Moscow, I announced that following a brief period I would ordain three men to the Melchizedek Priesthood. Family members and friends were welcome to remain for the ordinations. To my surprise, virtually every member and investigator stayed seated, quietly awaiting the ordinations of Andrei Petrov, Igor Kibiriov, and Aleksei Kostin. Each of these men received a blessing of great promise and subsequently served in the branch with uncommon skill and devotion.

Joan wrote of the problems experienced by members in Moscow in late 1990 from the perspective of her Russian friend Lucy, an Intourist guide Joan had met on a previous trip to the USSR:

> Lucy explained some of the difficulties facing the Soviet people at this time. Traditionally Moscow has been the city best supplied with consumer goods in the Soviet Union. With the easing of central control, regions and cities have been able to work out their own agreements on trade, and now Moscow is a city of shortages. She said that food-producing regions were not

interested in trading rockets produced in Moscow for food. She has not been able to buy butter, cooking oil, or eggs in the government stores for a month now. Other basics such as flour and sugar are also in short supply. The major cities have formed markets where prices are determined by the individual producer rather than the government, and these items are still available there but at a cost too high for most Soviets to afford. . . .

Gary said he heard on the news that on December 1 twenty-four items would be rationed in the Soviet Union and coupons would be necessary in order to purchase these items. Our missionaries will not be eligible for the coupons, so they will have to depend on members to supply them. So far the members have been wonderful. They realize the missionaries are vulnerable and do not have the same connections through which to get food. They say that in order to have food to eat in the big cities you need to have relatives or friends in the country to supply you.

So far there are no signs (other than very long lines) of the lack of food. The people look healthy and carry on with life's activities in a normal fashion. This situation will be especially difficult for the older people who are on pensions, however, as prices are undoubtedly going to be rising. Lucy said her mother's pension was only forty-five rubles a month. I look at these people (especially women) who have suffered so much already in their lives through the revolution, WW II, and Stalin's purges, and know that this current "revolution" will be especially difficult for them. I hope all of them have friends and relatives in the country!

Most believe that the necessary food is out there somewhere, but reasons for the poor distribution vary. Some believe in sabotage by those who do not want to change from the Communism of the past, while others think that food is being held back until prices rise so that a higher profit can be enjoyed. At any rate, the problems in the Soviet Union are immense at this time. Our missionaries have been able to survive well so far by eating at tourist restaurants and through the generosity of the members. Betsy's friends in Vyborg keep sending presents for us with anyone who visits the branch, such as delicious homemade jam and candies. We are moved by their generosity, especially knowing the difficult times they are experiencing.[1]

During November the first baptism by full-time missionaries in Moscow took place in the enormous circular Moscow swimming pool at Kropotkinskaia metro station, built on the former site of the Russian Orthodox Cathedral of Christ the Savior. I believe the devotion of multitudes of believing Orthodox exerted a sanctifying influence even on the pool resting upon the cathedral's foundations.[2] Elder Adam West baptized Mikhail Poniukhov and described Mikhail's (Misha's) early-morning baptism:

> We were both in white; and everywhere around us lay white, freshly fallen snow. The weather was –5 to –10 degrees Celsius (below freezing) and cloudy. There were about one hundred people in this huge outdoor pool. The air was so cold that the steam rising up from the pool's water was enough to give Misha and me complete privacy. . . . I baptized him with the Russian baptismal prayer, and thus it became both my first baptism and the first baptism by a Mormon missionary in Moscow. . . . We then came back to our hotel room by metro, and my companion Elder [Rick] Robinson confirmed Misha with a beautiful prayer.[3]

That same month Valentin Gavrilov, who later became a branch president in Vyborg, joined the Church. He wrote this account of his struggles toward faith:

> I was born and grew up in the city of Gorlovka, Ukraine. In our city there were very few Ukrainians, and it was rare to hear Ukrainian spoken. Most of the residents of the city had been sent by the Party after the war from all over the USSR to revitalize the Donetsk Basin. . . .
>
> I had never seriously thought about God. I was interested in anything to do with "the other world," in communication from "the other side," yoga, and various forms of magic. Once, at work I was told that some young American missionaries had shown up in Vyborg. They spoke Russian and visited with anyone who was interested. These rumors really caught my attention. I questioned my acquaintances and they explained that these Americans could be found on Sunday at the music school. I suggested to my wife that we drop by together to visit with these Americans, but she had more important things to do at home, so I went alone.
>
> To my surprise, the missionaries welcomed me and were very cordial, and paid me much attention. There I met a tall redheaded young man from Montana, Michael Layne, and a no less engaging but shorter John Webster from Utah. It turned out that Americans are just like us. . . . With great enthusiasm I questioned them about every detail of life in America—about buses, stores, food, schools, etc.

The Vyborg branch in 1991. Valentin Gavrilov is second from left on front row. His wife, Liudmila, is second from left in row 3 with plaid shoulder scarf

And then somewhat imperceptibly the conversation turned to religion. I told them I had never thought seriously about religion. On the question of the creation of the universe, I adhered to the Big Bang theory, and thought man most likely descended from monkeys, although the rest of the animals also had much in common—the same heart, lungs, liver, etc. They gave me a thin pamphlet—the Joseph Smith Story, and we agreed to meet the following week.

Discussing the universe, the creation of the world, and the origin of man was much more interesting than any particulars of life in the U.S. . . . The missionaries continued to plant in my soul seed after seed. What great wisdom is contained in the plan of salvation! And yet the ways of the Lord are incomprehensible, and it is not given us to know all truth. The culminating moment in my development came with my first prayer. How wise it was on the part of the missionaries—they were probably prompted by the Lord—to suggest that I myself ask the Lord, "Where is truth? Is it in the Book of Mormon, or in the hypotheses of contemporary scientists?"

This was my first prayer ever. I was still not a member of the Church. I was alone in a room. I knelt down on my knees and began to converse with God in a whisper, as if with a man. I asked him what I should believe in, how the world was created, how man was created, why does man live on the earth? . . . And then how great was my surprise when I literally sensed in my head an outside thought, clearly not my own.

What's more, it wasn't just one thought, but a stream of thoughts. With mild reproach I felt questioned: "What are you still asking about? Is it really not clear to you yet where the truth is? Could a handful of scientists, who are founded only upon certain materialistic facts, honestly reveal the process of the creation of the universe? Read my words and you shall know the truth."

At that moment I unequivocally knew that there was a God and that it was he who had answered me. I felt much joy and peace, and I knew I should read the scriptures.

After that there were many meetings with the missionaries. My family was very fortunate. We were taught by a remarkable person, Elder Bert Dover, from Arizona. It was very difficult for me to give up smoking, and I saw how Elder Dover suffered along with me. This gave me additional strength. I decided to get baptized quite simply, without any hesitation. . . .

My wife did not immediately accept God. Restrictions troubled her: no drinking coffee or tea, and then giving up ten percent of our earnings—we had only enough money for food. Engineers in Russia earn less than laborers. But somehow, gradually, thanks to the efforts of Bert Dover and Matthew Malovich, she also came to an understanding of the truth, and that is the most important thing. All the rest springs from an understanding of the truth of the gospel and the truthfulness of our Church.

I remember well how she worried the first time I told her that I had invited American missionaries over to our place. We live in a very old building, in an awful apartment, and to invite Americans to such an apartment was embarrassing! We spent a long time washing, cleaning, and scrubbing everything, and my wife prepared a lot of delicious food. We all enjoyed that first meeting with the American missionaries.

There were many guests at my baptism on November 24, 1990, and of course my wife and son. I myself was in somewhat of a peculiar state. I realized that something grand was occurring, but that nothing depended upon me any more. I had made my choice; I was giving myself completely into God's power, and whatever he determined, so be it. This state of being was surprising and very pleasant. I felt that God loved me and that now he would accompany me in my life at all times and in all places. My sole task was to not stumble, to resist the temptations of Satan, and to keep the Lord's commandments. Our friends, the missionaries, took wonderful photographs. And only now, a few years later, do I realize what an important step that was in my life.

The week following my baptism I struggled with a craving to smoke. It was very difficult. I sucked on candy, chewed gum, and nibbled on sunflower seeds. . . . And almost every hour I prayed to God that he would give me strength to refrain from this sin. The surprising thing was that within a week I could already calmly look at smokers, and within another week I even began to forget that I used to smoke.

Of course, for a long time I still felt that "something was missing," and I mustered all of my strength in order to chase away these thoughts. With time this became easier and easier. It was less difficult with alcohol. I rarely drank, only on holidays, so it was quite easy for me to give up alcohol. Within a month my wife and son were baptized, and we became a united family. At home together we read the scriptures out loud and discussed what we read. Gradually I began to notice that the relationships within our family became better. It became more interesting for us to be with each other.

It had always been difficult for me to make public speeches. Ever since childhood I have stuttered and often suffered greatly because of it. But I noticed an amazing thing—it was much easier for me to speak and give talks at church than in any other meeting. I felt the love of the Holy Ghost and of those listening to me. Within a year I received the Melchizedek Priesthood and a calling to be the branch clerk. The job was not complicated, and I was glad to be entrusted with this responsible job.

The greatest surprise for me was when I was called to be a branch president. Our branch was being divided in two, making it necessary to find a leader for the second branch. I prayed to God for a long time; I didn't consider myself a very suitable candidate. First of all, I stutter and therefore fear public speaking. Second, I was working at that time as an engineer in a factory from eight in the morning until six or seven in the evening, and there really wasn't time left over for church work. And third, I did not have a telephone at home (in Russia, getting a home phone installed is a very big problem). Nevertheless, I felt that God wanted me specifically to be the branch president. So I consented. At first there were many difficulties, great and small. But the Lord showed personal mercy on me.

I left the factory and opened my own private firm. I import and export goods to Finland. Now I plan my time myself and always conduct church meetings. Somehow I ended up with a home telephone, and now I can get in touch with the whole world. . . . My speech has improved, especially at church meetings. Most important, I am no longer afraid of public speaking, and now even if there is hesitation in my speech, I don't give it much thought. All of this I consider no less than a miracle accomplished by our Lord for me.

In April 1993 we all went as a family, the three of us, to the temple in Stockholm, Sweden. It was marvelous! It is difficult to find human words to describe this happiness, the happiness of uniting with God. The whole time I was there I wanted to fall on my knees and thank the Lord for this blessing. In the temple we sealed our marriage and family for eternity, and we were baptized for our deceased parents and many other people. Now we are saving money for our next visit to the temple. . . .

I am sincerely happy that I was able to come to a knowledge of the truth, and to the Church of Jesus Christ. I am infinitely grateful to our Lord for all the blessings which he has so abundantly showered upon me and my family.[4]

14

DECEMBER 1990

For just over half my three-year mission I had counselors in the mission presidency. At other times I felt that available priesthood leadership strength was even more badly needed in the frequently dividing branches and, eventually, districts. To compensate for this lack of counselors, I sought advice from branch and, later, district presidencies and from missionary leaders. In December 1990 I set apart Jussi Kemppainen and Dale Warner as my first and second counselors. These men provided exemplary service in strengthening members, freeing me for more work with the missionaries and general mission leadership.

On 17 December, we all rejoiced with Estonian Jaanus Silla when he received his mission call. Brother Silla became the first missionary to be called from any part of the USSR. One month after receiving his letter, he was to report to the missionary training center preparatory to his serving in the Utah Salt Lake City Mission. Although few expected that he could complete all the necessary arrangements, Elder Silla arrived in Provo right on time.

We were surprised when eight Estonians attending a Finnish youth conference as invited guests asked to stay with Latter-day Saint families rather than in dormitories with the other youth. The two who spent a few evenings with us explained they wanted to feel the spirit and observe the behavior of an LDS family. Except for Jaanus Silla, whose mother was already a member, none of their parents had joined the Church by that time. The youth wished to experience much that we take for granted: courteous relations, scripture reading, family prayer, and a spiritual core to everyday living.

We held our second mission conference in Moscow, a two-day Christmas gathering. As a group we toured the Kremlin with Joan's friend Lucy, sang Christmas carols, listened to inspirational talks, held a testimony meeting, and ended with a delicious farewell dinner procured and prepared by Pirkko Gibb, her family, and several other Church members. The food for the dinner was purchased over several days and weeks, not at the foreign currency shops but at Russian markets. The Gibbs' resourcefulness and generosity provided a heartwarming holiday gift for us all.

Joan's letter home recounts some of the generosity and love shown at this time:

> When Gary talked to the Primary leader in Leningrad, she said she felt the children would be so happy if they could get a piece of gum, a piece of candy, and a banana for Christmas. Because of the generosity of several people, they will be getting more. Konrad Nagele from Frankfurt is going to bring some candy for the children when he visits next week, and a friend of the Warners also sent some small candy. We plan to make little sacks with some Christmas fabric to put the goodies in and tie a ribbon around the top. In every branch with the exception of Moscow we will be able to bring bananas. . . .
>
> Members in Leningrad and Vyborg told us that flour, macaroni, rice, and cereal grains are now almost impossible to get. When we visited the Leningrad branch president in his home last week, his wife served us some fruit tea (canned cherries and hot water), bread, and boiled eggs. It was apparent that having these eggs was a special treat for them. In spite of all their difficulties getting food, they are *so* generous. The Vyborg Relief Society president insists that we come to her home for dinner when we go in January, and she continues to feed the missionaries with whatever she can find.[1]

Missionary Amy Barnett describes her Christmas 1990 in Leningrad:

> Both my companion, Sister [Stephanie] Carpenter, and I LOVE Christmas, and so the thought of putting together a Christmas party was more fun than work. We began by planning a Nativity scene for the main program. It became clear where we had to begin when we asked the Primary children if anyone knew the story of the birth of Christ. All we got in response were blank stares. We read through the story from the Bible and then assigned parts. The children reluctantly agreed to accept roles, for they still couldn't understand what we had in mind. We decided to hope for a miracle. . . . At first, it was just missionaries cutting, gluing, and piecing together ornaments for the tree and

hall. We were later joined by some of the faithful members and diligent investigators, and then the real ornament making began.

Elaborate ornaments and lanterns were skillfully crafted out of scraps of our leftover colored paper. Irina Nikiticheva even went from table to table teaching everyone how to make 3-D stars. It turned out to be a fun evening for everyone. The next night the missionaries met early to begin decorating the hall for the party. Half an hour later the trees arrived. Members placed two together in the center of the hall so they would look like one full tree. I was rather discouraged when I realized that the ornaments we made covered only about half of the tree, but soon the Relief Society arrived and covered the tree from top to bottom with shiny, sparkling ornaments and streamers. It was absolutely beautiful. Once we had removed the Lenin portrait from the wall, the room truly looked like Christmas. . . .

Our little Nativity scene surpassed all my expectations. The boys who played the wise men and the shepherds all took great care in making their costumes. They looked much more authentic than we did as children in our parents' robes. Ania and Aleksei played Mary and Joseph with such sincerity that the babe in their arms could have been real. Little Ania, our tiny, reluctant angel, stood reverently and even smiled on cue. I think we were all touched by the simplicity of this sacred event. We definitely got our miracle that night.[2]

At this Christmas season, many desired to contribute to meeting Soviet members' needs. My colleagues at Brigham Young University had cooperated with students, faculty, and townspeople to raise a first installment of three thousand dollars in a program called "Food for Russia."[3] A branch in Germany sent us three hundred dollars. Friends, family members, and others mailed contributions to help members in need. This unsolicited generosity showed the deep concern members felt for their brothers and sisters. One anonymous donor using the name Firestone wrote:

While watching the plight of the Kurds in Iraq I could not help but think of the starving Russians as well. Here is a check in your name. . . . My son is in the Brazil Salvador Mission and there is so much poorness there as well. . . . I would feel bad and so would my Father in Heaven if I did not share. . . . I decided not to give you my real name. The Lord will reward me openly if I do this in secret.

In the same envelope was a second Firestone letter dated more than a month later:

> Getting this money to you is difficult. I sent it by pouch mail and it was returned to me because there's no pouch mail to you. So I'll try again. I had such a good feeling when I sent it the first time that I have to keep trying. I just got word that our company is going to have a lay-off and I may be one of them, so I'm getting rid of this as fast as I can so I won't be tempted to use it. I love you two and hope it will help someone.[4]

When Elder Robert L. Backman visited Moscow as part of a delegation of Boy Scout officials, we met with missionaries and members. We also spent a memorable evening with the Andrei and Elena Petrov family in their one-room communal apartment. They invited us for dinner and discussion in the eight-by-ten-foot room where they and their eight-month-old daughter, Katia, lived. We spoke of their faith and aspirations.

As we were leaving, the Petrovs showed us the orderly but modest kitchen and bath they shared with two other families. Fortunately, they were on good terms with their neighbors; other Soviets, including some Church members, are not so fortunate. Instances not only of inconsideration, but of theft and even drunken assault complicate many lives. Yet as we read this December of the Christ Child's humble beginnings in a manger, we were reminded that often from modest circumstances arises true greatness.

PART IV

THE
FINLAND HELSINKI
EAST MISSION,
1991 TO 1992

15

JANUARY 1991

The year 1991 marked the turbulent end of the Soviet Union. It began violently the day after New Year with the central government's attempt to assert and preserve Soviet power in the Baltic republics and ended with the emergence of the Commonwealth of Independent States and Mikhail Gorbachev's December 25 resignation as president of the Soviet Union.

Earlier in the year, Estonian, Latvian, and Lithuanian governments placed barriers around parliaments, press and media centers, and other vital national buildings to hinder possible Soviet tank and troop movement. In Tallinn I squeezed between immense granite blocks more than five feet tall in front of the parliament and preventing all vehicular access. In many parts of the Soviet Union, but particularly in Moscow, massive pro- and anti-government marches and demonstrations continued. The prestige and authority of Gorbachev and the central Soviet government were waning while President Boris Yeltsin and the Russian Republic continued a rapid political ascent. On 13 January Soviet troops killed fifteen Lithuanian protesters in Vilnius, and Russia's President Yeltsin signed a bold mutual-security pact with the Baltic republics in which Russia pledged to defend any of the Baltic republics from Soviet government attack.

Meanwhile, Church attorney David Farnsworth consulted with Irina Saveleva about registering the Church in the Russian Republic rather than in the Soviet Union. Brother Farnsworth prepared papers that defined the Church's religious association to be led by a Russian president, counselors, and board. The association would become the legal entity of the Church in Russia, empowered to conduct official business, publish and sell printed materials, and invite missionaries and other guests to Russia. The registration process begun now resulted in Russian Ministry of Justice approval less than five months later.

In Leningrad the branch was finally divided. Iurii Terebenin, the first branch president, became the mission executive secretary. The new president of the Leningrad First Branch was city transportation engineer Viacheslav Efimov. This branch encompassed the central, northern, and eastern areas of the city. Kirov Opera chorus principal Andrei Khrapovitskii was called to lead the Leningrad Second Branch. That branch included Vasilevskii Island and the western and southern parts of the city. The Neva River divided the branches. The First Branch continued to meet at Novgorodskaia 9, and President Khrapovitskii secured for the Second Branch Sunday use of several rooms in a bright and ornate music school facility on Vasilevskii Island (Lieutenant Schmidt Embankment 31).

Brother Vladimir Batianov, another of the leaders involved in the division, described what occurred:

> The most difficult division was the initial one. At first we had one Leningrad branch and all members knew one another well. Suddenly we were informed that our branch would be divided. We wondered, What would happen to our friendships? Would we ever meet again? How would we make new friends? We had come to love one another. We were used to being together. And now we might end up in different branches with no assurance that we would see each other again! You can imagine how difficult this was. And when the division took place, we felt like part of our hearts had been torn from us.
>
> But then there were conferences at which we all met, shared our thoughts, and talked about everything. Many members have maintained these close relations right up to the present time. . . . We have some very active members who know their brothers and sisters in different branches, and who continue to call each other and keep up on what is happening.
>
> The second division caused far less pain. We now had some experience in how these things are done. We had come to realize that the division was necessary. The Church was growing, and divisions were a natural consequence. And when the time approached for the third division, we eagerly awaited the time when the change would be made. It was good for more people to receive callings in the Church, including more responsible callings.[1]

Meanwhile, in Moscow the mission rented a larger meeting facility in a studio theater on Spartacus Square near the Baumanskaia metro station. The historic building had a spacious entry hall, a marble staircase leading to the second floor where we met, large windows and comfortable chairs, classrooms, and two small rooms we were able to rent twenty-four hours a day. For the first time we could store our sacrament trays and printed materials rather than carrying them to missionaries' and members' apartments. We could also conduct branch business and hold leadership and auxiliary meetings at any time on Sunday or during the week.

In January the Area presidency gave us permission to purchase and distribute Finnish syringes and needles to our missionaries. Russian medical facilities were sterilizing and reusing needles, but not all needles were properly disinfected. Reports of AIDS contamination had begun to appear in Russian media. During this month an elder in Vyborg received an injection of painkiller following a concussion. Joan described the care he received:

> One of our missionaries was in the Vyborg hospital with a brain concussion as a result of a fall on the ice. Visiting him in the hospital was like taking a step back into the last century. Elder Layne was assigned to the best room in the hospital, as it was the only one with a private bathroom (toilet and sink). When Gary asked how far it was to the shower, the doctor told him that there were no showers or tubs in the hospital. The small room had three iron-framed beds without any adjustable features, one stool, and a couple of bedside tables. Nurses wear white lab coats and a white hat that resembles a chef's hat in height but is straight up and down instead of puffed at the top. The only food served by the hospital is porridge and bread. Families and friends supply the nutritional needs of the patients. Elder Layne assured us that he was getting very good care from the nurses and doctors. I imagine he is the first American patient in this small-town hospital. We had a report today that he is getting better now and will be released in a couple of days.
>
> Missionary health is a big concern, as the medical situation in the Soviet Union leaves much to be desired. Many hospitals do not have disposable syringes and needles, so the chance of contracting hepatitis and AIDS is greatly increased.[2]

Another missionary in Tallinn had received an injection before a doctor lanced an infected insect bite on the elder's leg. We felt we could not take the risk that these and other needles might be inadequately sterilized. For more than a year missionaries carried needles and syringes with them each day. Only rarely were the needles used, but knowing they were available was a comfort.

This month I was visited in Helsinki by a Russian member of the Church who had been instrumental in arranging comfortable meeting facilities and helping the Church to become registered in his city. He had accompanied singing during Sunday services and had introduced the gospel to future leaders of the Church in Moscow. Like a considerable number of our members, he had been (and still was) a member of the Communist Party and, in his case, of the city council. He had done virtually all of his work, as had other members, freely and generously, from the goodness of his heart. But then he learned that the Church had paid for legal, shipping, and certain other services, and he determined to submit his retroactive request for payment. Within a year he distanced himself from the Church when the mission did not compensate him for his services.

There may have been some who joined the Church from ulterior motives, looking toward financial and professional benefits or emigration to the United States. But they were few in comparison to those who accepted baptism because they felt the Spirit and embraced the gospel of Jesus Christ. I remain hopeful that many of those who fell away will choose to return, as some already have.

16

February 1991

In Moscow we generally stayed at the downtown Intourist Hotel. It was above the average Russian standard, though several decades old and inadequately maintained. Elements of organized crime and prostitution further corrupted the environment. Regardless, the location of the Intourist Hotel was ideal—two hundred yards from Red Square, the Kremlin, and a hub for three major subway lines.

While interviewing and holding training meetings with missionaries and members, on two successive days I saw waves of Russian demonstrators march down Tverskaia Street, recently renamed from Gorky Street, a six-lane thoroughfare from the international airport to the Kremlin. The protesters continued to Manege Square, just north of the Kremlin. There was no shouting, no bands, few placards, only the sound of thousands of shoes creating a staccato rumble on the pavement. At the square the participants held rallies featuring speeches and chants. On the first day, marchers opposed Gorbachev's policies, especially an announced average 60 percent rise in prices of most goods and services to begin 1 March. On the second day, a similar number demonstrated in favor of him and his initiatives. The marchers on both days seemed sullen but peaceful, yet they provided sobering, menacing evidence of deep dissatisfactions. Similar demonstrations were held throughout 1991.

The most tragic day of our mission occurred 23 February 1991, instantly transforming every other personal or mission adversity into relative meaninglessness.

In October 1990 Sister Marta Gutierrez, a young Nicaraguan two years out of medical school, had been transferred from the Finland Helsinki Mission to Finland Helsinki East. She had come to the USSR at age sixteen to study medicine for five years in

Moscow and Kiev, and she knew Russian better than most of our other missionaries. She was a vivacious and devout sister, but recent information from Nicaragua had deeply troubled her. A change in her country's laws appeared to require that she resume her medical practice within months or complete additional years of training later. On 5 February we spoke at length about her options, and although concerned, she had decided to remain in Russia on her mission.

In the early afternoon of 23 February she and her companion, Sister Carrie Madsen, emerged from the Leningrad Red Guard subway station and attempted to hail a taxi to take them to an appointment. Several taxis stopped, but, as was common, refused to accept them as passengers because the sisters' destination was not in the direction the drivers were traveling. Suddenly a speeding van[1] swerved to miss an elderly man shuffling across the street and struck Sister Gutierrez directly, hurling her against a stone building twenty-five feet away. Sister Madsen, brushed by the van and dazed, rushed to Sister Gutierrez, cradled her in her arms, and, summoning all her faith, prayed fervently for the powers of heaven to preserve and restore her companion. But Sister Gutierrez was dead, killed instantly.

Members and missionaries mourned the passing of a righteous and dedicated young woman. In a meeting with the missionaries in Leningrad, I emphasized Spencer W. Kimball's comforting perspectives from his article "Tragedy or Destiny."[2] Missionaries recalled Sister Gutierrez's superior knowledge of Russian, the esteem in which she was held by the members, her effectiveness in teaching investigators, her happy disposition and warm personality, and her love of her Savior, Jesus Christ. Many mentioned their sympathies for her mother and relatives and remarked on the joyful reunion of Sister Gutierrez and her father, who had passed away when she was young.

Grieving branch members met to remember and honor Sister Gutierrez. They also gathered at the site of her death to sing hymns and place flowers at the corner of the building where she had lain when the ambulance arrived. Members held a somber memorial service around her coffin prior to her body's being flown to Nicaragua. We gradually resumed our lives, grateful for having known Sister Gutierrez.

In February we held our mission's first leadership training seminar for all eighty-eight leaders of the branches in Estonia and Russia. The Kemppainens, Warners, several missionaries, and Joan and I had prepared for weeks for this meeting. In the two-hour opening session, nine Russian and Estonian leaders spoke on aspects of leadership that each exemplified. I then emphasized that a good Church leader is a caring shepherd, a beacon of righteousness, and a well of inspiration.

After a refreshment break during which informal discussions arose, all afternoon was devoted to training for priesthood and auxiliary leaders. Each American or Finn who led a session distributed essential material from Church handbooks translated into Russian. This material outlined the aims of the organization and the means available to accomplish them.

Those attending from Tallinn and Moscow traveled overnight by train to reach Leningrad in time for the leadership meeting—from Vyborg the electric train trip required approximately three hours. After the meetings the leaders took overnight trains to return to their cities for Sunday responsibilities. We were concerned that we might have asked too much of the leaders, but when we later visited the branches, the most frequent question was, "How soon can we arrange another leadership meeting like the one recently held in Leningrad?" Of course too many such meetings would have quickly become a burden, but the leaders wanted to learn their duties and serve well. They were more than willing to endure inconveniences and expense to receive counsel from mission leaders and to compare experiences with their fellow leaders from other branches.

During this period, a new problem was becoming acute. When missionaries had traveled often to Helsinki to obtain new visas and hotel vouchers, we sent boxes with copies of the Book of Mormon and other materials back with them for missionaries and members in their cities. Now that missionaries were remaining longer in Russia and Estonia and traveling less frequently to Helsinki, supplying these items became a severe problem. Whenever I visited a city I took mail to the missionaries and as many other materials as possible, but other travelers and I could no longer transport all that was necessary. So, in February, we tried shipping our first boxes of the Book of Mormon to Tallinn and Moscow.

The Finnish transportation companies had no trouble delivering materials to Soviet Customs in any city. The problems arose when missionaries and members attempted to obtain the books from customs. A bewildering array of forms, authorizations, official stamps, declarations, and payments routinely required at minimum a full day of punishing effort. One would have to be there to understand how long one must stand in line, with some patrons exercising special privilege and stepping in front of you at every stage. Customs officials would leave for an hour or more without explanation or apology. Further, procedures changed often without notice, necessitating starting certain phases over. Often those in charge were gratuitously rude. It was difficult not to feel angry and dehumanized at the end of such a day. Those who had the dreaded assignment of retrieving materials from Soviet Customs deserve special commendation for their diligence, patience, and endurance. Given the choice, I am confident any of them would have preferred to cross the plains.[3]

On the other hand, the Church had no unusual problems in getting into Estonia and Russia eighteen hundred boxes of food, half for members and half for nonmembers. Each box weighed approximately twenty-six pounds and contained flour, rice, macaroni, cooking oil, cereal grains, powdered milk, dried fruit, and vitamins. Each Church member was eligible to receive one box. Additional boxes were available for families with young children or elderly parents living with them. The purchase of most of the foodstuffs was made possible by German, other European, and some American fast offering funds; milk and vitamins came from American welfare storehouses.

The nine hundred boxes distributed within cities in which the Church had branches were apportioned by consulting city agencies that maintained files of underprivileged children, especially large families, and dependent elderly. Although the boxes were given without charge, a letter inside each one invited those with the means and desire to contribute fifteen rubles to the local branch's

Russian townsfolk receiving humanitarian aid packages

fast offering fund, about the cost of the box's contents when those items had been available on the Russian market.

Peter Zarse, high councilor in the Frankfurt Germany Stake, and many other German members had obtained high-quality food, packaged everything in conveniently sized boxes to which they affixed handles, and arranged transportation. Relations between Germany and Russia had been troubled for centuries, often erupting into vicious wars. Yet German Saints and others responded with enthusiasm to the opportunity for helping the Soviets.

Soviet citizens who received the packages were deeply grateful, for many felt themselves destitute and helpless. Their living standard continued to fall for the next several years, yet in time they learned to compensate. The help provided through the Church was vital because of the people's real need for the food and because of the important psychological boost it provided. What particularly amazed me was how, even in their sudden indigence, several spoke of helping others nearby now and of looking to a time when they could assist others elsewhere in the world. Both

Church members unloading humanitarian aid packages at facility in which Leningrad branch met

nonmembers and members wrote letters to the Church expressing sentiments similar to these from an eighty-seven-year-old Vyborg woman:

> I thank you from my heart for your attention and concern for me in my old age and loneliness. Warm thanks for your package, which was very important to me because I am weak and cannot go to the stores. . . . During my entire life no one has ever given me anything, though I have shared what I could with others. And now God has seen me in my loneliness and helped me. Thanks to dear God, and to you, good people. I offer your church 15 rubles from my small pension. May the Lord preserve you.[4]

Meanwhile, Church membership continued to grow. The following letter from Dmitrii Mokhov, a young man who was baptized in February, provides a glimpse into the spiritual search of a number of Russians:

> Until I joined this Church, I lived as many other youths do who are my age. I had friends, my wonderful parents, and a job which I enjoyed. It seemed to me then as though I had everything

With the Mokhov family. Clockwise, beginning with the Browning children: Jon, Katie, and Betsy; Dmitrii Mokhov; mother, Vera Mokhov; father, Boris Mokhov; Natalia and Anna Mokhov; Joan Browning; Anastasiia Mokhov; and Gary Browning

that one needs for a good, peaceful life. Additionally, I'll acknowledge that I had been concerned with questions about God. My knowledge of him was so inadequate that you could liken my state to a first-grader who goes to elementary school for the first time, taking with him a great interest and a great desire to understand all the new things that are told to him.

With such feelings, I went to church for the first time. I found out about it through my sister. . . . One autumn day missionaries visited her school. The evening after their visit, she told our whole family about the new things she had learned. It was a very interesting discussion about a "new" church. We unfortunately had never heard anything about it before. What we had learned interested all of us, me in particular.

The first day I was at church, the atmosphere there amazed me. It left a deep impression on me which served as the reason I decided to continue associating with the missionaries. There were many happy, smiling faces. Although I was seeing everyone for the first time, it seemed as though everyone there was a close acquaintance.

As soon as I had heard the first three discussions, I decided for myself that I would be baptized into this church. I particularly wish to thank all the missionaries for the very difficult and yet very worthwhile task of learning our language and also for the love with which they taught me the discussions. With every discussion I found out something new for myself. I saw the kind and happy faces of the missionaries, and I heard the testimonies of their experiences with prayer and service to God. And with great joy, I thought about how all of this could be in my life if I were to follow the example of Christ. I understood that I can live with our Heavenly Father, and that he loves all of us. For that reason, I could hardly wait for my baptism.

I prayed a lot to find out that the Church and the Book of Mormon are true—and I can confidently say, "YES!" My baptism day is one I will always commemorate—almost like my birthday. . . . I am so happy that my sister was baptized with me and that our whole family supports us in this. One of my younger sisters might also be baptized. Only after that will we be able to tell ourselves that we are on the right path![5]

Over time all four children and both parents of the Mokhov family were baptized. The father has served as a branch and district president in Moscow and has been employed as a Church materials management specialist.

Aleksandr Goncharov, a son of Galina Goncharova, the first Russian baptized in Moscow, also joined the Church in February 1991. He wrote:

Once a new instructor came to our school to teach us history. She was an older lady and a very interesting person. She knew Old Slavonic (it is a very old language—related to Russian), which is hard to understand and especially hard to read. She would often read to us from old books she had borrowed from an archive. Those texts were not only hard to gain access to, but also dangerous to include in an academic course without prior approval.

One time she brought a Bible to class. That was the first time I found out about religion and Christianity. It was always very quiet during these classes because it was new to us. . . . It seems to me that the Holy Ghost was there during these classes. It was quiet and no one argued. The feelings of inspiration lasted with me long after the classes ended. I really enjoyed those lectures. That is how I found out about Christ and his sacrifice for us. I can still remember it all. When I close my eyes, I can see the whole picture. But there was one thing I just couldn't understand: Why would people kill a man who never did anything bad to anyone, and why didn't any of the countless people he helped, help him?

Some time later, after the appearance of Gorbachev and perestroika, many foreigners, mostly Americans, started visiting

Russia. One of these visitors gave me a small Bible. I began reading it little by little. I was somewhat uncomfortable reading it because it was so small and because it had been illegally transported into the country. I was interested to find that when I showed my Bible to friends at school, they all wanted to borrow it so they could read it themselves.

A little later, a friend of my mother's (who was from Utah and was working at the American embassy [Dohn Thornton]) invited her to go to a church meeting on Sunday. Mother was very interested and had been searching for the truth—she had been having a lot of problems with me, my brother, and my father. It was then that this friend said to her, "You know, Galina (that's my mother's name), I have seen that you are really interested in seeking for the truth. For that reason, I have decided to invite you to church."

When she returned home that Sunday, we all sat down together and asked her a lot of questions, to which she answered: "It was my first time there. I don't know why it was the way it was. Go to a meeting and see for yourselves." I have to mention that for a Russian in those days to wake up early on a Sunday was unheard of. Our culture has been, more or less, built around the idea that you work and study from sun-up to sun-down six days a week. But on Sunday you relax and stay at home and do whatever you want. Usually, we would sleep in and watch TV until one o'clock in the afternoon. All of my classmates and I had such a schedule.

Nonetheless, in three weeks I prepared myself ahead of time (that is, I made sure I had a full night's sleep) and went to the church meeting. There were still no missionaries in Moscow at that time. What I first noticed at the meeting amazed me: people were smiling and greeting each other. They were interested in how I was doing and even asked me how I had slept (Mom had told them earlier that I hadn't been to church because of my love for sleep). There were eight people there from the embassy and also a large family from Denmark. It didn't take long to meet everyone even though we couldn't say anything in English. We went every Sunday thereafter—never missing once.

We were so interested that every week we also attended a kind of fireside or family home evening where we read the Book of Mormon together and shared our feelings and impressions about what we had read. It was so fascinating that, forgetting about everything else, I would hurry to the meetings to talk about the Church and find out more about it. . . .

Summer began, and I left for a summer camp. I was there for

quite a long time. When I came back home I no longer wanted to go to church. It was probably because I didn't want to change my life and obey the commandments. It seemed to me that life would be easier my way. But not much later, I began to feel that I had been mistaken. I felt that I needed to be baptized and receive the Holy Ghost, whose spirit was always at our meetings. I started to pray and attend church meetings again. I was later baptized (a little over six months after my mother's baptism) on the 17th of February, 1991. I can't even express all the feelings I have, but I know it was a true baptism and I am 100 percent sure that it was the right step in my life.[6]

17

MARCH 1991

All the branches developed steadily. During my visit to Vyborg in March 1991, some 140 people attended sacrament meeting. The music school had become too small, and a division of the branch seemed imminent. In Leningrad I held a two-branch leadership meeting at which all the priesthood quorums and auxiliaries were well represented.

With all that was happening, Joan tried to make certain our family was not forgotten. Occasional trips with the children, such as the one she described here, were invigorating:

> We took a day and drove to Lahti, a city about an hour and a half from Helsinki. The city is located on a large lake and is surrounded by hills high enough to provide skiing opportunities in the winter. It was a truly memorable day. After looking around the city we drove along the lake, passing several ski resorts. We stopped at one that had snow sculptures doubling as slides for children to play on. The snow was perfect for cross-country skiing, and we went on some trails that are used for European competition races.[1]

On Saturday, 23 March, a meeting of great significance for the Church in all of Russia was held at the Moscow Spartacus Square facility. Thirteen representatives, three more than the ten required, gathered to participate in the founding meeting of the Church's Russian Religious Association. Iurii Terebenin served as chairman for the official founding meeting.

From Vyborg, Andrei Semionov and Tatiana Turutina attended; from Leningrad, Iurii and Liudmila Terebenin, Viacheslav Efimov, Irina Maksimova, Vladimir Batianov, and Svetlana Glukhikh; from Moscow, Andrei and Elena Petrov, Galina Goncharova, and Nina Leonteva; and from Sochi on the Black Sea, Vladimir Fiodorov, who served as secretary. President Dennis B. Neuenschwander and

I represented the two missions (Austria Vienna East and Finland Helsinki East) having Church responsibility for Russia west of the Volga River.

An inspirational highlight of the meeting occurred as the thirteen Russians shared their conversion stories and testimonies. I could not conceive of a more faithful and worthy group of founding members.

Church attorney David Farnsworth carefully explained how the association would benefit the Church through its status as a legal entity with the ability to address very important temporal issues. He emphasized that the association was not an ecclesiastical organization. The mission and branch presidents would continue to preside until a stake was formed. Moscow attorney Irina Saveleva further discussed the association's statutes, powers, and spheres of activity. To facilitate communication with Russian government officials, a Church member in Moscow was needed as president of the association, and the group approved the Area presidency's nomination of Andrei Petrov for that position.

Another historic moment for Moscow occurred the next day. On Sunday, 24 March, the Moscow group became a branch with Andrei Petrov as president and Albert Walling and Daryl Gibb as counselors. When Albert Walling had become the Moscow group leader seven months earlier (August 1990), we both agreed that one of our principal aspirations would be to help prepare a capable Russian brother to become the first Moscow branch president. One month after Brother Petrov was baptized in September 1990, he was called to serve as Brother Walling's assistant in the group leadership.

Now the time had come for a Moscow branch to be formed. Other groups had called themselves branches, but this was the first officially designated branch in the Russian capital. We both felt that Brother Petrov was prepared to lead the new branch. Brother Petrov asked that his mentors, Brothers Walling and Gibb, continue serving with him.

During this month a long, generally accurate, and complimentary article on the Church appeared in the prestigious and widely read Russian weekly newspaper *Literary Gazette*. The article, entitled "Apostles of Prosperity," portrayed family, pioneer spirit, self-reliance, hard work, and prayer as appealing ideals for today's Russia. One message was that the LDS Church, "possibly the most American manifestation of the spiritual life of America," could teach Russians valuable lessons of immediate relevance.[2]

Beginning in the 1980s, other generally positive material about the Church had appeared as chapters of scholarly books and as articles in the popular press,[3] but this *Literary Gazette* article gave the credibility and prestige comparable to that which a *New York Times* feature would provide in the United States.

Until the 1980s, many Russians obtained their information about the Church from two sources, both encyclopedias. The most readily available was the *Great Soviet Encyclopedia,* which treated the Church in two largely dismissive paragraphs. It provided a few lines of historical information, brief reference to Church teachings, including polygamy ("abolished only in 1890,") and stressed the close ties between Mormonism and ethical priorities of capitalism—industriousness and frugality.[4]

The highly regarded but rare prerevolutionary Brokgauz-Efron *New Encyclopedic Dictionary*[5] devoted two long pages to the Church. In addition to giving a concise history of the Church, it treated several distinctive Latter-day Saints teachings, including the Godhead, degrees of glory, ordinances, Church governance, tithing, and continuing revelation. This article was comparable to the best western encyclopedia articles on Mormonism of the time. But few Russians had access to this respected reference work.

Many Russians who knew something of Mormonism had formed their earliest perceptions from the television adaptation of *A Study in Scarlet,* Arthur Conan Doyle's first Sherlock Holmes book, which had been published in 1887. The translation and later television adaptation of this book were immensely popular in Russia. Utah Mormons were characterized as fanatically devoted to tyrannical leaders.

Now Russian media representatives were eager to receive and dispense accurate information about the Church. Several producers of Russian television programming contacted me for material suitable for Russian television. Church Public Communications personnel assured me that films were in production and would soon become available. By the end of our mission some were beginning to appear, including selected Church public service messages and Tabernacle Choir telecasts.

The mission, meantime, had grown considerably. Joan's letter home summarized developments:

> The Finland Helsinki East Mission now has thirty-two missionaries, double the number we had when we arrived in July. By May we will have forty. There are now two branches in Leningrad, each having between seventy-five and eighty members. The branch in Vyborg has the same number of members, but for the past month the sacrament meeting attendance has been 140-plus people trying to squeeze into a room that comfortably seats half that number. The four missionaries there go to church and are able to entirely fill their week with appointments made on the spot. This is very helpful, as few in the town have telephones. There are now about forty-five to fifty Russian members in Moscow. They meet with a variety of Latter-day Saint foreigners, mostly Americans, who work in the city.[6]

18

April 1991

Through the efforts of Marina Saarik in Tallinn, in April 1991 the Church received the first congregational invitations and visas for all the Estonian-speaking missionaries—the two Russian-speaking missionaries would serve for a time in Estonia and then return to Russia in rotation. And the Estonian visas were valid until the missionaries returned home! All those who had spent so long working on visa issues recognized what an achievement this was. We looked forward to the time when the Russian Religious Association could do the same in behalf of the more numerous Russian-speaking missionaries.

In a letter home written in early April, I described conditions in the two Estonian Church units and the economic trials in the country:

> Currently the Estonian branch has sixty-four members with an average sacrament meeting attendance of twenty-seven members and twenty-three nonmembers. Generally fourteen attend Relief Society, twenty-seven are at Sunday School, two in Primary, and three in Young Women. Through March 1991 the branch had fifteen baptisms this year. . . . A vivacious fifteen-year-old girl is encouraging her father (battling vodka and smoking) and mother (with strong ties to the traditional Estonian Lutheran Church) to accept the Church. All the other members are young single girls, single women, a few young single men, and three or so middle-aged men. . . .

> In the Tallinn Russian group (approximately one-half of the Tallinn city population is Russian), two missionaries are accomplishing the Herculean task of beginning the Church from the ground up. Last October there were only two Russian members who had joined along with the Estonians. At that time two Russian-speaking missionaries arrived in Tallinn and arranged for the Russians to meet separately on Sunday, although joint social and family home evening activities are held.

141

Earlier, Russian-speaking investigators had visited church meetings in Tallinn, but generally had not continued to attend because they could understand very little of the Estonian service. For weeks and months the missionaries struggled to find investigators and those courageous enough to join a fledgling and foreign-based organization. Now the group has thirteen members, with an average sacrament attendance of thirty-eight. Today, sixty-two Russians were at fast and testimony meeting. . . .

Economic and political conditions continue to deteriorate in Estonia and Russia, among other places in the Soviet Union. Food is even less available now, prices have risen dramatically, and the ruble keeps falling in buying power. However, now the missionaries are receiving bank rates of twenty-seven rubles for one American dollar! Two years ago Joan and I paid over $1.50 for *one* ruble. But it is sad to see economic paralysis, political impotence, and popular disillusionment spread all over Estonia and Russia. The countries, potentially among the finest of the world, are in the death grip of a moribund structure that resists burial. Everyone who brings the topic up insists that the worst is yet to come, possibly this fall.[1]

Until this month I had trained each missionary district leader (we did not yet have zones) in his own city during my monthly visits. In April we held our first all-day training session for the district leaders. With missionary leaders packed tightly into a small Leningrad hotel room, I discussed the vision I had for our mission, and each of them spoke on an assigned topic: guidelines for successful service with branch leaders, goals, accountability and reporting, observation and feedback, district meetings, companion exchanges, and mission morale. How impressed I was with these leaders.

For Vyborg, Joan suggested a very wise temporary solution to overcrowded Sunday meetings. Because we had only one available facility at the time and because I did not, in any case, feel assured that we should divide the branch quite yet, we created an additional sacrament meeting. Half the branch attended sacrament meeting first, all branch members joined together for the other meetings, and then the other half of the branch held their sacrament meeting last. Because we were divided into groups during the middle meetings, the facility remained adequate, and all who attended seemed content.

Vyborg is a relatively small city, and transportation to church services does not require the time it does in Leningrad or Moscow. This circumstance lessened the urgency to divide the branch. Dividing the branch along geographic lines for sacrament meetings, however, did help prepare the members for that first, and always traumatic, division.

Late in the month the Young Ambassadors from BYU arrived in our mission. Their firesides and concerts awed everyone. It was uplifting for our Soviet youth to be in the presence of exemplary Latter-day Saints who displayed such professionalism and wholesomeness.

At each concert missionaries received several particularly good referrals. Investigators often remarked that the inspiring performance of the Young Ambassadors contributed to their decision to join the Church. Members, who so often were denigrated by their associates for joining a little-known church, felt more confident after meeting the Young Ambassadors. City officials and other influential guests were pleasantly entertained, favorably impressed, and more inclined to give the Church a fair hearing.

As always, this BYU performing group was recorded and telecast on the most widely available Soviet channel, influencing thousands who would hear again of the Church and decide whether to listen further. On this trip the Young Ambassadors performed to enthusiastic audiences in Leningrad, Moscow, and all three Baltic republics.

Challenges appeared inconsequential in comparison with the joy of serving such valiant new Latter-day Saints as Sister Olga Garasimishina:

> I am Ukrainian. I study in Vyborg at the medical institute. Even though I am very far away from home, I feel almost as if I were a native of Vyborg. Here I have been reborn. Here I have found a dear family. But unfortunately, either this winter or next year, I will have to leave and go back to my home in Lvovschina. But how will I live there without our Church? Without brothers and sisters? Who will baptize my friends, family and all those who come to a knowledge of the truth?
>
> Kiev is far away from us. I will be able to go there, of course,

but not very often. Every Sunday, I go to church here as if it were to a hearth, so that I might be warmed by the fire. How will I be able to exist without it when I am at home? I cannot imagine life without this family which is so special to me. Of course, the Comforter, the Holy Ghost, will be with me. I will also have my faith and the scriptures. But what about my brothers and sisters, and the sacrament and hymns? Where will all this be?

When I was home this summer, I felt it was very important that the Church be where my home is. When Sunday at 11 o'clock came, I was sitting in a field and reading my scriptures. But at that moment, I thought about how everyone in Vyborg was getting together just then, and I wanted so badly to be with them. I sang all the hymns by myself (I could sing them with my full voice—no one could hear me). I began to feel better. But I won't be able to do this much longer. It was very hard. How great was my joy when I made my way to Kiev and had the sacrament for the first time in three weeks!

I know you understand. I want very badly for The Church of Jesus Christ of Latter-day Saints to be in Lvov. What can I do for my people? What do you suggest I should do? How can you help me? We have very good people here, and probably 80 percent of them are believers. But the true faith is in one church only. It is our Church. I know that it is true because it is a living church. It is all of us people. We are members of the body of Christ—and his body is our Church. I want all my people to be "grafted in to this vine." I want them to be happy. I hope you will help. I will pray for everything I've written about.[2]

Sister Garasimishina later served a full-time mission in the Russia Moscow Mission. While in Vyborg she received her call with assurance that further information would be forthcoming. She returned to her native Ukraine and awaited communication. When nothing more arrived, she packed a bag and set off by train for Moscow. In the capital she stayed with an old friend while attempting to locate the mission office. After a few days she saw two sister missionaries, who took her to the mission office and introduced her to President Richard Chapple—and Sister Garasimishina commenced her mission.

19

MAY 1991

For almost a year I had been concerned about recording a history of the branches developing in Russia and Estonia. During May 1991 an appealing solution appeared. Months before, Elder John Webster had contacted each of the early members in Vyborg and invited them to write a few paragraphs about their conversion and growth in the Church. He collected these sheets, added pertinent portions from his own and other missionaries' journals, and attached photographs. The result was a collection of first-person accounts that captured the essence of the birth and establishment of the Vyborg branch. Much the same approach was later taken with success in Tallinn by Katrin Roop, in Leningrad by Liudmila Terebenin, and in Moscow by Dohn Thornton and Daniel Souders.

Early in May, BYU president Rex E. Lee and Sister Janet Lee visited Leningrad and Moscow. In Leningrad an audience of approximately 350 people was impressed with the Lees' perspectives on the role of faith, prayer, and education in the life of a Latter-day Saint. For a long time after the meeting, Leningraders posed questions to the university president about American education generally and BYU specifically. Many would eagerly have gone to the United States to study, had their resources allowed.

In Moscow the branch met on Saturday, as happened once or twice each year. Earlier in the month all Russians had had holidays from work to commemorate the victory over Nazi Germany. In exchange for free days on Thursday (the actual V-Day holiday), Friday, and Saturday, Russians were to work on Sunday. In addition to the Lees' excellent addresses at this Saturday meeting, the Young Ambassadors sang three inspirational songs, and two members of their group spoke. In the afternoon, President Lee, Randy Boothe (Young Ambassador musical director), Edwin Morrell (Young Ambassador tour manager and former president of the

145

Austria Vienna East Mission), and I were interviewed by Soviet Central TV concerning BYU, the Young Ambassadors, and the LDS Church. These extensive interviews were interspersed among the Young Ambassadors' musical numbers when their concert was telecast, again providing the Church an exceptional media opportunity that complemented other efforts to open doors and hearts to the gospel.

Brother Aleksandr Kudriashov learned of the Church through attending a Moscow Young Ambassador concert. This is his story:

> I grew up in a working class family. I lost my father early on (in 1941 he became missing in action during the war), and I don't have any brothers or sisters. I was raised alone by my mother in humble circumstances. Because of our difficult economic situation I went to work at the age of sixteen in order to help my mother.
>
> My mother is a believer and often attended the Russian Orthodox Church. Soviet propaganda attempted to confuse and destroy my belief in God, so when I started school I stopped attending church. As a result, when I became an adult I constantly experienced difficulties in spiritual matters. Belief in God was condemned and persecuted, but I always believed that God loved me. He has helped me many times in difficult moments of my life. I have continually recalled a precept of my mother: "Always remember God and love him with all of your heart." I am very grateful to God for helping me through the trials that have beset me and for helping me find happiness in life.
>
> I simultaneously worked and studied in school and graduated from the Institute of Engineering and Construction. . . . I started as an apprentice metalworker in a factory, and after graduation from the institute I worked as an electrical equipment repairman.
>
> I am married; my wife's name is Galina Kuzmina. I have two sons, Aleksandr [later to become a Moscow branch president] . . . and Dmitrii. . . . During the summer of 1991 at a Young Ambassadors' concert in Moscow, I met some missionaries who told me about The Church of Jesus Christ of Latter-day Saints. While taking the lessons from the missionaries (Elders [Bradley] Weyland, [Michael] Price, and others) and while attending a branch as a friend of the Church, I felt with my whole soul that this was exactly what had been missing all of these years—interaction with brothers and sisters who deeply and sincerely believed in and loved our Savior Jesus Christ.

*Aleksandr Kudriashov and son Aleksandr visiting the grave
of their mother and grandmother, Easter*

The missionaries had a great influence on me. These young people were bright, clean, and deeply faithful. They were strengthened by a solid understanding of the scriptures and were always prepared to help in any way, no matter what the problem. Their sacred faith has led many people in Russia into the bosom of our Church.

On July 13, 1991, I was baptized. It was a joyful and great holiday for me. I chose the place for my baptism myself. It was in the magnificent nature of the Silver Grove on the shore of the Moskva River canal.

As I continually went to church, [branch] family home evenings, and picnics, I made many new friends—brothers and sisters, the numbers of whom were continually increasing as the church itself was growing, thanks to the missionaries and the selfless work of our leaders. My faithful attendance at church and study of the scriptures, the Bible and Book of Mormon, have influenced my spiritual growth.

My first calling was to be the second counselor in the Sunday School. After our branch was divided, I was called to be the Rizhskii branch clerk. As a direct result I feel I received my greatest blessing—visiting the temple in Stockholm, Sweden.[1]

Joan described the Lees' visit to Leningrad in connection with the Young Ambassadors' tour and other efforts to foster good feelings toward the Church:

We went on a tour of the city with the Lees and then to a former palace where the Leningrad city offices are located. We were given a tour of the most significant rooms used to greet important guests and also visited the restored chapel used by the royal family. The purpose of our visit was to deliver a geiger counter to a member of the city council who is helping make arrangements for the Church. . . . The city is anxious to check areas around Leningrad, since there are nuclear power plants in the vicinity. . . .

President Lee is hopeful that he will be able to arrange a scholarship program that will allow a few Church members to attend BYU. A great problem will be to choose students who will return to the Soviet Union. You can't blame the people for wanting to leave the difficult situations in their own country, but we would hope that those who attend BYU will choose to return and strengthen others. Several of our strong members have emigrated, and I am sure that others will follow if they possibly can.

The Young Ambassadors also performed in cities where the gospel might soon be preached. Joan recounted the story of a concert in Tartu, Estonia:

Last Friday we took the ship to Tallinn with the children. The Young Ambassadors were scheduled to have their final concert there on Saturday evening and this looked like the best chance for the children to see the performance. On Wednesday we received word that the YA schedule had been changed and that the Saturday concert would be held in Tartu, a city nearly 200 kilometers from Tallinn. On this note we tried without success to make arrangements to take our car over on the boat. The Tallinn missionaries bought bus tickets for us on Saturday afternoon so we spent three hours traveling across the Estonian countryside. The homes and farms reminded us of our trips to

Poland rather than of typical Russian scenes. A chimney with a stork and its nest reinforced the feeling.

We had time to walk around the town of Tartu before the performance and saw part of the university. . . . The town is really quite charming, and since it is the second-largest city [107,000] in Estonia, it is likely that missionaries will be sent there as the mission grows. The YA concert that evening was completely sold out, so we sat on folding chairs in the aisles. The audience loved the show and applauded until several encore numbers were performed. The Young Ambassadors were very excited about their experiences performing in the Soviet Union. They were filmed for television by five different stations and have provided many referrals. One person has already been taught and baptized in Leningrad as a result of their concerts there a few weeks ago. . . . The YAs were enthusiastic despite the fact that the group ended up in low-class hotels, often without hot water, and with less than desirable food. The general problems in the Soviet Union and the breakdown of the central economy resulted in very inconsistent treatment as they traveled from town to town.

Since the last train and last bus returning to Tallinn from Tartu left just about the time the concert started, we arranged with three taxi drivers to drive us and the missionaries back to Tallinn following the concert. The cost was 250 rubles per taxi (less than $10). We arrived back at our hotel after midnight, and it was light most of the way home. Even when the sun went down there was still light on the horizon.[2]

On May 18 and 19 our mission held its first all-mission youth conference in Leningrad. President Jussi and Sister Raija Kemppainen planned the conference, and they, the Warners, the Russian branch leaders, and Joan and I served as adult activity leaders. From Vyborg came twenty-six participants; from Moscow, twenty-four; from Leningrad First Branch, twenty-two; from Leningrad Second Branch, twenty-three; and from Tallinn, fourteen; to this group of one hundred and nine were added six participants from mission headquarters and twelve other speakers. We met in Leningrad State University facilities at Petrodvorets (Peter's Palace) while university students were on spring vacation.

The Kemppainens organized the conference around the theme "I Am a Child of God." They showed slides and told stories of a recently married Finnish Latter-day Saint couple as babies, children, school pupils, missionaries, while dating, and at their temple marriage. Later two youths from each branch provided insights on thorny questions besetting them, such as ridicule from friends, temptations to cheat, break the Word of Wisdom, or engage in premarital sex; and on recognizing the Spirit and gaining a personal witness. Three workshops followed, through which three groups of youth rotated: one with branch president Andrei Semionov and Relief Society president Irina Maksimova on the contributions of the Word of Wisdom to physical health and on morality and spiritual power; another with President Kemppainen designed to make certain the youth became acquainted with and trusted each other; and the third with President Dale and Sister Rene Warner featuring crafts and cultural enrichment.

Following dinner, each branch presented approximately thirty minutes of singing, dancing, poetry reading, or skits. The skit I recall most vividly, given by the Tallinn youth, was composed of three brief scenes. In the first, the husband appeared intoxicated and was verbally abusive, and both husband and wife shouted insults at each other. In the second, the husband slouched on a chair and watched TV while a neglected wife struggled to maintain her composure in the kitchen. But in the third segment a handsome husband dressed in suit and tie returned from work, embraced his wife, and sat down with her at the table to enjoy dinner. Before eating they asked a blessing on the food and then, while sharing the meal, asked about each other's activities of the day, showing sensitivity for the other's concerns. I was particularly moved because there were no full Latter-day Saint families in Tallinn at that time. These youth portrayed that for which they hoped.

Each youth received a CTR ring (in English to lessen the cost) and an explanation of its meaning. The evening ended with a dance. At 11:00 P.M. we had a closing prayer, and the youth, to our surprise, went to their dormitory rooms and to sleep without a murmur. On Sunday morning they were taught in separate groups on the subjects "I Am a Young Man of God" and "I Am a Young Woman of God." Then in a combined meeting one youth from each branch spoke on the conference theme. Finally youth and their leaders bore testimony. After a meal we bade each other farewell and left for our homes. The Kemppainens, Warners, and Joan and I returned to Helsinki.

At the border between Russia and Finland we had an unusual experience. The border guards noticed on the back seat of our van a Russian translation of a *New Era* article by Joy Saunders Lundberg entitled "The Strapless Dress."[3] We had just received several translations from the Vyborg translator and were taking them to Helsinki for duplication and distribution.

In Lundberg's story, an Oregon farmer, alone while his wife helps with a new grandchild in Utah, is concerned lest his daughter appear immodest at the school dance. He carefully and quite successfully sews straps on her gown. Later the girl feels grateful that he cared for her enough to shield her from being too much "in the world." At the border, while we all waited outside the van, two young guards sat inside it for ten minutes, reading the story to each other, nodding approvingly, obviously agreeing with what they read. They then complimented us on the story and with broad smiles waved us on our way.

On 28 May 1991, the Church's Russian Religious Association was registered, legally recognized and approved, by the Russian Republic Ministry of Justice. David Farnsworth, Andrei Petrov, and I attended a ceremony with several high officials from the Ministry of Justice, including Mr. Eduard Gatseptian, who now was the chief specialist at the Ministry of Justice and who had been the man responsible at the Russian Republic Council on Religious Affairs for facilitating the original Leningrad registration just eight months previously.

President Petrov made a presentation summarizing the origin, purposes, and distinguishing beliefs of the LDS Church and presented the officials with additional copies of Church materials in Russian and with Tabernacle Choir tapes. David Farnsworth represented the Area presidency in officially expressing greetings and appreciation for the good work of the ministry. Now the Church was a recognized legal entity that could conduct business, print and distribute Church materials, and issue invitations for missionaries to serve in Russia. We soon discovered that the cooperation of the USSR Ministry of Foreign Affairs was necessary before visas could be granted. This was a potential problem, for the

Association's registration was through the Russian Republic, but the visas still came only through the USSR Ministry. Events over the next few months eliminated this concern.

During this month missionary work was begun in Zelenograd. Zelenograd is administratively a part of Moscow but is fifty kilometers northwest of the capital proper. This city of nearly five hundred thousand inhabitants was a military, scientific, and educational center, long closed to foreigners and most Russians alike. Missionaries began to work in Zelenograd after a Zelenograd high school student named Denis Shirokov was baptized in the United States and returned briefly from study abroad.

Denis was confident that interest in the Church would be great in Zelenograd, and Elder Kurt Wood was designated to commence work there. His extraordinary labor in Zelenograd inspired others who followed him and led eventually to the formation there of a Russian branch.

May baptisms in our mission included that of Anastasiia Maslova, a sister who in time became a fine missionary to Canada:

> I was born and raised in Moscow. I have a very small family, just my mother and I. My mother and father divorced when I was very young. My mother raised me essentially by herself. We are very close. I graduated from a music pedagogical college, after which I worked for a year in a school as a music teacher. My specialties are choir directing and playing the piano and accordion. . . .
>
> Before becoming acquainted with the Church, I had no religious convictions. I can't say I was an atheist, though. . . . I remember reading often in our history books that there is no God. That was the Communist perspective of Marxism and Leninism. I remember how my mother would ask, "Why do you think there is no God?" I would answer, "That's what it says in my textbook. My teacher told me." My mother would say, "But do you really think we descended from the monkey?" I was not baptized a member of any church, but my mother really helped me to think and realize there is a God. She prepared me for the truth.
>
> I met the missionaries when I was a student in 1991. . . . I directed a women's choir. Once we gave a concert, believe it or not, for several missionaries. There were ten missionaries, eight elders and two sisters, all from America, with the exception of one sister from Poland. After we sang for them they began to tell

us about family home evenings and their families, using the unfamiliar word "Mormons." ...

After the concert, my friend and I invited some missionaries to my house. They came and told us about the Church and led the first discussion. At first everything seemed curious: they didn't drink tea, they didn't drink coffee, what did they drink? ... They invited us to church and, although I wanted to go, I was afraid. I didn't want to go alone so I took five friends with me and immediately liked the services. They were warm, and people welcomed me as if to say, "Where have you been for so long?" It was wonderful. I think the fact that it was the first Sunday of the month, Fast Sunday, also played a great role. People at the meeting shared their testimonies. Seeing men cry when they spoke about Jesus Christ touched me deeply. After the meeting I felt a real sense of joy and I couldn't understand why. The following week seemed long. I couldn't wait to return. We met with the missionaries and they taught us the discussions. I had met them in March, and in May of 1991 I was baptized.

The only thing difficult for me to accept, probably simply because I didn't understand it, was when the missionaries would say The Church of Jesus Christ of Latter-day Saints is the only true church. When they would say the word "only," I felt somewhat angry inside. "How can you say 'only'? All churches are good; all of them teach about God." Even for some time after my baptism I didn't completely understand it. I didn't tell anyone; I just tried to understand it myself. With time I realized that if there is one God, he must have one truth, and there cannot be many true churches. I know that all churches are good, but only one is true. I know this is our Church.

I remember when I came to church the first time, I was impressed by the happiness and smiles on the faces of those attending. ... Perhaps you have noticed that very few people on the streets smile here in Moscow. I know there are few reasons for people to smile these days. What I realized clearly when I came to church, accepted baptism, and continued to participate was that I now felt within me an enormous happiness. At first I didn't understand why I felt this great joy. Then I began to sense why. As I worked with the sister missionaries, and talked with people at discussions or on the streets almost every week or even every day, I began to feel a need to engage in this work. I decided to serve a mission because I wanted people around me ... to also feel this happiness, to have a reason to smile, even when it is difficult, when there is no money, or even work, to still see purpose in life and be happy in any situation. . . .

My mother was a great support to me, although she is still not a member of the Church. . . . She encouraged me to go to church. Each time I went she asked me what I had learned. . . . She was always interested and loved the members of the Church and the missionaries. . . . She even said once, about six months after my baptism, "You spend so much time with the missionaries, don't you want to go on a mission yourself?" I guess in some way she even began to prepare me for a mission. . . .

I attended the temple for the first time in Provo. . . . The temple had a great influence on my life. When the missionaries would tell about the temple, it always seemed so pure and unaccessible to me. I never thought I'd be able to go to the temple. We didn't have one in Russia. I didn't know whether I'd be able to save enough money, but I always had a great desire to go. I loved to hear about the temple and look at pictures of it. . . . When I received the opportunity to attend the temple, I was frightened at first—it was so unfamiliar. I wasn't sure I was worthy to enter. . . . But, it was a unique experience. I know the temple is truly a house of God. . . .

The strongest impressions from my mission are connected with the honor I felt when seeing the changes that occurred in people's lives. That was the greatest miracle. There were several brief moments in discussions when I would think, "If I hadn't decided to serve a mission, I wouldn't have met this person, I wouldn't have taught this person, I wouldn't have heard this testimony, I wouldn't have seen how this person came into the Church. . . ." On my mission I began to learn how to feel more, to understand more with my feelings what the gospel means in my life, and why this Church exists, and what the Holy Ghost is.

I missed Russia a lot. It was difficult for me. This may sound strange, but it was on my mission that I became a Russian patriot. Earlier I didn't have a very high opinion of Russia and her government. All of it was, in some ways, offensive. I still see shortcomings, but I am glad I am a Russian. . . . Many people would ask me if I were going to return to Russia. There were many offers to stay, but I understood I went to Canada as a missionary, as a representative of Jesus Christ. It was an honor for me to serve there, but I was happy to return to Russia. I understand I also have a mission here—to help members of the Church and to teach my friends.[4]

20

JUNE 1991

I telephoned Leningrad early one morning in June 1991 to ask about the health of a missionary suffering from apparent intestinal problems and learned that another missionary, Sister Carrie Madsen, had just undergone an emergency appendectomy. The Semionov brothers, Andrei and Pavel, both physicians and both members of the Church, maintained a vigil at her bedside to ensure she received the best available care. Sister Madsen was characteristically imperturbable and confident. With her faith, priesthood blessings, and the help of the Semionovs and other attentive Russian medical personnel, Sister Madsen recovered rapidly, despite considerably less than ideal physical circumstances.

During the month of June, President Albert Choules of the Europe Area presidency, together with his wife, Sister Marilyn Choules, visited Tallinn, Moscow, and Leningrad to hold missionary and member meetings. A highlight for the missionaries in Moscow occurred as Elder Choules shared with us glimpses into his personal "Gardens of Gethsemane," including the passing of his first wife following their mission in New York and his own recent battle with cancer, from which he was still recovering. We were all moved and uplifted by his assurance that the appropriate response to affliction is the Savior's, "Thy will be done," followed by a determined and humble effort to conform to that will.

In Leningrad, Elder Choules bore a memorable witness to the gift of prophecy. Much earlier he had received in a patriarchal blessing assurance that he and his family members would serve as missionaries to the Lamanites, on the isles of the sea, to Italy, and in Russia. The Choules family had served in the other lands, and now he was privileged to preach the gospel of Jesus Christ in Russia.

A large delegation from Vyborg traveled three hours each way

*The Tabernacle Choir
in front of the Moscow
Bolshoi Theater*

by electric train, sitting, when a seat could be found, on hard wooden benches to participate in the meetings. Several of the youth attending had taken part in graduation celebrations the evening before until the early morning. After only two hours of sleep they arose to leave for Sunday conference in Leningrad.

What an immeasurable blessing our mission experienced with the visit of the Tabernacle Choir to Moscow and Leningrad. Thanks to the tour organizers, members of the Church obtained tickets for the concerts in the resplendent Moscow Bolshoi Theater and Leningrad Philharmonic Hall. Elders Russell M. Nelson, Dallin H. Oaks, and Hans B. Ringger accompanied the Choir and spoke at firesides and after-concert dinners. These elegant dinners for national and city dignitaries were sponsored by several wealthy and generous donors and arranged by Beverly Campbell, director of the Washington, D.C., office of Church Public Affairs and Communications.

At the June 24 dinner in Moscow, Aleksandr Rutskoi, vice-president to Boris Yeltsin (both of whom had been elected by a landslide less than two weeks earlier), made public the May 28 registration of the Church in the Russian Republic. Vice-president Rutskoi welcomed the Church's efforts to assist in the spiritual regeneration of Russia. Elder Nelson presented the Russian state through Mr. Rutskoi a porcelain statuette of a child's early steps from the encouraging mother to the outstretched arms of a welcoming father.

Many important government contacts were made at the dinner and during the next day's visits to government representatives in their Moscow offices at the Ministry of Foreign Affairs, Supreme Soviet, and USSR Council on Religious Affairs. An especially rewarding visit was the meeting of the two apostles and the Europe Area president with Patriarch Aleksii II, leader of the approximately eighty million Russian Orthodox Church members, and his personal secretary and advisor, Father Matvei. The patriarch received the group warmly in his modest reception hall at Chistyi Pereulok [Pure Lane] 5 in downtown Moscow. Father Matvei, having served in the United States, translated from English into Russian and I from Russian into English.

The patriarch asked probing questions about the aspirations and distinguishing features of the LDS Church. He averred that our efforts were welcome as long as our Church did not seek converts from among his Orthodox members. Elder Oaks responded diplomatically yet candidly that as a rule, those who become interested in the LDS Church are believers in God who belong to no church or who are disaffected members of a church that has not met their spiritual needs. I was impressed by Patriarch Aleksii's detailed recounting of his recent trip to Belorus and by his deep feelings of sorrow for these suffering people. He recalled four twentieth-century disasters which had befallen them in greater measure than any other people: Stalinist repression, the ravages of World War II, militant atheism, and Chernobyl's deadly radiation.

Elder Nelson spoke of this meeting in general conference, illustrating a point on the need for tolerance of other's beliefs as we proclaim the good news of the Restoration in "mildness and meekness": "Patriarch Aleksii was most gracious in sharing a memorable hour with us. We perceived the great difficulties endured for so many years by this kind man and his fellow believers. We thanked him for his perseverance and for his faith."[1]

Later that day, 25 June, the General Authorities gathered at the Kremlin. For the Russians as a people, the Moscow Kremlin ("fortress") is a premier symbol of secular and spiritual history, unity, stability, strength, tradition, resilience, creativity, and beauty. Largely constructed during the twelfth through the fourteenth centuries, the majestic Kremlin walls, intersected by twenty distinctive towers, enclose the heart of Moscow and, indeed, the heart of all Russia. Close to the Water Conveyance Tower, nearest of the towers to the Moscow River, Elders Nelson and Oaks entreated God in behalf of the Russian people. As from this spot Russians had for centuries drawn life-sustaining water for Kremlin inhabitants, now these two latter-day apostles earnestly desired to offer living waters of the Spirit, the fulness of the Restoration, to those whose heritage it is to cherish the inimitable Kremlin.

Elder Nelson expressed gratitude for the opportunities of the recent past and future. He offered to the Lord a moving prayer of recommitment of the Russian Republic

> for the furtherance of Thy work, indeed as Elder Francis Marion Lyman did nearly eighty-eight years ago. Wilt Thou cause the light of Thy gospel to reach the hearts and the souls of the people of this republic and of this great union. Wilt Thou thwart the efforts of the adversary who would make it difficult for Thy work to prosper.[2]

This apostolic prayer greatly moved and heartened all present.

Three days later, nearly six hundred people, including the Choir and over two hundred American members and friends, attended the Choir fireside in Leningrad. As in other firesides and interviews, Choir members who knew Russian spoke, an ensemble of Choir members sang, and Church leaders provided inspirational messages. At this fireside Elder Nelson shared his personal perspective on the history of the Church's efforts to become established in Russia.

Members of the Choir, nearning the end of their European tour, had brought bags of extra food, toiletries, and clothing to be given to the members and missionaries. A considerable mound of gifts gladdened the hearts of scores of Leningraders, including missionaries who rejoiced at the familiar peanut butter, instant soup, candy, and other items long missing from their diet. While awaiting distribution, the largesse was stored briefly in missionaries' bathtubs.

Russians have always admired things monumental. The

massive size and artistic grandeur of the Tabernacle Choir produced an indelible impression. Central TV taped the concerts and
telecast the music, interspersed with interviews from General
Authorities and Choir members, to millions of viewers on at least
two prime-time occasions, the first being on Friday evening, July
19. Many learned that to be in the presence of these good and
gifted Tabernacle Choir members is to yearn to become better oneself. Nothing could compare with the Choir in majesty and mag-
nitude, and the Russians were blessed immensely by these two
memorable and ennobling concerts.

A missionary in Moscow described in the mission newsletter
a baptism that came about through a Tabernacle Choir referral:

> One of the greatest blessings of my mission was to see the
> Sidorov family baptized. They were a referral from the
> Tabernacle Choir. A member of the Choir [Annette West] by
> chance met the eldest daughter of the family on the metro. The
> Choir member spoke no Russian and Natasha spoke almost no
> English, but that didn't stop the Choir member from giving
> Natasha an Articles of Faith card and her home address.
>
> Natasha wrote to the Choir member, and soon enough the
> referral slip was sent to our mission. It sat in our Moscow street
> guide until one night about two months ago. . . . These people
> are prepared. When we met with them, they already seemed like
> Latter-day Saints. During the first discussion the Spirit was
> strong. We committed them to a baptismal date at that time,
> and they did all within their power to keep that date! The father
> and mother both work, but they got their baptism day off so the
> whole family could be baptized together. These folks are rocks![3]

Other referrals, such as the one to Valentina Malygina, came
through those who accompanied the Choir and contributed to
extending its powerful influence:

> I grew up in a family where parents never spoke of God, but
> when I recall my own life, I remember that I thought of him
> often and asked for help. But I was never baptized. When I was
> twenty-five, I really wanted to read the Bible, but it was difficult
> to obtain. I read much in our classical literature on biblical
> themes, but I was not able to read the Bible itself.
>
> And then I, a grown woman with a daughter, went to
> a birthing center to bear a second child. The doctors told me
> the child appeared to have strangled in the womb and, by all

Valentina Malygina

indications, could not be saved. I began to pray and ask God to help me give birth. Suddenly the midwives attending me shouted loudly. A doctor ran to me from an adjoining room and helped me give birth quickly. My son was alive! Now he is eleven years old. From that time I have known that there is a God and that he loves us.

When I was thirty-five years old, my children and I were baptized into the Russian Orthodox Church. In my prayers I spoke with God, but in the Orthodox cathedrals, for some reason, I could not feel the Holy Spirit. Thus, I went to church very rarely. But then the Mormon Tabernacle Choir came to Moscow. And two Mormon women, Norma and Mary, came with the Choir as tourists. They stayed with my family and talked much about their church, but I understood little. My friends also had Mormon tourists staying with them. They received a Book of Mormon, and I really wanted one, too.

After a few months, missionaries came to visit my family— Norma and Mary had given them our address. They told us about The Church of Jesus Christ of Latter-day Saints. My daughter and I started to attend the branch that meets at the metro station Skhodnenskaia. Here we felt joy from our nearness to God and to the members. The achievements of the missionaries who came to us from across the ocean are astonishing. They intrigue us by their youth and deep faith.

But still I could not agree to be baptized. What I was concerned about was that the Church had come to us from the American continent. But later my daughter and I understood we couldn't get along any longer without our Church. Now we have been in the Church for a year and a half already, and we can't imagine how we could live without it. Our life is richer spiritually, and we now have a reason to live. And from our elders we have learned to be happy.[4]

In addition to those influenced by the Tabernacle Choir visit, others found the Church through continuing media exposure. One of them was Sister Olga Borodina, a sister in Moscow who would strengthen many by her faith, insight, and eloquence:

Papa died in 1991. That same year but prior to his death I had become acquainted with the Church and was baptized. My discussions with the missionaries continued for a long time. I studied everything new with interest and received a confirmation of that which had long been in my heart. I spoke with Sister Chudyba for a long time about death and what happens after it. At first I could not believe that everything would be just the way she described, but she succeeded in convincing me. We had that conversation just before I left on a trip to see my parents.

Within two days I was already explaining all of this to my papa. He listened with interest about our Church and about everything new I had learned. I told him about my conversation with Sister Chudyba and concluded with the thought that now we did not need to fear death. We would definitely meet again, but we would have to wait a while for that meeting. Laughing, I said, "Now you can die peacefully. We'll meet again anyway."

If only I could have known that would be our last conversation, that within four days he would die from a burst blood vessel in his brain [a stroke]. The knowledge I had helped me to take care of the things that needed to be done and to give support to my mother. It was a convincing example of how the Church helps, and of the correctness of its teachings. . . .

One day, after I read in the newspaper that a representative from The Church of Jesus Christ of Latter-day Saints had come to Moscow, as well as a short description of the teachings of the church, I told my husband it was very close to what we believed in our own family. Within a few months there was another short article in the paper, and I told my husband I wanted to become acquainted with that church, but wondered how I would be able to find it in such a big city. He responded, "Don't worry, if it's meant for you to be there, you will find this church."

Once again, within a few months I got a phone call from my friend who told me her neighbor had taken her daughter to a Mormon meeting, but she didn't know anything more than "Baumanskaia" subway stop. The next morning I got up very early and went to Baumanskaia. For four hours I walked around to every place where there could be a meeting.

Eventually I found the right place, and the first person I met was Elder [Adam] West. The second person who impressed me was Elder [Bradley] Weyland. On that particular day he was the teacher. After the meeting the sky seemed bluer and I felt happy.

Since that meeting I have missed church very rarely, only due to illness. The Church entered my life naturally, although I wasn't actually baptized immediately—it wasn't until three months later. Again I wanted to be certain I wasn't making a mistake. Even now I can hardly believe that the Church is not a wonderful fairy tale—it is my life. I have received the marvelous opportunity to work on perfecting myself spiritually. My children don't need me every single minute now, and therefore I can do a lot of work for other people. . . .

I am grateful to the missionaries for their work, for their examples, and I am also grateful to the parents of our dear missionaries. I love them all so much and I don't know how I was able to live before. It's too bad that although we had been Mormons in our hearts for so long, we only discovered [the Church] three years ago.

I am now the district Relief Society president. It's a very demanding calling. My husband's role in my calling indicates what a support our husbands are to us. I am very grateful to him for his help and his friendly counsel. I am grateful to him for his understanding of what the Church means in my life.

To my great sorrow, my family members do not attend church with me. There are reasons for that. However, my husband and children are interested in everything that happens at church. I am convinced that my patience and my example will help them make the right decision, and I simply need not to overly worry about it. I do not doubt that God loves all of us and that he will not abandon us.[5]

21

July 1991

In July 1991, reflecting on a year in the mission field, I again considered the pressing need for introductory materials about the Church. I once more requested a brief and inexpensive pamphlet outlining the Church's origin, distinctive characteristics, contemporary relevance, and benefits for members. The Tabernacle Choir had provided us with several hundred exceptionally beautiful and thorough introductory booklets about the Church and Choir that could be distributed on important occasions. I also repeated a request for a video about the Church suitable for broadcast on Soviet television.

Further, we needed more translations of the teachings of current Church leaders for our members who were avid readers and constantly asked for the words of the living prophets. I was consulting with Russians in Leningrad about starting a mission journal to contain selected material translated from the Church magazines.

Early in the month I spoke to a group of American Latter-day Saints who had traveled with the Tabernacle Choir on its recent Eastern European tour. Following my presentation on the history and development of the mission, some asked what could be done to facilitate the Lord's work in Russia. Explaining that mission presidents are asked not to solicit funds for their individual mission projects, I avoided a direct request but affirmed that our greatest need was for additional printed materials. Later, members of the group spoke with Church Development officers Thomas Rasmussen and Rex Guyman about making arrangements for a gift to our mission. Working with businessman Richard Hughes, this group eventually delivered two computers, a laser printer, a photocopy machine, and a scanner to our mission. Each mission office was authorized to have one computer purchased with Church funds, and this computer as a rule was occupied all day long. The donated equipment was crucial to our ability to translate, print, and photocopy an array of basic Church materials.

Beginning in July I spent considerable time reviewing a collection of hymns in Russian provided by the Church Translation Department. I also sought and received evaluations from Russian Latter-day Saints Svetlana Artiomova in Helsinki, Olga Tambrei in Tallinn, Mikhail Sorokin in Leningrad, and Vadim Viazmin in Moscow. Although all considered these translations an important step and an appreciated indication of good will, they were often inaccurate, and the natural Russian cadence frequently contradicted the hymns' musical rhythms. Much had been accomplished, but we agreed that more work was needed.

Late in September, permission was given for poet and Church member Vadim Viazmin of Moscow to retranslate the hymns. He began his assignment well and accomplished much, but the project faltered when he moved to the United States. Efforts were made in Salt Lake City, Frankfurt, and Moscow to prepare a Russian hymnal, and a booklet of thirty-five hymns and ten children's songs was ready in 1994. Until that time we used photocopies of a dozen hymns, most of them translated by Elder Kurt Wood, a gifted missionary and a graduate in Russian from Stanford University, with ample counsel from native Russian Latter-day Saints.

With our missionary force growing relatively rapidly, we needed to encourage and guide development in Russian language and proselytizing skills. With suggestions from others I prepared the rudiments of a formal Russian language study program and a skills achievement course adapted from the effective Finland Helsinki master missionary program. The course relied on the scriptures, the missionary study guide, and missionary discussions. Elder Adam West prepared a reading schedule for language study and weekly quizzes to pace the missionaries and verify understanding.

During July I was authorized to call two assistants to the president, Elders Michael Layne and Adam West, and three zone leaders for Tallinn, Leningrad-Vyborg, and Moscow.[1] These brethren and their successors served well and lessened my administrative burdens.

Finland Helsinki East missionaries in Tallinn, Estonia

Joan's letter home provided this overview of the July mission conference in Tallinn:

We decided to take the van on the ferry with us so that we could bring supplies. We had it loaded so full that there was barely enough room for the Warners and us to squeeze in. We brought boxes of Books of Mormon and *Gospel Principles* because Moscow was completely out and we have not been able to arrange a shipment there; lovely brochures printed for the Tabernacle Choir visit . . . ; one hundred pounds of salt water taffy sent by an anonymous person in Provo so the Russian members could learn about the 24th of July holiday and have a memento from Utah (in small ZCMI bags); two thousand needles and syringes to give to the Leningrad hospitals that provided health care for our sick missionaries; Nintendo, transformer, and TV to keep Jon entertained; and treats for the conference, including a microwave oven to cook popcorn. We had no trouble whatsoever at customs other than having to wait a long time in line.

Thursday was spent entirely on language training. Gary taught the Russian missionaries, and Brad Woodworth taught the Estonian ones. In the evening some of the missionaries went to a gym to play basketball and volleyball while others gathered to talk and sing. The Friday morning session concentrated on mission business, including the introduction of a new program called the Master Missionary Program to encourage the missionaries to reach specified levels (bronze, silver, gold) in language and missionary skills. Two assistants to the president (APs) were introduced, and an organization of the mission into zones and districts was explained.

In the afternoon we had guided tours of the Old Town and some time for shopping. The Russian missionaries fell in love with Tallinn because of the relative abundance of hard currency goods and better stocked stores with Soviet goods than they have seen lately in the other cities. A small station selling gas to boats close to the hotel sold bananas for foreign currency, to the delight of the missionaries who haven't had any for months. Several of the elders bought Soviet suits since they cost less than fifteen dollars and Tallinn did not require a resident card in order to purchase one. Watches seemed to be another hot item. One store had pocket watches on chains for four dollars, so many of the missionaries, along with Jon, are now sporting them. Sister [Rene] Warner and I bought over thirty-five pounds of strawberries for $7.50, washed them in the bathroom sink, and served strawberries and cream that evening (with cream brought from Helsinki in our ice chest). In Helsinki strawberries cost about five dollars a pound, so we loved every bite and the missionaries did, too. The evening consisted of songs, games, and a skit by the Leningrad missionaries.

Yesterday morning the program included zone reports, AP talks, a president's message, and a testimony meeting.[2]

On 29 July, President Jussi Kemppainen telephoned me to report that Moscow television was broadcasting a series of films of several BYU performing groups. The films had been made while the students toured in Russia over the years. Also included were segments from Church and BYU videos, and interviews with BYU president Rex Lee and various artistic directors. Immediately upon the completion of this program, cameras were turned on at the Moscow Sheremetevo 2 Airport to cover the arrival of United States president George Bush for a summit meeting with Soviet president Mikhail Gorbachev. At the conclusion of this summit, they signed an important treaty providing for mutual reductions in strategic nuclear weapon arsenals. The films of BYU performers had been telecast to represent good will towards the United States, portray wholesome American ideals, and incline Soviet public opinion toward cooperation with the West.

Oleg Rumiantsev, a Moscow branch president

In July Oleg Rumiantsev joined the Church. He recorded his testimony as follows:

> My life can be divided into two parts: the first being my life before I became a member of the Church, and the second, my life after baptism. The first part of my life . . . lacked that which gives us a personal relationship with God. An understanding of the greatness of our Heavenly Father's plan . . . gives us the opportunity to make correct choices between right and wrong, that is, "to choose the right."
>
> The opportunity to obey our Heavenly Father through faith has helped me to receive answers to the many questions which have arisen prior to and following my baptism. I am thankful to the Lord for not abandoning us in our misfortune, and for choosing a man through whom the Church of Jesus Christ, his gospel, and the Priesthood could be restored in their fullness. I am thankful for the Prophet Joseph Smith.[3]

22

AUGUST 1991

In a letter in August 1991, I summarized the development of the mission:

> Our mission continues to grow, although we have slowed down a little during the latter part of the summer. . . . Without dividing the two Leningrad branches or the Moscow branch, we are beginning three new groups in each of those huge cities (over five and nine million inhabitants, respectively). The two branches in Leningrad and the Vyborg branch now have just over one hundred members each. In Moscow there are eighty-six Russian members and approximately twenty-five Americans. The Estonian-speaking branch in Tallinn has eighty-five members, and the Russian-speaking branch there has thirty-two.[1]

This month, Elder Richard G. Scott of the Quorum of the Twelve Apostles, his wife, Jeanene, and their son Michael, who had just completed his mission in Sweden, toured three of our mission cities: Moscow, Tallinn, and Vyborg. The final minutes of our flight to Moscow and early minutes on the ground were accompanied by a spectacular thunder and lightning storm with torrential rain.

Elder Scott, undaunted by this hostile reception, seized every opportunity to teach and train the missionaries, members, and me. He was tireless and unswerving. I firmly believe that his vigorous efforts to strengthen us all were essential in helping us endure the challenges that arose later in the month.

Elder Scott's focus with the missionaries included the First Presidency's June 1991 document, "Fundamental Considerations in Proclaiming the Gospel," which emphasized a balanced approach in missionary work for proselytizing, retention, and activation. He taught us how to read the scriptures perceptively. He urged us to perform at a higher level, noting that "the work has gone well here, but it can go substantially better." In Moscow near the Kremlin and in Tallinn in the park adjoining the parliament, Elder Scott offered prayers of thanksgiving and blessing on the peoples of the Russian and Estonian republics. While Elder Scott instructed the brethren in priesthood leadership meetings, Sister Scott taught the sister leaders, and their son Michael courageously contacted Russians on public transportation and on the street, and accompanied our missionaries to their appointments.

In a stirring meeting with four Moscow branch leaders—all we could produce on short notice during the dacha ["summerhouse"] season—Elder Scott patiently and cordially emphasized the need to love the Savior and his teachings. The powerful resources of the Church can assist members to grow close to their Savior. Elder Scott delineated the path to personal revelation and spiritual growth and spoke warmly of his good friends the living prophet, the scriptures, and Jesus Christ.

I was concerned that the pace and the discomforts of the trip would fatigue the Scotts. I felt particularly anxious when we traveled by train together in a small second-class sleeping compartment from Tallinn to Leningrad. My concerns proved groundless. Like our other General Authority guests, Elder Scott and his family were most gracious.

In a letter home, I recalled Elder and Sister Scott's kind words about Joan:

> So that Joan could be with the children on the first day of school on August 11, she left right after the closing prayer of the Moscow sacrament meeting, returned alone to the hotel by subway, got her suitcases, took a taxi to the airport, flew to Helsinki, found her car, and drove home to the children. Hearing Elder and Sister Scott express admiration at her courage and strength reminded me once more, as has happened often on this mission, of what a remarkable woman she is.[2]

Early Monday morning, 19 August, Joan's twin sister, Jane Shawen, telephoned us from Spokane, Washington, to ask about Gorbachev's "resignation." This was the first we had heard of what, we learned that evening, was an attempted coup by USSR vice-president Gennadii Ianaev and seven other hard-line Communist officials calling themselves the Government State of

Emergency Committee. I immediately telephoned my assistants and directed them to call the zone leaders. They were to call the district leaders and review security precautions. They were told not to participate in any way in political or related activities, congregate in groups of Americans, remain out past 9:30 P.M., speak English outside of the apartment, or wear name tags. Elder Hans B. Ringger called and asked me to remind the missionaries that, if necessary, they could take refuge in the American embassy or consulate. I called the APs again with this important information.

During the day President Jussi Kemppainen and Joan called me at the mission office frequently with updates: Gorbachev was under house arrest in the Crimea, tanks were moving toward Red Square, a state of emergency had been declared in major Russian cities, large gatherings were prohibited, curfews established, all opposing political and unofficial press activity was forbidden, all political parties except the Communist Party had been banned, and more. During the day I attempted to conduct urgent mission business. By afternoon a few worried parents began telephoning for information and assurances.

In a Russian TV telecast from Moscow, the leaders of the rebellion lied about Gorbachev's health and disposition and about their motivations for appropriating power. They claimed Gorbachev's health would not permit him to continue to lead; citizens needed more time to debate the Union Treaty (according to which, among much else, the six republics most determined to become independent states could withdraw from the Soviet Union and the other nine would gain considerable independence); and that only they could fight crime and inflation effectively.

Elder Ringger continued calling to counsel, inquire about conditions, and verify that no missionaries or members were known to be in danger. As circumstances became clearer, I called missionary leaders to request that all missionaries remain in their apartments until further notice. I also called all the branch presidents to provide encouragement and support. It was clear that if the hard-liners returned to power, the repercussions for those Russians who had joined and now led a church considered American could be serious.

The leaders and members themselves were exemplary in their

courage and faith. On Monday evening in Tallinn, the Estonian and Russian members met for their usual group home evening, this time without the missionaries. Several members fully expected that the missionaries would be compelled to leave the country. They affirmed to each other the depth of their new religious convictions and pledged to continue the Church alone, if necessary.

On Tuesday, 20 August, I again called missionary leaders and several companionships to gather current information. All reported that they were in frequent contact with each other and that no problems had arisen, although I later learned that two pairs of elders had found themselves in a dangerous situation after an unwise picture-taking session from the roof of their apartment building. Russian military officials interrogated and reprimanded the missionaries in their apartment and departed.

During the day, President Bush advised that United States citizens now in the Soviet Union "should consider leaving the country as soon as they safely can." But Elder Ringger assured me (and I others) that Church leaders were in contact with United States government sources that would assist them in deciding to evacuate missionaries, were the necessity to arise.

On the late-evening Russian news, I was dismayed at first to see a brief segment near the end of the program showing a handful of poorly armed Russians and others barricading themselves around the Russian Republic White House, the Russian legislature building. They spoke passionately about their determination to follow Lithuanian patriots' example to defend freedom against usurpers. Then I realized that seeing this segment on Soviet TV meant the leaders of the coup had only limited powers of censorship.

I did not anticipate that thousands, inspired by the example of the few, would rally to their cause. All during the night and the following day, supporters of perestroika streamed to the White House to express their solidarity with Yeltsin and their defiance of Communists. Boris Yeltsin's dramatic statement, delivered atop a tank before an estimated 150,000 cheering supporters at the White House, created an unforgettable symbol of resistance and strengthened popular opposition to the coup.

I was continually astonished at how easily I could call in to

Russia from Helsinki during the coup. Usually I had to dial several times before getting a free line, especially if I telephoned after 7:00 A.M. Also unexpectedly, missionaries with whom I spoke during the rebellion informed me that government stores had more food than they had seen since their missions began. Apparently the insurgents hoped to purchase public support with groceries and other favors held in reserve for this day. But the news media began reporting increasing support for Yeltsin and Gorbachev.

By Wednesday, 21 August, the coalition of Communist reactionaries was rapidly disintegrating. I gave permission for each missionary to telephone parents to reassure them. By evening Yeltsin was in a position of considerable power, and Gorbachev was preparing to return from his forced isolation in the Crimea. On Thursday Gorbachev arrived in Moscow, and the tanks and soldiers, several of whom had joined the Yeltsin side, withdrew from the city.

In the evening of 22 August Gorbachev appeared at a news conference and presented his doleful version of the story, reaffirming his commitment to reforming (but not abandoning) socialism, his firmly preferred social order. But the mood of the man in the street, emboldened by the recent days' citizen victories, was inclined to repudiate socialism, Communism and, hence, Gorbachev. Rather, the citizens began more fully to enthrone Boris Yeltsin, their new hero who, from a tank turret, had given voice to the hopes of his countrymen for a better life.

During the coup attempt, on Tuesday, Estonia and Latvia declared independence from the Soviet Union. Lithuania had already done so in 1990 and now reaffirmed that decree. Over the next few days, Ukraine, Belorus, and Moldavia followed suit. By the end of the week, Russians and others removed several statues of enshrined Communist leaders. On Saturday, Yeltsin signed an order banning the Communist Party in Russia and ordering police to seize Party assets, including records and property.

On Monday, I had wondered whether it would be prudent for our branches to meet until the political climate settled down. But by Sunday, 25 August, all LDS branches met with a great sense of relief and appreciation, and missionaries had resumed serving in all aspects of their calling without more than usual concern for safety.

Elder Adam West recalled in his journal at the time that in January 1991 on successive Sundays both Moscow assistants to group leader Albert Walling, Daryl Gibb and Andrei Petrov, had spoken with memorable power on Genesis 18. In this chapter Abraham inquires of the Lord whether he would preserve Sodom if as few as ten righteous people could be found. The Lord affirms his willingness. Brothers Gibb and Petrov had assured Church members worried about their futures during uncertain times that if they and others were to strive for righteousness, the Lord would preserve them and their land. Elder West and others sincerely believed that the Lord had done so during the recent perilous days.

One week after the failed coup, the national legislature banned Communist Party activities and approved an interim government to form a confederation. By the end of the year this confederation became the Commonwealth of Independent States. The legislature ratified the independence of the Baltic states. On my trips to Estonia, I observed curious changes: experienced Soviet border personnel sitting side by side with "student" Estonian officials dressed in distinctive blue-gray uniforms in passport and customs areas, new Estonian names and flags on boats and buildings, more open expression of national pride in Estonian culture and history, and an inclination to disregard current economic deprivation in light of robust expectations for a brighter future.

Early in August Antonina Reziukova was baptized in Zelenograd, where she became a dedicated Young Women leader. She wrote of her spiritual toils and triumphs:

> I want to testify of the truthfulness of The Church of Jesus Christ of Latter-day Saints. I was a believer even before meeting the missionaries, but belonged to a different church. I had no doubt that God lives, but that missionaries had come to Russia with their own church and their own teachings—that I questioned. . . . I did not want to leave my own church because it was in that church that I was born and grew considerably. I did not want to leave my brothers and sisters. . . .
>
> Listening to the missionaries, I understood that everything they said was correct, that to be in their church would represent the right decision, and the Holy Ghost gave my heart happiness.

Yet both churches, it seemed to me, correctly taught how we should exist and what we should do. Later, I found out the difference—the Book of Mormon helped me. But for some reason I was unable to trust this book—I considered it the teachings of man. Who could help me with this question? God and prayer, of course. Only God and prayer saved me from my doubt. I asked Jesus Christ with only four words: Is this church true? In such a manner, I continually repeated the selfsame words from prayer to prayer.

Having come home from work one beautiful day, I decided to lie down and rest a bit. I didn't sleep, but I was very drowsy. . . . I heard a tender and quiet voice. I heard four words, "The Church is true." At that moment, I was rather frightened because I had never had such an experience. I can still hear that voice as though it were speaking today, but at that time I wondered whether perhaps something was wrong with my mind.

The days went by, and I became a member of The Church of Jesus Christ of Latter-day Saints. Occasionally, I met brothers and sisters from other churches who said they were very concerned about me. They said they suffered, knowing that I had gone astray in religion, that I had ended up on a devious path. They tried to demonstrate this to me by proving all their words with verses from the Bible. I began to feel the winnowing of the devil as doubts arose. But the Savior never abandons his children, and he sent his Comforter through the Bible and the Book of Mormon. . . .

But the devil is not dozing. He is constantly directing people to me who will challenge my faith. And the more faith I have, the more spiritually powerful people he sends, through whom he can tempt and try me with the aim of snuffing out my spirit. And again there are trials—prayer after prayer. But again and again, God rushes to my aid.[3]

23

SEPTEMBER 1991

At the 1 September 1991 fast and testimony meetings throughout the mission, members and missionaries emphasized their gratitude that the deep anxiety felt during the attempted coup had been replaced by promise and opportunity. Missionary work continued to proceed well. Many Russians were elated at being able to express their freedom of conscience and elected to exercise that right as their hearts perceived truth.

Our mission was blessed this month by the arrival of another senior missionary couple, Elder Joseph and Sister Pauline Pace. Though elderly even for senior missionaries, they were filled with youthful optimism, determination, vision, and wisdom. Elder Pace had been mayor of San Jose, California, and a medical doctor. He developed good relations with doctors and directors at leading Russian medical institutes and complexes. Sister Pace was experienced in music, Relief Society, and teaching. They became among the most fearless and successful finders of investigators in our mission.

Elder and Sister Pace provided this perspective on their mission:

It was December 30, 1990, when we were called to go to the Finland Helsinki East Mission. We entered the MTC July 4, 1991. Russian is a very difficult language, but the MTC is an incredible spiritual feast. September 4 we flew to Helsinki. Following a briefing by our mission president, we took the overnight train to Moscow.

We found a pleasant apartment close to a metro station, overlooking the Moscow River. It was on the eighth floor and had a lift, two rooms plus small kitchen, a bath, and a balcony. As we were unpacking, apprehensive because of our fragile language capability, we heard a voice say in perfect English outside our door, "May I help you?" So Irina Liudogovskaia came into

175

our lives. She became a dear friend, eventually a Church member, translator, and lifeline to whatever our needs were.

Irina Liudogovskaia lived with her parents and twenty-year-old daughter on the same floor as we did in the apartment building. Her husband had passed away twelve years earlier. She worked for the Institute of America and Canada and traveled in all those countries. . . . She was a computer operator and secretary. She believed the gospel and accepted each principle as we taught her, but she said, "I can't be baptized, because I can't hurt my parents who had me baptized as a baby under dangerous circumstances." We finished the sixth discussion, and she continued attending church every week.

Following an operation during which she hemorrhaged a great deal, she received a priesthood blessing and was healed. She asked to be baptized as soon as she was well enough. She is now the Relief Society president in her Russian branch. She is also the pianist, and she works full-time for the Church as a principal translator. When General Authorities speak in Moscow, it is Irina who translates for them. . . .

Eventually, I had an office there in the Kremlin Hospital in Michurinsk. My wife and I taught English to a class of doctors two afternoons a week. Medical teaching was in the form of clinical conferences with presentations of cases, after which class members could ask questions. I helped the Russian doctors who took turns presenting cases with their pronunciation of medical English. . . .

With our limited knowledge of Russian, we had to be creative in finding those to teach the gospel principles to. The community calendar in a free English weekly newspaper opened the door for us. Each week it ran an announcement of where and when The Church of Jesus Christ of Latter-day Saints would hold church services in Russian and in English. It then listed Elder Joseph Pace and our telephone number. People would call us. We set up appointments and taught in our own apartment. Who called? Russians, Africans, people from Iraq, etc. The Russians who spoke English generally were up-and-coming and well educated. Those converted would become the leaders that were so badly needed in the explosion of Russian branches—when we arrived, there was one branch; when we left, there were eight.[1]

Following are parts of a letter from Sister Irina Liudogovskaia:

I'd like to share with you a few of my memories of how I came into the Church. This is especially important to me today, April 20 [1994], because today for the first time I went to the temple in Friedrichsdorf [Frankfurt], where I'm spending a week on business at the invitation of the [LDS Church] Office of Translators. I have many wonderful impressions of Germany. But the strongest, of course, is of my visit to the temple. Right now it's difficult for me to understand all of my impressions. . . . The endowment ordinance was wonderful. It seems to me that people should attend the temple as often as possible, for it helps one to become better and to remain true to the covenants made with the Lord.

I sense how much I have changed since almost three years ago when I first attended an LDS Church meeting. Initially I went there with my neighbors Joe and Pauline Pace, who had invited me to attend. It was interesting and great practice to speak English with them. In general, what they told me and what was said in church on Sundays was appealing. . . . At that time many things baffled me, so I asked a lot of questions. Joe and Pauline were the main influence on me in the beginning. I just couldn't understand why at their age they felt it necessary to go so far away—to Russia. After all, it was very difficult for them physically. Wouldn't they have been better off to stay home near the television and rest—certainly they had earned that right.

At first [Elder and Sister Pace] brought me to the International [English-speaking] Branch. It was very interesting there. I met fascinating people. Nevertheless, with time I realized that my place was in the Russian branch where I could be with my Russian brothers and sisters, and help them. There I received the calling to be Relief Society president. Soon the Church started to enlist my help in translation work.

The most wonderful thing about our Church is the opportunity to serve the Lord freely, converse with others about him, and find true brothers and sisters in Christ. I never had any brothers and sisters of my own, but now I have so many. We spend a lot of time together. We meet every Monday with three families from the branch—parents and children. We talk about the Lord, drink Mormon [herbal] tea, and then study English. I look forward to these Mondays, and pray that no one will become ill and prevent us from meeting together.

The main thing that has changed is that I have found peace in my soul. I have stopped worrying about every little thing. It has become easier for me to live. I know much that I didn't know before. Even when I had to undergo an operation, my brothers and sisters were with me. Joe came to the hospital twice and anointed me with consecrated oil. I came through the difficult operation very smoothly, and soon returned home.

Each week I impatiently await the following Sunday. I know that I will go to church where I will see many people I love. The Church is growing in Moscow and all over Russia. We pray that our country will finally find peace and rest, and that Christ will come to us again, and most important, forever.[2]

Joan described a visit to the Mokhovs, a family in Moscow whose children were members. Of interest is a common Russian custom of carefully preparing for winter. Many families spend summers away from the cities growing food at their dachas, which complicated our efforts to maintain contact with members and investigators.

The Mokhovs live in the nicest apartment I have seen in Moscow. It consists of two two-room apartments that have been joined together so that they have two bathrooms and two kitchens. The rooms are larger than usual and are sunny and delightful. The boy has a room of his own, and the three girls share a room. In addition to the parents' bedroom, the other room is used as a combination dining room–family room. Since apartments are usually very small, rooms are generally multipurpose, with couches that make into beds at night. The children's rooms are set up this way but the parents' room actually has a double bed in it. The second kitchen is used as a utility and storage room.

The previous evening the family had returned from their dacha outside of the city where they have been tending their garden all summer. The balconies of the apartment had apple slices drying and baskets of produce ready to preserve for winter use. We had a delicious dinner prepared from vegetables and fruit from their dacha: green beans, cucumbers, tomatoes, beet salad, pickles, plums, apples, potatoes, squash, carrots, and juice made from a local berry. They had purchased only meat and ice cream for the meal.[3]

On 6 September, Leningrad officially became St. Petersburg again. Also this month, the Church's year-old registration in St. Petersburg was allowed to lapse. The Area office reasoned that because the Church was registered according to law throughout all of the Russian Republic, individual city registrations should no longer be required. Attorneys in Moscow and Frankfurt agreed that the Church had complied fully with the letter and the spirit of the law in the Russian Republic.

Nonetheless, political leaders in cities and districts within cities still wanted all churches and other associations registered locally, regardless of the national law. To grant building permits and conclude land usage agreements, the city, in effect, required registration. Quite clearly, city officials believed that local legitimization of a church would shield them against criticism from citizens and churches that opposed granting a new church privileges, even those guaranteed by law. This issue complicated municipal relations with the Church all the time I served. In 1993 the Church decided to follow Russian custom where necessary, though clearly not required by law, and register local Church units.

During September, the first Russian-speaking branch in Estonia was organized with Anatolii Diachkovskii as president of the youthful and spirited branch. In addition, Elders James Webb and Matthew West, Estonian-speaking missionaries, began to serve in Estonia's second-largest city, Tartu, home of the respected Tartu University. Their first sacrament meeting was held on October 8 with the two missionaries and three investigators.

In September three new groups were organized in St. Petersburg and three in Moscow with missionaries as group leaders. The groups were begun because the number of missionaries in our mission was growing rapidly, and more areas in which missionaries could serve were urgently needed. We also hoped eventually to develop branches conveniently located to more members in order to facilitate attendance. Having already divided the Leningrad branch—with considerable member consternation—only this past January, we did not want to divide the branches again so soon. We considered it preferable to identify promising areas and begin groups with very few or even no members. In every case members living near a new group were invited to attend the group's meetings but were allowed to continue attending their branch. In the course of a few months, most "older" members chose to join the groups. Generally within six months these groups had become branches, and new groups were being formed.

In September the Valerii Mariev family and Aleksei Akimov, working as volunteers with others, produced the first of occasional issues of our Russian-language *Liahona*. Eventually the Area was able to provide the Russian Latter-day Saints with the Church international magazine by the same name, the first issue of which appeared as our mission ended in June 1993. Copies for distribution to all members arrived several months later, after surmounting difficulties of epic proportions at Russian Customs.

Joan commented on our mission and family in September 1991:

> The philosophy of the Area presidency on missionary work is to "build from centers of strength," which means that we have files of referrals for Russians living in areas other than Moscow, Leningrad, and Kiev. After the Church is well established in these cities, missionaries will be sent to the somewhat smaller cities. We have fifty-six missionaries now in Russia and Estonia, and Vienna East has about twenty in Kiev. We do have some members who live in other cities. Most were baptized either abroad or while visiting Moscow or St. Petersburg. It is very difficult to keep people committed when they are unable to attend a branch or ward, as you can well imagine.
>
> In spite of this, Church literature is always appropriate, and it is sad that we can't promise to have two young men in suits deliver it to them. I imagine that within a few years there will be several missions in Russia and hundreds of missionaries, but we have quite a few problems to solve before this can happen. We are still struggling with the visa problem, housing, communications (mail, phone, etc.), banking, translation and delivery of Church materials and an unending list of challenges. Hopefully another year will put several of these difficulties behind us. In spite of this, we now have around 400 members in Russia and 100 in Estonia. . . .
>
> Sunday in Tallinn was a busy day as we tried to attend meetings at both the Estonian and Russian branches. The Russian branch was organized Sunday with thirty-seven members. We met the new branch president last winter when we visited his wife, who had recently been baptized. We were impressed with him and commented that he would make a good branch president. . . .
>
> The office continues to have more work than is humanly possible to do, so we now have two missionaries from the Finland Mission for a couple of hours a day to help take care of some of the details. The Warners will be going home in January, so we are wondering who their replacements will be. . . . Couples are especially valuable in leadership training, so we are thrilled to have another coming.[4]

24

OCTOBER 1991

Joan and I attended our second mission presidents' training seminar, this one in Prague, Czechoslovakia, in October 1991. It was wonderful to visit with mission president colleagues again, hear the uplifting presentations of the Europe Area presidency and Elder Dallin H. Oaks, and spend a few days away from mission pressures.

Joan briefly described the conference:

> The conference was excellent and taught us ways to improve the missionary work in our mission. Elder and Sister Oaks were with us for a couple of days and gave excellent advice. We had two sessions for wives that focused on common problems wives and families face in this calling. We had a bus tour of the city and also enjoyed a morning to walk around the magnificent old section of the city on our own. All in all it was a marvelous experience that will sustain us for some time.[1]

On 8 October I received a letter in English from a Latvian man baptized in Holland and now returned to Latvia. He requested more information about the Church and expressed an interest in carrying on a correspondence on topics relating to the Church. I was delighted to learn that a member of the Church was now living in Latvia, but I worried about the time a regular exchange of letters might require. Two days later a letter arrived from a woman in the United States married to a Latvian man. She wished to communicate with Latvian members, if any existed, and share her feelings and her knowledge of the Church. Again a blessing had been provided to answer an immediate need.

Attorney David Farnsworth sent a fax with the wonderful news that the Russian Religious Association of the Church finally had Ministry of Foreign Affairs authorization to extend visa support to missionaries. Ministry of Justice approval had promised visa authorization, but only the Ministry of Foreign Affairs could actually grant it. This meant that the Association, with Andrei Petrov as president, could now formally invite missionaries to Russia and that Russian embassies and consulates would grant visas upon receiving the official invitations. The Finland Helsinki East Mission would acquire the completed invitation from the Religious Association, and Salt Lake City personnel would submit the invitation to and receive the missionary visa from the Soviet/Russian consulate in Washington, D.C., New York, or San Francisco for United States citizens; a Finn would receive a visa from the Russian embassy in Helsinki, and so on.

Although much work remained to change over our missionaries from the private invitations obtained by Church members, to have new missionaries receive visas before arriving in the mission was a bounty of immense proportions. Sister Rene Warner, Joan, Andrei Petrov, and I worked long hours to complete the transition, but a future without the time-consuming and expensive process of obtaining visas any other way appeared glorious. To quicken the operation, Elder Dale Warner arranged for an impressive official association seal, and Joan prepared attractive letterhead stationery using the computer.

The Lord had blessed us in this area as he had in many ways. I am reminded of his blessings in the following letters from two men baptized this October who became priesthood leaders in Zelenograd: Oleg Svitnev and Viktor Shitulin. Brother Svitnev recounted:

> Faith in Jesus Christ and in his resurrection, and the knowledge the missionaries gave me, led me to be baptized by water and of the Holy Ghost. I testify it truly was the Holy Ghost who helped me make the correct decision when in one of the discussions with Elders [Kurt] Wood and [Mark] Pingree my wife and I, with tears of happiness in our eyes, set a date for baptism.
>
> My whole life has changed and been filled with meaning. Worldly success and failure concern me little. Now I live with prayers to my Heavenly Father, Jesus Christ, the Holy Ghost, and thoughts of love for them and my fellow men. . . . I feel at home with my new friends, members of the Church. . . .
>
> The power of the Melchizedek priesthood and the Holy Ghost also assist me in my temporal affairs, and in serving my

Oleg (second from left) and Liudmila (far right) Svitnev at the Stockholm Sweden Temple with President Reid H. and Sister Donna Johnson and an interpreter (far left)

Heavenly Father and fellow beings. Remarkable, beneficial changes in my life and in the lives of my branch members confirm this. Indeed, "blessed are they that hear the word of God, and keep it."[2]

Brother Shitulin shared his gratitude for the blessings of the gospel.

I am so happy I belong to the Church. It seems to me as if all of my life to this point has prepared me for joining our Church. From my childhood I have been taught to love others and all living creatures. I have been intuitively living the Word of Wisdom, and I have always felt as though a Higher Being has directed me. I feel as though my meeting with the missionaries was planned from above. But I will always be thankful to them and to those people who brought the Church to our country. I pray for God's blessings to be with them.

Much has changed in my spiritual life since my baptism. Before, I was often unsure of myself and continually sought for something to hold on to. I was upset by my disappointments and was jealous of others. I have now found a firm foundation. I know it benefits me to be able to turn to our Heavenly Father with a clean heart and ask for his counsel and his help. And I know he will give me an answer and will send the Holy Ghost to me. . . . I know Heavenly Father loves me and always blesses me. Now I no longer worry about temporary setbacks, nor do I elevate myself in the presence of success. Faith helps me to overcome adversity. . . .

When I partake of the sacrament, I imagine myself in the midst of Christ's disciples during the Last Supper. I imagine Jesus offering us the bread and water so that we might remember him. The sacrament gives me new strength for the whole week, and I am unable to live without it.

The restoration of the priesthood brought a great power. I am grateful to bear the Melchizedek Priesthood, and to know that through me the power and the will of God can be realized. When I bless the sacrament, confirm new members of the Church, bless and heal the sick, I feel the power of God pouring out through my hands.[3]

25

NOVEMBER 1991

As Christmas neared we began receiving more offers of help for Church members in our mission. Many proposed sending in boxes of clothing or food for us to distribute. The difficulties were in transporting boxes to our mission cities without their being opened and pilfered and then in deciding to whom of the needy we should present the gift. Hurt feelings and jealousies of members who only heard of the gifts could outweigh the advantage to the one or relative few. For that reason we generally recommended that donors send such gifts as sacrament table cloths, baptismal clothing, pictures for Primary and Sunday School lessons, English CTR rings, Young Women jewelry, and money to purchase Bibles in Russian for converts.

Our practice was to ensure that each individual or family baptized had a copy of the Bible, the Book of Mormon, and *Gospel Principles.* Generous sponsors had donated funds for copies of the Book of Mormon, and we appreciated additional contributions for copies of the Bible. One donor sent a check for two thousand dollars for Bibles at the very time we needed the money. Later, Russian Bibles became more available and the cost less prohibitive, and only occasionally was it necessary to furnish Bibles to new members. Members of the Brigham Young University community and others contributed money to our fast offering funds and sent vitamins for all our members. The vitamins were a welcome supplement to the uneven diet of the members during the winter months.

With the encouragement and leadership of Elder Joseph and Sister Pauline Pace, and with Europe Area presidency authorization, the Moscow International Branch was created on 10 November 1991 with Elder Pace as its first branch president and Sister Pace its first Relief Society president. The branch was formed to address the needs of English-speaking expatriate members who did not know Russian. A steadily growing number of businesspeople, attorneys, embassy employees, and students formed the bulk of the branch membership. Some of them had found that having regular Church association exclusively in Russian was inadequate. Expatriates were welcome to attend Russian-speaking branches, but we encouraged Russian members, who were badly needed in their own branches, to attend those branches rather than the international branch.

Many stayed after the services to discuss common problems and possibilities for improvement. One of those was Grigorii Fomin from Nizhnii Novgorod. He first met with missionaries at the time of the Tabernacle Choir concerts. Brother Fomin made three subsequent trips to Moscow to hear the discussions. Now he was prepared for baptism and eager to help establish the Church in his home city. A determined Brother Fomin, suffering from spinal impairment, walked on crutches with difficulty. Here are excerpts from the story of his life and conversion:

> I was born November 11, 1930, in the village of Vasilkovo, Yaroslavl region. . . . My mother . . . numbered Orthodox priests among her ancestors. . . . [She] was a faithful woman who prayed to Holy Mary. She did not reveal her faith openly at that time, since believers were severely persecuted. I was not baptized in the Russian Orthodox Church, and during my lifetime remained outside any religious organization right up until the time I came into The Church of Jesus Christ of Latter-day Saints.
>
> My father was a follower of Tolstoy's religious and ethical teachings. Among his books was Count Leo Tolstoy's *Reading Circle*. My father completely abstained from smoking and alcohol. This had an influence on me. . . . My mother had poor health, and it was difficult for her to take care of household chores. We children were very diligent in our efforts to help. When I was eleven, I fell ill with typhus and was close to death. . . . During World War II (1941–45), I worked together with other rural children in the fields and the meadows. . . .
>
> At that time the peasants' strong spirit of industriousness, goodness, and cooperation had not been crushed by the collective farm system. The marvelous natural beauty surrounding Kostroma also helped one to endure difficulties and fortified the soul. And my own spiritual disposition allowed me to feel the influence of my parents, especially of my mother and her

relatives. The spirit of their intelligence was free from any narrow political prejudices. This is the spirit of acknowledging that which is good and wholesome in every people. . . . Side by side with Russian spiritual values, I comprehended with my heart and mind the talented strains of international culture. . . .

My early education was in the field of teaching. I graduated from a physics and mathematics school in Krasnodar and I worked as a physics teacher. Then I transferred into construction work, first at a Samarkand cinema supply factory and then at a Kostroma excavator factory. I enrolled in a correspondence graduate program with the Moscow Institute of Engineering and Construction. In 1967 I received a university degree in technical sciences. Guarding my spiritual character, I did not become a member of the Communist Party. . . .

At the age of twenty-seven I married Galina Tolokonova, a sincere person, good-hearted and hardworking. A son, Andrei, and a daughter, Anna, were born. Everything was progressing nicely, but suddenly something unforeseen occurred. My wife's health deteriorated. For a long time the doctors were unable to correctly diagnose her. Acting upon an incorrect diagnosis, they operated on my wife, and she died on February 20, 1967, at the age of thirty-six. . . .

I am convinced that Heavenly Father helped me to endure. In the interest of my children I moved from Kostroma to Nizhnii Novgorod and received a teaching position at an engineering institute of water transportation. Over many years I conducted courses in technical disciplines. The loss of a loved one leaves its mark for many years to come. . . .

Years passed. The children grew up, and another trial came. During the course of many years I had been bothered by a pain in my spinal column. Once [in 1984] when the ailment worsened while I was in the hospital, the lower part of my body became paralyzed. An operation was performed on my spine. Some time later I had yet another. But attempts to return my spine to its former condition were unsuccessful. After a seven-month stay in the hospital, I was faced with the question, "Am I really destined to become a terrible burden on my daughter and son?" I asked for help from Heavenly Father and felt a surge of determination not to give up.

At first I took only a few steps on crutches. It was months before I was able to go as far as the nearest vegetable stand on our street. After several years, a significant amount of independence returned. I began to use city transportation, though not without risk. . . .

My path to The Church of Jesus Christ of Latter-day Saints went through definite stages. . . . In about 1987 I chanced to watch a television program from the series "Traveler's Club," directed by Iurii Senkevich. On one occasion he told of the Western United States, and about the state of Utah and Salt Lake City. He showed film clips illustrating the trek of the Mormons and how they manifested extraordinary industry in cultivating the land. I think that when they looked beyond their labors to the mountains rising up to heavenly realms, they were buoyed up by a flood of inspiration and new strength. After all, this was their promised land as the prophet Joseph Smith prophesied. . . .

I was struck by the faithful spirit of these people for whom despair and hopelessness simply ceased to exist. This television program was again brought to my memory when later, in the fall of 1990, I read a book entitled *Across the United States of America* by G. D. Timokhin and published in Moscow in 1980. I had a desire to feel this faith professed by the Mormons more strongly. . . . I decided to write to the leaders of The Church of Jesus Christ of Latter-day Saints. In my imperfect English I wrote about my admiration of the Mormon pioneers' spirit of steadfastness. . . . I asked them to send me literature reflecting the Church's operating principles. I gave a little information about myself. The only address which I had available was that of an Orthodox priest, Father Viktor Potapov, who conducted a religious program on the airwaves of the radio program "Voice of America."

In an accompanying note I asked Father Potapov to help in forwarding the letter to The Church of Jesus Christ of Latter-day Saints. I later thanked him for his help. Fortunately the letter found its way to the Church and later to the Finland Helsinki East Mission. In the beginning of March 1991 I received a package from the mission mailed from Vyborg. In the package was a Book of Mormon and *Gospel Principles*. There was a letter enclosed from the mission president dated February 15, 1991. He responded to my inquiry about the Church and invited me to forward my impressions and any questions arising from my reading of the enclosed books. In the beginning of April, I answered this letter. . . .

On May 20th I received a second letter from the mission president with an enclosed drawing of the nearest branches of the Church to attend in Moscow and other cities. I went to Moscow on Sunday, June 23, and met with the considerate Elders [Bradley] Weyland, [Richard] Chapple [an American

Grigorii Fomin (center, right) with Elder Russell M. and Sister Dantzel Nelson and their Russian missionary son, Russell M. Nelson Jr., in 1993

professor studying in Moscow and later president of the Russia Moscow Mission], and [Andrei] Petrov. In the evening a church meeting was held at the Hotel Cosmos. The next day I attended a concert of the Mormon Tabernacle Choir. It was a miracle to receive the Lord's blessings conveyed through song.

One day later, Elders Weyland and Franklin conducted a spiritual discussion with me in the theater on Spartacus Square. Over the following months I made several trips to Moscow. Elders Franklin and Nelson cared for my spiritual preparation. . . . And so I came to the ordinance of entering into the Kingdom of God. On November 11, 1991, the exact day I was born into this life 61 years ago, I was baptized by Elder Russell M. Nelson Jr. and received the laying on of hands for the reception of the Holy Ghost by Elder Dale Franklin. . . .

On April 28, 1992, a member of the Europe Area presidency and the Second Quorum of the Seventy, Elder Albert B. Choules, and president of the Russia Moscow Mission visited Nizhnii Novgorod. I am grateful that with all that they had to do of an official nature there, they found the time to visit me and to conduct a spiritual discussion in my home. I was ordained to the Aaronic Priesthood by them. I saved the bouquet of roses that stood on the table that day.

And then came the wonderful day. The mission president,

along with Elders Russell Nelson, Weldon Dodd, Robert Couch, and Tommi Sankala, arrived on July 21, 1992, for the opening of missionary work in my city. They were received by the deputy mayor of the city, B. Dukhan. I rendered assistance in arranging for apartments for the missionaries. The first sacrament meeting of the group was held at my apartment on July 26. . . . On November 29 I was ordained to the Melchizedek Priesthood.[1]

Joan described the problems Russians were experiencing or anticipating in November 1991:

The food situation in Moscow was especially bleak over the [Revolution Day] holiday, as people stocked up on bread in case the bakeries were closed. This created a shortage, so lines for bread were long. I noticed there was not a line at one grocery store which I passed, so I walked in to find that the only thing they had to sell was gallon-sized bottles of juice. Beginning the first of December, ration coupons for several items, including bread, will be issued in Moscow. In St. Petersburg we saw long lines outside of grocery and department stores, but did not have a chance to actually go into any stores. The branch leaders indicated that the members are getting along so far, but felt that the situation would worsen during the winter, and that they would appreciate help then.

In Moscow just across from our hotel, people stood in groups holding items to sell. For the most part, they were selling cosmetics from French firms such as Estée Lauder and Lancôme, whose stores in Moscow sell their products for rubles, but where the lines are especially long. One man had some dried fish and another had a loaf of bread to sell. Just inside the door of a small department store a lady stood holding a dress that she was trying to sell. Prices are rising so rapidly that some people are turning to capitalism automatically in order to meet their expenses.[2]

We received the first seven missionary invitations from Andrei Petrov through the Church's Russian Religious Association. These were for missionaries arriving soon in Helsinki. Sister Warner processed them at the Soviet embassy in Helsinki and obtained seven visas! We were startled to discover that the visas were only valid for two weeks. Once in Moscow, the missionaries worked through the Church's attorney there to renew the visas for the remainder of their missions.

Now we began to change over from the missionaries' private

Sister Rene Warner, in front of the Soviet Embassy, Helsinki, Finland, holding the first visas obtained through the LDS Russian Religious Association

invitation visas to Association invitation visas. At first the ruling was that all forty-plus Russian-speaking missionaries would have to return to Helsinki for their visas. Later in the month, Andrei Petrov informed me that the Foreign Ministry officials decided, as a one-time exception, that they would validate missionary visas in their offices and present them to Andrei Petrov for distribution. It took until January 1992 before all missionaries in Russia finally had received Russian Religious Association invitation visas, but those visas remained in effect until the end of each person's mission.

Among the seven new missionaries who arrived in November was a senior couple, Alton and Kathleen Donnelly. Elder Donnelly had been a professor of Russian history at the State University of New York at Binghamton. His background enriched his service incalculably. He later served as counselor in the St. Petersburg mission presidency. We all appreciated their warmth, strength, and steadiness.

The mission was greatly blessed this month by the visit of Elder M. Russell and Sister Barbara Ballard and Elder Hans B. and Sister Helen Ringger. We flew together to St. Petersburg, where Iurii Terebenin and Viacheslav Efimov met us with an Intourist bus, which they had rented for three days—with a driver—for twenty dollars. At the all-mission missionary meeting, Elder Ballard urged the missionaries to remember that pioneers of any day must be strong and obedient. He reminded us that in 1925 there were virtually no members of the Church in Latin America, and now there are millions. He promised us that if we and others performed our labors well, the results in Russia would be similar. Our members are like a new, budding flower and we are to be gentle and patient with them, Elder Ballard added, but we must be certain that false doctrine is not taught—otherwise, we would soon become a false church.

At the all-mission member leadership meeting the next day, more than one hundred leaders were trained using very basic concepts and materials in small groups. In late afternoon Elder Ballard spoke on the need for a restoration and Elder Ringger on the blessings of home teaching. Elder Ballard also answered questions, such as the following:

"When will the Church build buildings here?"

"As conditions permit, but remember, Jesus taught three years without a building—you, not buildings, are the Church; the Church is where the priesthood and ordinances are."

"What do we say to those who accuse us of joining an American religion?"

"We are an international church with members in one hundred and thirty-five countries."

"When can we go to a temple?"

"The main criterion is worthiness; one day a temple will be built in Russia."

In the evening fireside, Elder Ringger gave an outstanding talk, comparing the majestic nineteenth-century palace hall in which we met to the glory of a good life. As an architect, Elder Ringger could vouch that this hall resulted from careful planning and exact execution of the plans; likewise, there is a divine plan that will produce eternal beauty in our lives. That plan includes repentance, baptism, and endurance to the end. Elder Ballard placed our lives in an eternal perspective, including our development in God's love before our birth and the eternal implications of living our lives according to God's will today. On Sunday a general meeting was held for Church members from St. Petersburg and Vyborg and any others who were interested. After the meeting we flew back to Helsinki just in time for Elder Ballard to speak at a fireside.

During November sixteen-year-old Oleg Belousov joined the Church in Zelenograd. Here is the story of his conversion and growth in the gospel:

The Church of Jesus Christ of Latter-day Saints—this name meant very little to me when I first heard it in the summer of 1990. I learned of it from my sixteen-year-old Mormon friend from America, Noah Davidson. He came to Russia with some of his friends on a student exchange. Thanks to Noah, I found out about this religion and the Book of Mormon, which power I could have never imagined at the time. . . .

It would be wrong to say that my family and I didn't believe in God, but on the other hand, we were not strong believers, either. Nonetheless, we had already been engaged in a difficult search for some time. We wanted to join a church, but didn't know which one to join. We were surrounded by many incomprehensible churches and religious sects, all of which claimed to be the only true church in the world.

Then, at the very time which was so hard for us, a small branch of The Church of Jesus Christ of Latter-day Saints was established in Zelenograd. I can distinctly remember even now, how by pure coincidence an issue of the Zelenograd newspaper *Gorozhane* turned up in my hands two years ago. In this issue there was an article entitled, "Mormons—Guests of Zelenograd." I was so happy to see this article! At that moment I thought to myself, "Maybe this is our one chance to draw nearer to God, and most important, to gain an understanding of him."

It has been a year and a half now since my parents and I became members of The Church of Jesus Christ of Latter-day Saints. I can't say that our path has been easy, or that the principles of the Church have never evoked doubt in us. Of course they have. As it turned out, our family visited the Church at the very time of its establishment in Zelenograd, and it is likely that the lack of people in the branch aroused doubt (if

Oleg Belousov

not worse) in our souls. But now, two years later, I understand that by the wise plan of our Heavenly Father, we became members of the Church. And since then, we have seen before our very eyes the swift growth of the Church and the strengthening of the faith of its members. For me, this is proof of the truthfulness of The Church of Jesus Christ of Latter-day Saints.

It would surely be a mistake to underestimate the great work which has been done here by the first missionaries: Elders [Kurt] Wood, [Michael] Van Patten, and others. Their talent, deep faith in God, and confidence in the truthfulness of the Church planted in my heart a deep conviction and faith in God and his love for all people. With every new day I become all the more convinced that God loves me and that he helps and directs me in this difficult life.

My life has completely changed since the moment of my baptism in this Church, and I can now say that I have truly made a correct decision, for by becoming a member of the Church, I have found out the meaning of life on this earth. It has amazed me what incredible concern and attention the Church gives to the youth. I am surrounded by kindness and warmth when I am with the members of the Church, and I am positive that I would never have experienced that had I not joined The Church of Jesus Christ of Latter-day Saints.

I am thankful to my Heavenly Father for restoring his Church through Joseph Smith in the same form that it was during Christ's life. I am also thankful that Russian people can join the only true Church and find out about the fullness of the gospel of Jesus Christ and through him, return to our Father in Heaven.[3]

26

DECEMBER 1991

Early in December we toured Tallinn, Estonia, and St. Petersburg and Moscow, Russia, with Elder Dennis B. and Sister LeAnn Neuenschwander. In each city they held training meetings for missionaries and member leaders and firesides for all. With members, Elder Neuenschwander focused on developing love of God and fellowman (including self) through faith, repentance, baptism, and the gift of the Holy Spirit. Sister Neuenschwander spoke on the history and significance of the beloved children's hymn "I Am a Child of God."

Many missionaries commented on Elder Neuenschwander's much-admired clarity and firmness as he taught about missionary discipline. He also gave instruction on unique Latter-day Saint contributions to the understanding of the Creation, Fall, and Atonement; on bearing testimony and teaching by the Spirit; and on building relationships of trust with investigators.

Elder Neuenschwander urged missionary leaders to follow the example in Exodus 18 of those who sustained burdened leaders by lifting part of the load from them. Solve as many problems as possible before passing them on to the next level, he advised. Become an enthusiastic advocate of the mission president's decisions and initiatives. He also helped leaders understand how important the baptismal interview is in determining worthiness and in teaching the significance of the ordinance.

In mid-December, Elder Douglas and Sister Lois Dewey arrived in Helsinki to prepare to replace the Warners as the office couple. The Deweys became loyal friends, proficient in administration, and decisive in the success of the mission.

Seven months after the first, a second all-mission youth and young adult conference was held in St. Petersburg. Branch president Viacheslav Ivanovich Efimov and other Russian Latter-day

Saints played the major organizing and executive roles, with Elder Dale and Sister Rene Warner providing support and counsel.

Joan described the conference and some of the hardships still facing members at this time.

> The youth of the mission held a conference December 20–22 at a health resort about one and one-half hours by train outside of St. Petersburg. . . . Betsy attended the conference, along with 150 Russian and Estonian youth. Betsy had hoped to practice her Russian, but a couple of girls from Moscow who speak English well quickly sought her out to practice their English instead. One morning the group was served hot cereal cooked in milk, and bread with cheese. The youth were excited, as they have had very little milk and less cheese in the last couple of months. Extra trays of cheese quickly disappeared as the youth packed some away to eat on the train or to take a taste back to loved ones at home.
>
> The branches held Christmas parties during the holidays. In St. Petersburg the leaders decided to hold one party for both branches and the groups. About 450 people attended the party, including 110 children! Needless to say, refreshments and candy for the children were in short supply. In Vyborg the party was also very well attended. During December the attendance at church meetings was not as high as usual, probably due to the fact that people were spending hours in food lines in order to get enough to eat. . . . Frankfurt will be sending a truck on January 18 with boxes containing staples similar to the ones sent last year. This year there are more members and fewer boxes, however. The next few weeks should reveal if higher prices will have any effect on solving the shortages or only create added suffering.[1]

Our Christmas missionary conference was held at the same St. Petersburg Oktiabrskaia Hotel at which I had stayed the first evening I spent in Russia in 1963. The sixty-two missionaries enjoyed a tour of the city and of the Hermitage. We reviewed our 1991 performance, established goals for 1992, including a greater emphasis on teaching families and potential priesthood holders who were needed to lead new branches, heard messages from mission leadership, watched videos of October general conference and *It's a Wonderful Life,* followed by testimonies. Joan gathered critical visa information from all the missionaries, and I reviewed emergency evacuation procedures.

*Finland Helsinki East missionaries at Aleksandr Column
near Winter Palace, St. Petersburg*

During our mission, we received occasional and always uplifting letters from Sister Shirley McMichael of Macon, Georgia.
Never married, she had served three full-time Church missions
and now cared for her elderly mother. Since early November 1989,
she and Brother and Sister Graybeal, from Riverton, Utah, had
been sending packets to Slavic peoples, beginning in Belorus. They
had sent almost three thousand parcels containing a Book of
Mormon, *Gospel Principles*, and the *Joseph Smith Testimony* pamphlet to whoever requested the information. As Sister McMichael
wrote: "It has been the great joy and happiness of our lives to have
sent these to a hungry, sweet people."[2]

On 8 December the leaders of Russia, Ukraine, and Belorus
proclaimed a Commonwealth of Independent States open to the fifteen former Soviet republics. Eleven joined—but not the three
Baltic states or Georgia. By decree, in mid-November, Russia's
President Boris Yeltsin had taken control of Soviet natural
resources, banking, and money. In December he asserted Russian
control over the foreign ministry, KGB, and parliament. On 25
December 1991, Mikhail Gorbachev resigned as president of the
Soviet Union, and the Soviet Union ceased to exist. Control of its
massive nuclear arsenal was transferred to Yeltsin.

Among those baptized in December were many who strengthened the Church significantly. The two men and the woman
whose accounts appear here served as branch presidents and Young

Viacheslav Baltovskii

Women leader. Brother Viacheslav Baltovskii recounted his search for the gospel and his growth in the Church:

> One day I happened to get a Bible. I really liked Jesus Christ. . . . I had no doubts about his divinity. The Gospel of John became my favorite book, perhaps because so much is said about the Holy Ghost there.
>
> Once while walking down the street, I suddenly asked myself, would that which I was studying, T'ai Chi-Chuan [meditation and martial arts], save me? I unexpectedly received the answer, "No!" This frightened me because I relied on T'ai Chi-Chuan and thought it would deliver me from the difficult situations of life.
>
> Furthermore, the Bible directly pointed out my sins and transgressions. One revelation alone from the Gospel of John led me to fear and trembling. I knew I had to change. The year 1988 was a time of change both in the nation and in my life. . . . I turned to Christian churches, that is, to those churches that believed in Jesus Christ. Of course the Orthodox Church was the first one I looked into. Much of it was strange to me, but mainly I could not agree with the church that monasticism was higher than marriage. I truly believe that holy and pure relationships

exist between man and woman, and that great wisdom and a mystery of God are concealed therein. Even the scriptures speak of this more than once. My soul did not want to give up this belief for anything.

I investigated other churches as well, but they didn't satisfy me. Their interpretation of some parts of the Bible didn't seem right to me. Now I can more precisely define my feeling. I didn't sense the joy that comes with the fullness of the gospel.

While exploring the Bible during the three years before I became acquainted with The Church of Jesus Christ of Latter-day Saints, I noticed that there was much that Jesus Christ did not say there. He even says this himself in John 16:12, "I have yet many things to say unto you, but ye cannot bear them now." I continued to have many other questions. I felt in my heart that there was yet more knowledge besides the Bible, and I definitely wanted that.

Nevertheless, I decided to be baptized in the Orthodox Church, as I wished to be saved from my sins. I really hoped that baptism would change me. I also thought about giving up smoking. But as before, I did not receive complete satisfaction, and the same heaviness remained. I continued to learn about other churches and read various literature. I tried to meet believers. In this manner I found myself on a Catholic pilgrimage in Poland. We walked two hundred kilometers from Warsaw to Czestochowa. The two weeks I spent there helped me understand much. During that time a feeling formed within that the Lord does lead us by the hand from our very birth, if that's what we want. However, the Catholic Church did not satisfy me either.

One wonderful day I was riding on the metro and reading the journal *Science and Religion*. This journal often covered unusual teachings and mysteries, as well as various churches. In that issue there was an article about the Mormon Church. It was called "The Mystery of the Gold Plates." I was acquainted with many wise teachings (from the world's point of view), but I was not impressed in this instance by "wisdom." As I began to read and ponder, I was visited by a feeling of unusual joy and freedom, and inside I exclaimed, "I've found it!"

I don't think I'd ever been so happy or felt so free and light. The entire burden that had been such a weight all those years fell from my shoulders. There was much more I liked in the article. However, there were some things that as an Orthodox patriot I was unable to accept, such as the Article of Faith that speaks about the New Jerusalem being built on the American continent. But the feeling I'd had at that point so softened my heart that I was even able to agree with that. I decided to find this church no matter what.

Unfortunately, however, neither the Church's address nor telephone number was listed in the article. I tried to call the editor, but was unsuccessful. About two years later I was riding the escalator in the metro. A girl standing next to me was reading a newspaper. On the back side of the paper was an article entitled, "Mormons in the USSR: Who Are They?" I managed only to find out the name of the newspaper and the edition before the girl went on her way. The escalator ride was over, and I had probably frightened her a little with my animated interest in her newspaper.

I went out onto the street and could not find that newspaper anywhere. It was an earlier number. Suddenly a desire arose within to get on a trolley bus and go. Where and why I did not know. But when the trolley bus reached Pushkin Square, it was as if something pushed me off. I walked along the pedestrian underpass. There were lots and lots of different newspapers being sold here. And lo, a miracle—I found exactly what I had been searching for. I read the article with excitement, and this time there was an address as well as the time of church meetings. It said that the Mormons met on Sundays at 10:00 and Wednesdays at 6:00 (why Wednesdays I did not know). It was 5:00 on Wednesday, October 16, 1991, so I decided to go to Spartacus Square. It was right there in a theater that the first branch of The Church of Jesus Christ of Latter-day Saints met.

There I met the first member of the Church in my life. It was Sister Carrie Madsen, who introduced me to Elders [Chad] Hutchings and [Dennon] Ison. It was they who held the first discussion with me. They were great. Even though they were just preparing to leave, they took off their coats without hesitation and showed they were interested in me. I am very grateful to them, because after the first question about whether I believed in God, they listened to my profession of faith for forty minutes. Their Russian wasn't perfect, but the whole time I felt like they heard me and were listening attentively. After that it was easy for me.

But what they said astounded me even more. They told me more about the gospel, and my joy became greater and greater. Other testaments of Jesus Christ, the premortal life, Joseph Smith's search for truth and his visions, the priesthood, and temples—all this not only answered my questions, but additionally brought me much joy, knowledge, and ever more questions.

I was especially astounded beyond belief when I learned about eternal marriage and its foreordination. I simply leapt for joy.

The missionaries asked me to pray about the Book of Mormon. I came home, closed the door behind me, and having sat down at the table, I opened the Book of Mormon to Moroni 10:3–5. After reading it again and making certain of my feelings and desires, I called upon God. I would not say that I saw a light, but I sensed one with my whole being and heart. This feeling of tranquillity, joy, and peace left no room for doubt that the Book of Mormon is the word of God and that the scriptures are true. This witness helped me to be at peace with those things I had disagreed with. . . .

I now knew I had to keep the Word of Wisdom. The most difficult part was giving up tobacco. I smoked only when I was thinking, and I was always thinking. I usually smoked a pack a day. The missionaries who taught me the discussion even fasted with me, but my first two attempts to give up smoking were unsuccessful. One day I happened to run out of cigarettes, then found two more a little later. My father and I were visiting my older sister, but I had stayed alone in the car to wait for him and decided to have a smoke. At that moment an unusual feeling of great power came over me, and I suddenly knew that if I were to throw these two cigarettes away right then, I would never smoke again. I threw them out, and I smoked no more.

It wasn't easy, and already the next day I wanted to smoke again. It was hard. I couldn't do anything. Sometime around 5:00 I almost gave up, although I remembered the witness. In a weakened condition, I fell on the sofa and involuntarily began to pray. Suddenly something very pleasant, warm, and tender surrounded me. My torment eased and the desire to smoke left forever. I bear witness that God freed me from tobacco, and that I did not do it by myself. It was his strength that set me free.

Then came the day of my baptism. For me it was a holiday. Those who had helped me learn about the Church were near me. After I was confirmed a member of the Church and had received the gift of the Holy Ghost, the first thing that I saw when I opened my eyes was a light. This light was everywhere and it was very bright and joyful. I looked around. The missionaries who had confirmed me were surrounding me. I no longer thought of them as Americans, rather they were like my own people, and I loved them sincerely. I had never been so happy. I felt like smiling at everyone in the metro. Later as I read the Book of Mormon, I wanted to go out and proclaim to people: "Come and partake. This is what you must partake of . . ."

The university branch was closer to my home, so I began to attend it. . . . Our branch was like a family. No one was more important than anyone else. It was as if we all sat together around a large campfire—and that fire was Jesus Christ. . . . We enjoyed unity, friendship, and spiritual discussions where we would learn even more about the gospel. . . .

I had various callings. The first calling I received was to be the Sunday School president. Due to my inexperience in leadership, I took everything upon myself at first—both the lessons and the preparations to conduct Sunday School. But gradually I learned my role. That was followed by a calling to be president of the priesthood quorum. At that time I was trying to go out with the missionaries to discussions. I shared my testimony and it grew. During these discussions I gained tremendous spiritual and psychological experience. I advise all brothers and sisters to take advantage of this opportunity to grow spiritually.

I thought about a mission and planned to become a missionary. But I was already twenty-six when I received the Melchizedek Priesthood. Within two months I received my next calling—to be a branch president. Each time before I received a calling, there were difficulties and trials. This time, especially, things were difficult for me. . . . [Upon learning the missionary branch president would be moving to a new branch:] Suddenly I felt the powerful influence of the Holy Ghost. At that moment I knew that I would be the president of my branch, and I spoke in my thoughts with the Spirit as with a man. . . .

A month after I was called as president of the branch I visited the Stockholm temple for the first time. . . . As I first approached the temple I felt that I was not alone. Although I didn't see anyone, there were still several people who were standing near the doors of the temple greeting me. I didn't see them, but I clearly felt them. I stood still for ten or fifteen minutes. The influence was so sweet and awe-inspiring that I didn't notice anything around me. Next to me stood Natasha Mokhova, who is always very lively, but she stood quietly and was under the same influence. That which I learned in the temple is impossible to convey. I received many answers to my questions. But the main thing was the feeling I had. My mind became clearer. The course of my life became clear and I had a better idea of what I should do.

Even after the temple I really wanted to go on a mission and planned to do so, despite the fact that my leaders were telling me that it was more important to start an eternal family. In the end I realized my mission is here at home. After all, the Church has three missions: to proclaim the gospel, perfect the Saints, and redeem the dead. That means my main work is to help my brothers and sisters to become better and to help them complete the work for their dead. Furthermore, I should always be a witness for Christ. When I am at discussions with the missionaries or when I talk to people on the street, with or without the missionaries, I feel happy. . . .

With conviction I declare to the whole world that the teachings of The Church of Jesus Christ of Latter-day Saints are the teachings of God the Father, his Son Jesus Christ, and the Holy Ghost, who are one great God, and that salvation comes only by faith in Christ and through his mediation.[3]

Sister Anna Malkova recounted her remarkable search for truth:

I didn't believe in God. I felt that there was a force of Good or Love, or whatever you call it, that watches over the world and keeps it from collapsing. This seemed to suffice, but it didn't really concern me. About five years ago everything became very tedious. My studies were uninteresting, getting acquainted with new people was boring, watching movies, and even spending time with my friends was all very tiresome. I began to think: Who am I? What am I? What I am doing here? What is it for?

I read everything: Buddhist books, Hare Krishna books, articles on extra sense, Riorikhs' books [scholars of Eastern religions and philosophies], the Bible, and many others. . . . I chose Christianity because only in it did I find love, although I was still unable to understand Christian meekness. I began to wander again as I investigated many different confessions, churches, and sects. I really liked the Orthodox Church with all its solemnity and sacredness. I read about the lives of many saints, which touched me to the very depths of my soul. They were humble, loving and patient, and through their trials they gained wisdom and helped those in need.

Still, I could not understand or love "contemporary Orthodoxy" with its impossibly long and incomprehensible church services, which have a kind of "ostentation." I liked the simplicity and happiness of the Catholics. Finally I decided that it was not important which church a person attends, but that it is most important to have a relationship with God.

When Slava [Viacheslav Baltovskii] mentioned that he had met with the Mormons, I decided out of curiosity to go with him to a discussion with Elders Hutchings and Ison at the Spartacus Square facility. If you had asked me about five minutes after the discussion what it had been about, I probably wouldn't have been able to tell you. I hardly heard a word. I sat and took in everything that was around us. I felt peace and joy. We set off for home. In our subway car there were many people with tired faces and swollen eyes. I felt so sorry for them. The joy I had inside me was like a fountain. I smiled, not knowing what for. I laughed, not knowing why. And for the first time I really felt that these people around me were indeed my brothers and sisters. I felt as though I loved them, that I could help them, and that I wanted to help them.

After every discussion I went home filled with happiness, knowing that my Father in Heaven was happy for me. As I prayed about the Church and Book of Mormon, joy and peace entered my heart, but I was afraid to admit to myself that I had already received an answer. I prayed, and tears fell from my eyes like a summer rain when the sun shines. The third time, I was finally able to believe that God Himself was answering me.

I don't know whether I would have been able to overcome all my doubts if it hadn't been for the love and support I felt (and have never encountered anywhere else) in that branch. It was my home and my family. . . .

The morning before my baptism was terrifying. I was afraid that maybe I had made a mistake or I wasn't ready. And even when walking into the water, I wasn't sure I was doing the right thing. But then, all my fears, together with all my sins, remained in the water. I came out of the water clean, bright, and a little stunned. I felt with all my being that I was clean before God and that he had forgiven me of everything. I lost my sense of reality and looked at everything as if from above.

When the elders placed their hands on my head during my confirmation, I felt, as it were, that a beam of fire was entering into me, penetrating my whole body and filling me with light and beauty. Unfortunately, I submitted myself so completely to this feeling that I heard virtually none of Elder Poole's blessing. I remembered only isolated phrases. I wrote "unfortunately," although I'm not sure I regret it. It was such a beautiful, new, and unexpected feeling for me. I am very happy that I have the memory of this feeling and that it returns to me almost every time that I think about my baptism.

I recently read that communion of the Holy Ghost with the spirit of a person leaves the strongest impression, even stronger than it would be if one were with Jesus Christ himself. Association with the Holy Ghost leaves an indelible print in one's memory and one's soul that is impossible to forget. I testify that it is not possible to forget such a thing. My memory of this keeps me from feeling peace if I am straying from the Lord, and impels me to seek him once again.[4]

Anatolii Pushkov, a father in Zelenograd, told of his and his family's conversion:

I believed in God before I found out about The Church of Jesus Christ of Latter-day Saints, and I had a testimony that God lives and that he helps me. Before finding out about the Church, I already knew many scriptures from the New Testament and had heard many sermons on TV from Christian preachers speaking about God. However, I didn't know where I could find a more full knowledge of Christianity. . . .

When I learned of The Church of Jesus Christ of Latter-day Saints, I was ready to receive the gospel of Jesus Christ. It happened like this. At the time a friend of my wife, now Sister [Antonina] Reziukova, invited my wife, Tatiana, to a meeting of the Zelenograd branch in the beginning of September 1991. Elders [Kurt] Wood and [Russell] Nelson invited her to hear the discussions about the Church, and she agreed. Thus, the missionaries found themselves in our home, and as a family we listened with rapt attention to the first discussion about the wonderful Church of Jesus Christ of Latter-day Saints.

My wife and I heard all of the discussions, and we decided to be baptized. Our daughter, Margarita, heard only two of the discussions and chose not to hear any more. The baptism didn't take place on the appointed day, however. My wife had fallen ill and was hospitalized. After my wife recovered, I left on a business trip. By that time, our daughter had decided to be baptized also. We waited for her to hear the remaining discussions. Then Elders [Michael] Van Patten and [Mark] Pingree were serving in the Zelenograd branch. The day for baptism was set for the 29th of December, 1991. Our whole family was baptized.

After our baptism, we shared our testimonies in our family. As it turned out, each of us had felt the Holy Ghost and a great change inside. For me, baptism was a great testimony that God lives. During the confirmation, I felt the influence of the Holy Ghost very powerfully. . . .

I tried to keep from missing a single Sunday meeting. I read the Book of Mormon and the Bible, and had many conversations with the missionaries. I was blessed by God. During this period, my understanding of the teachings of Christ grew rapidly. This was a wonderful and miraculous time. A strong faith grew, and my testimony was strengthened.

Tatiana, Anatolii, and Margarita Pushkov. Anatolii has served as a Moscow branch and district president

The Holy Ghost helped me and stayed with me. The meetings on Sundays were and still are a great joy for me. There I become immersed in the word of God, and I have the opportunity to serve my brothers and sisters. On the 5th of July 1993, I received the Melchizedek Priesthood and was ordained to the office of elder. [Subsequently Brother Pushkov was called to serve as president of the elders quorum and then of a branch in Zelenograd.]

I am so thankful to my Heavenly Father for giving me the opportunity to serve other people and to serve him. I am thankful for the blessings he gives me when in his service. In less than two years, I have obtained knowledge that has changed my previous perceptions of life, the universe, and science. When I compare my life before and after my baptism, I don't even recognize myself. I was truly born again of the water and of the Spirit, and I testify that Heavenly Father loves us and that our Savior, Jesus Christ, lives and guides his Church through prophets on earth.[5]

27

JANUARY 1992

Early in January 1992 Joan and I received a letter over President Ezra Taft Benson's signature informing us officially that the Finland Helsinki East Mission would cease to exist in early February 1992. Two new missions would be created from our former mission: Russia St. Petersburg (Tallinn, Tartu, Vyborg, and St. Petersburg), and Moscow. President Charles and Sister Susan Creel would preside in St. Petersburg, and we would lead in Moscow. Joan began preparations to move our family for the final year of our mission.

We deeply regretted leaving one part of our mission but were pleased by the opportunity to devote more time to the other. At a family home evening we told our children that we would be moving to Moscow, probably at the end of their school year in May. Like us, the children had enjoyed living in Helsinki, but they also wanted to be with our missionaries and members and began looking forward to the move.

Children's contributions to a successful mission can be immeasurable. I noted this month that Betsy finished typing English equivalents and accent marks for a list of the five hundred most commonly used Russian words sent to me for the missionaries by my BYU colleague Don Jarvis. She and her sister Debi had spent hours preparing for duplication Church hymns that had just been translated into Russian. Katie and Jon stamped "Not for Sale" messages in many hundreds of copies of the Book of Mormon in Russian, so that we could take them into Russia without paying high customs fees. Betsy and Jon drew illustrations on poster board for my talks to youth. And Katie's fervent testimonies during our evening meetings with newly arrived missionaries were inspiring and memorable.

The children had generally remained in Helsinki with a variety of sitters when Joan and I traveled to zone conferences, usually twice a month. Jon especially suffered from these separations, often developing severe pains in his stomach and attacks of juvenile arthritis. Betsy completed high school, attending three different high schools in two foreign lands. The children will forever be grateful for their experience, but much was required of them—and they gave in full measure, and sometimes beyond.

A magnificent Finnish missionary couple, Erkki and Mirja Silvenoinen, arrived in our mission to serve in Estonia. They were well experienced in the Church, had studied Estonian, and were indomitable and joyous. Their humble, patient, and good-natured service among the Estonians made a crucial difference in the development of testimonies, of administrative acumen, and in the general growth of the Church in that country.

Two new branches were formed officially in our mission in January 1992: one in Zelenograd and another in Vyborg. The Zelenograd branch was formed 19 January 1992 with Oleg Svitnev as president and Viktor Shitulin as his first counselor. The second Vyborg branch grew naturally from the earlier division of sacrament meetings. During January, Valentin Gavrilov was sustained as the branch president in the second branch.

Joan writes of humanitarian assistance that arrived at this time:

> A truck with food packages from the Church left Frankfurt on Saturday, January 18th. Each member will be given a fifteen-kilo package and there will be extra ones for each branch to distribute on the basis of need. Again the recipients will be invited to contribute to the fast offering fund if they wish. Because food prices have increased since the project was organized [on January 2, state subsidies of most goods and services were eliminated, causing prices to soar], the estimated cost per package is low—based on last year's prices. From what we can tell, the price increases have not stimulated greater supplies. They have only increased discontent among the people.[1]

Toward the end of January the Martynov family was baptized. This family has contributed immensely to the development of the LDS Church in Moscow. The father, Sergei, has served as branch

Tatiana and Sergei
Martynov and their
children at the Stockholm
Sweden Temple

and district president and as a member of the mission presidency.
Excerpts from an interview with him follow:

I was born in Moscow and have lived there almost all my
life. . . . I have worked as an architect and designer, and directed
an architectural firm. . . .

I have always been a believer, although maybe not a con-
scious believer. I don't know whether . . . I believed in God the
Father and God the Son, but I believed in goodness and justice.
And I really sought for confirmation that goodness and justice
exist on the earth. I sought for someone who could embody this.
Mortals are generally unable to serve as an example of supreme
goodness and justice. They are not perfect, yet I sought for perfection. . . .

In connection with my education as an artist and designer,
I studied eastern cultures quite extensively. I studied Buddhism.
. . . I looked into Orthodoxy and Catholicism. . . . My paternal
ancestors were Russianized Poles. They were Catholics, so
Catholicism was closer to me than Orthodoxy. . . . I already had
a firm knowledge that Jesus Christ was our Savior. I knew this.

Like most Russians, I learned [about Mormons] from books.
Here books about Mormons speak of polygamy, the founders of

JANUARY 1992   **211**

the Church in America, and the persecution of the early members. That they were persecuted and driven out of [the midwest] in the recent past, aroused my curiosity and I became interested in finding out more about this church. . . .

In 1992, I noticed by chance a brief paragraph about the Church in a Moscow newspaper. . . . It stated that the Mormons met on Spartacus Square. . . . I decided to go see for myself who these Mormons were. . . . It took me a while to prepare myself, but after about two or three weeks, I committed and went to the meeting. I was rather amazed at the simplicity of the service and the kindness shown to all newcomers. People came up to me, sat by me, and smiled at me. I felt needed there. I felt good there. I attended sacrament meeting and partook of the sacrament.

I was impressed by the Book of Mormon. I read it several times. At first I read it as a scientific work. . . . I don't remember when it was that I began to read the Book of Mormon with my heart instead of my head, but it was then that I began to understand why it had been written. . . .

It is difficult to talk about the feelings one experiences for the first time in the temple. [Our] trip to the temple richly blessed our family. I had always loved my wife and children, but in the temple, it became clearer why we love each other, why our Heavenly Father loves us, why Jesus Christ endured such pain, and how he expressed his love for us through his sacrifice. This understanding of why we love each other gave [us] the means to further strengthen our family, to come to know each other better, and to feel more confident that we have chosen the right path.[2]

PART V

THE RUSSIA MOSCOW MISSION, 1992 TO 1993

28

FEBRUARY 1992

On 3 February 1992, the nineteen-month-old Finland Helsinki East Mission was divided into the Russia St. Petersburg and Russia Moscow Missions. The new St. Petersburg mission began with 43 missionaries and 574 members; the Moscow mission had 28 missionaries and 186 members. Joan and I enjoyed greeting St. Petersburg mission president Charles Creel and his wife, Sister Susan Creel, who stayed with us in Helsinki en route to their mission field. They had been serving in Kiev as a missionary couple. We were impressed with their vigor, confidence, good sense, and warmth. After a dinner at the mission home, President Creel and I spent a day discussing the St. Petersburg mission.

The Creels left for St. Petersburg the next day without a mission office or home. At the same time, their capable office couple, Elder and Sister Wright, formerly serving in Frankfurt, arrived in Helsinki. They operated the St. Petersburg mission office from our Helsinki facility for two weeks, until they, too, moved to St. Petersburg. During the time they were in Helsinki, Joan and Sister Wright purchased more than forty boxes of office and household supplies and equipment, which were shipped to St. Petersburg by truck on 18 February.

In the meantime, Frankfurt Physical Facilities representative Gary Packer located an adequate office and apartment combination in a hotel appropriately named "The Sea Gull," where the Creels lived and worked until the completion of their mission in July 1993.

During February I made several trips to Moscow, mainly to work with Frankfurt Physical Facilities representative Jeno Toth in locating a mission office and home for the Russia Moscow Mission. Considerable time was required to scour newspaper listings, meet with fledgling real estate entrepreneurs, travel long distances to examine dozens of possible facilities, and discuss

215

terms and conditions with proprietors not used to negotiating agreements and, hence, indecisive but often outlandish in their expectations.

Much of what Jeno, Joan, and I examined was pitiful in condition and location. But many missionaries, members, and friends worked to help us find a prospective mission office and home. The first proposed office, on Merzliakovskii Lane, was soon deemed too small and became, instead, a fine facility for officers of the Russian Religious Association and Moscow ecclesiastical leaders. In the largest of its five rooms, twenty members could fit around tables and along the walls for leadership training and auxiliary activities. The mission office was found in mid-March.

The future mission home consisted of two adjoining apartments, each with three rooms, a bath, and a kitchen. The apartments were in a Stalin-era building (hence of better construction than later housing) and located on Dmitrii Ulianov Street. This street intersects at right angles the Leninskii Prospekt thoroughfare to the city center from the southwest and continues across to Moscow University and Sparrow Hills one and a half miles from the mission home. The building is a sprawling thirteen floors with hundreds of apartments. The entrances to the building were, like most Russian entryways, often dark and odoriferous, with damaged stairs and frequently inoperable, tiny elevators. But the Frankfurt Temporal Affairs office arranged for a Danish firm to completely renovate the apartments before our family moved in. Remodeling was to be completed by 1 June.

Although plans were being made to divide the one Moscow branch and three tiny groups into five branches, at that time the only official branch had been meeting since December 1991 in a quasiprivate science high school facility at Donskaia Street 37 near the Shabolovskaia subway station. For the first time there was ample classroom space and an auditorium large enough for sacrament meetings. By the time I visited the branch in mid-February, the leaders had located a piano but still had no microphone for sacrament meetings. President Andrei Petrov conducted the sacrament service masterfully, although the meeting began late because the person assigned to prepare the sacrament did not arrive on time.

That Sunday more than 150 attended sacrament meeting and

approximately sixty were in the adult Sunday School class. A rather aggressive and presumptuous Russian emigré who had been living in California upbraided the Russians for their passivity and pessimism. The Russian class members answered her calmly and persuasively, demonstrating a depth of thought and authentic optimism that enlightened and silenced their accuser. Several enthusiastic BYU student volunteers teaching English in Russian nursery schools helped with Primary and other age groups.

Following church services I held a leadership training meeting for fifteen branch leaders. Most of the meeting was spent discussing the reasons to divide branches when they become as large as ours in Moscow. Understandably, in every city members vigorously resisted this first division of their close branch family. As they adjusted and observed the advantages of division, generally they were far less hesitant about further divisions.

Later I interviewed investigators and members, including two women concerned that the LDS Church did not sufficiently honor the Virgin Mary. Venerated Russian tradition attributes to Mary numerous miracles in preserving the nation from enemy attacks and interceding on behalf of worthy individuals in dire straits. I spoke with two recent converts about requirements for serving a mission. Another man explained that he wanted to be baptized but could not marry the woman with whom he now lived because he would first need a divorce from his estranged wife, which would likely mean loss of his apartment. Andrei Petrov and I also spoke at length about the branch and the Russian Religious Association.

During February four students from the missions in the former Soviet Union—one each from Tallinn, St. Petersburg, Moscow, and Kiev—were invited to attend BYU for a year and then return home to share their experiences at the university. The translation office in Frankfurt sent us a few attractively printed lessons from priesthood and auxiliary manuals translated previously by our members.

Early in the month, for the first time, the missionaries in St. Petersburg received their support funds sent from Germany through a local Russian bank. Unfortunately, several subsequent efforts to transfer money through Russian banks were less successful. The best method remained for visitors from Frankfurt and Helsinki to carry considerable amounts of cash into Russia on their visits.

Joan's letter home described additional food assistance that came from Germany during this month.

> A food shipment was delivered to the Russian and Estonian Church members during the first week of February. . . . The truck was delayed by customs officials as it traveled through Lithuania and Latvia, so the deliveries were over a week late.
>
> Nothing was heard from the Russian truck driver after he left Frankfurt until he finally made the delivery in Tallinn. I for one was concerned that the entire shipment might have been sold to black marketeers. Another load of food packages will leave Frankfurt at the end of this week. The boxes have temporarily eased the members' pain. Some in Vyborg commented that the boxes arrived when they were in desperate need and had nowhere else to turn. Neither flour nor cooking oil has been available there for two or three months.[1]

All the letters we received on our mission were appreciated, but two in February were of particular significance to me. One was from a General Authority who recently had attended a conference in Nicaragua and heard about members of the Gutierrez family, some of whom had joined the Church after Sister Marta Gutierrez's death one year ago this month. The family, I learned, was consoled and faithful. I deeply appreciated this reassuring, comforting letter from one whose schedule was extraordinarily demanding. The second letter was from a woman whose friend in the Tabernacle Choir had told her that after the Choir's trip to Russia she prayed for Joan and me by name every day. These much-appreciated words of support and confidence buoyed me up during challenging times.

Among those baptized in February were three young men who soon served the Church well. Brother Iurii Sushilin, who became the regional Physical Facilities representative, shared this story of his conversion:

> I met the missionaries for the first time in 1991. Before that time I knew very little about the Mormon Church. Several times in various religious periodicals I read about the church, but the information given was scanty—only that such a church existed, that it was established in the nineteenth century, its founder was Joseph Smith—but that was all. I didn't know anything else.
>
> My conversion, however, happened rather quickly. I met the missionaries in November or December of 1991. I remember it

well. There was an entire group of them standing in the metro singing hymns and handing out invitations to their Sunday meeting. I walked up to them and listened for a few minutes. A missionary named Elder Poole came up to me and gave me an invitation to their church service to take place the next day. Since Sunday was my day off and I didn't have anything planned, I decided to go to the meeting. I was very interested in learning more about the church.

I can't say that I believed in God, but I knew about him, since my mother was an Orthodox believer. At home we had icons, and she often prayed. But she did not force her views upon me. Besides, it was a difficult time, since in society antireligious propaganda labeled belief in God a weakness. In addition, I was a member of the Communist Party. Since the Party propagated atheism, I thought that I shouldn't believe in God. Still, I never tried to convince my mother that she was wrong. I considered belief in God a personal decision.

I wish to say that before meeting the missionaries, I felt the need to know more about God. For approximately a year, I tried to regularly attend meetings of the Russian Orthodox Church, but I did not derive satisfaction from them. Eventually, I stopped attending Sunday services.

After attending my first LDS meeting, I had a strong feeling that I should attend them more often. I needed to learn more of God. By this time I had already begun to believe firmly in God, and knew that faith in him was a necessity. . . . I believed in the [LDS] Church I could receive answers, and that is exactly what happened. The missionaries began to present the discussions and I began to learn more and more. . . . For me, the most important issue was to know for myself that this church is true. I wanted my own witness. For some time I was unable to receive it, but before my baptism I received this strong testimony. Since that time I can firmly say I am a member of the only true Church of Jesus Christ. . . .

I was baptized in Moscow in February 1992. It was a bright, sunny day and I remember it well. Several of us were baptized in a swimming pool. Members of the Church, many my acquaintances and even my friends whom I invited, were at the baptismal service. Elder [Lane] Rousseau baptized me and Elder [Cameron] Poole gave me the Holy Ghost. . . . After my baptism, I was called to be a Sunday School teacher. The calling was very unexpected and I didn't feel prepared to teach others. But after I accepted and began to prepare lessons, I understood that this calling was necessary for me, and that I could manage. . . . I was a teacher for about six months. After that I was called to be the second counselor in the Serpukhovskoi branch presidency. . . .

Some time later, President Mokhov asked me to be the second counselor in the district presidency. I thought for a long time about whether or not I could fulfill such a calling, but in the end I decided to accept. I figured that the district president must have prayed to know who could fulfill this calling, and if he received the answer that I could, then I should accept. I have been the second counselor in the East District presidency of the Russia Moscow Mission now for already over a year. I love this work and this calling. I am very thankful to President Mokhov and God for this calling. . . .

At the end of February of this year [1995], I visited the temple. A group of members traveled to the Stockholm Temple. This visit made a great impression on me. I will strive to be able to go again. . . I know that attending the temple is essential for every member of the Church, even if it is once a year. It facilitates our spiritual growth.[2]

Brother Valerii Kolesnikov, who became a branch president, recalled the answers to lifelong questions and the fulfillment of a forgotten dream:

I first began thinking about God around the age of five. I remember asking my grandmother about him. I don't remember exactly what she said to me, but I recall that her answer was so convincing that for the rest of my life I found myself wondering, "Who is he?" and never, "Does he exist?" There were times when he seemed to me to be a remarkably severe, angry, and ruthless being. If we were to talk about what The Church of Jesus Christ of Latter-day Saints has given me, then I would say that it is an assurance that God is impeccably pure, exalted, and full of love and compassion toward all living creatures. . . .

When I first attended The Church of Jesus Christ of Latter-day Saints, my spiritual condition, as they say, left much to be desired. I was disappointed with the Russian Orthodox Church, or rather, I was unable to feel comfortable there. I was not able to find my place in the world, either. By this time, I had read much religious literature and already had my own picture of what the True Church should be like. Figuratively speaking, it was as a mountain standing firmly on the ground, its summit reaching up into the heavens. . . .

I had intended to leave Moscow and move to Ukraine so that I could be closer to the Dnieper River and to nature, and contribute to the spiritual rebirth of my homeland. I thought that maybe the true church was not on the earth and that maybe every church represented only a part of the truth. And perhaps the true church exists in a purely mystical way as the sum total of the souls of all true followers of Jesus Christ, they who lived as he did and proved their loyalty to their convictions by dying for them. . . .

I acquired an issue of *Christian News* because I wanted to maintain my ties with other Christian organizations and keep current on various trends of Christianity. Once I opened the twenty-third issue of this publication in which I found a section entitled "New Confessions." My eyes flew uninterestedly past a brief article on the "Molokans"; . . . I then moved on to an article entitled "Mormons." . . . I had scarcely read the first lines when my heart, or rather something much deeper from the very center of my soul, suddenly responded to the words which, it is clear to me now, were written by the very same power as the one which was helping me to understand them, and not only understand, but receive them into my heart.

At the end of this article there was an address and several telephone numbers. Having forgotten in my excitement that it was still only Saturday, I darted off to the listed location. The man on duty at the facility informed me that Mormons meet on Sundays. The next day, I again went to the theater on Spartacus Square, and as soon as I saw the faces of the two missionaries standing at the entrance to the meeting place, a voice inside me told me that I had finally found my friends, that I had found those who live by the very same ideals for which my soul had been longing. For the first time in my whole life, I felt as though I was among my own kind. Surprisingly, I had never met any of those church members before, but nonetheless, I had the feeling that I had known everyone there from a long time before.

After the meeting, I left my telephone number with Elders [Chad] Daugherty and [Michael] Van Patten, and the very next day we met in my apartment. If we were to talk about the role of the missionaries who brought me into the Church, I would have to say now that God fashioned everything in the very best way. It is not a coincidence that the dependable and devoted Elders Van Patten and Daugherty were my first missionaries. . . .

At this, the end of my letter, I would like to briefly tell of the blessings I received in the temple in Sweden. A little over twenty years ago I had a vision in which I saw myself dressed in white. I was among others who were also dressed in white. I had forgotten about that vision, despite my quite good memory,

Andrei Lokshin at his translator's desk with his parents,
Galina and Aleksandr. Aleksandr has served as president of a Moscow
district and of the LDS Russian Religious Association

until the very moment when I passed through the veil into the
celestial room of the Stockholm temple.[3]

Andrei Lokshin, a young man who became principal translator
for the Church, shared his testimony:

> Once, an experienced engineer told me: "One's first job is
> like one's first love." And I understand him because I also feel
> that way. I recall that I, as my Russian literature teacher had
> hoped, intended to become a journalist and that my work would
> be in some way connected with literature. Could I have ever
> known where I would find myself working when I first started
> out as a student of the Highway Transportation Institute? . . .
> My work today has become my life, love, and calling. Some-
> times I think that I came to this earth for this very reason. . . .
>
> The more time that goes by, the more I understand that one
> of the fundamental teachings of the gospel is that God has a mis-
> sion for us. It fills me with immeasurable joy when I think about
> how we all belong to one and the same Church—a Church
> which has been established in truth and in the eternities, a
> Church which is formidable and stable, as regiments bearing
> banners, bringing the good news of the gospel to the worlds of
> the living and the dead.
>
> We belong to one Church and we labor for God and his

Church. I need nothing more than this. I am not worried about which degree of glory I will attain after my time on earth is over. Whether I think about it or not, it will be decided. I hardly care what my salary will be. I don't even long to go to America! The only thing I need is to work for the Church and in the Church. . . .

The Church is taking its very first steps in Russia, although sometimes it seems as though these words are merely an attempt to vindicate its temporary setbacks. I am sure that a great future is awaiting the Church, that a Book of Mormon will be in every library, that all Russia will find out about Mormons from the mouths of the missionaries and from the examples of the members of The Church of Jesus Christ of Latter-day Saints themselves, and not from Sir Arthur Conan Doyle's *A Study in Scarlet*. I never would have written these words without faith in the truthfulness of the Church, in the Prophet Joseph Smith who was chosen of God, and in the truthfulness of the Book of Mormon.[4]

29

MARCH 1992

By March 1992 free market forces had begun to operate well and consistently in Russia in only a very few places. One was at the lone McDonald's restaurant (two others were open by mid-1993), and another was at Izmailovskii Park, where on weekends sellers set up tables or rented booths. One Saturday Joan and I visited the park, where scores of Russians and others take exquisite merchandise to sell: fur hats, shawls, stacking dolls, oriental carpets, linen, lacquer boxes, balalaikas (a stringed instrument), porcelain, rare coins and antique metal hardware, books, paintings by contemporary artists, flags and banners, and military uniforms and other paraphernalia. On that day in March, as usual, the Izmailovskii Park merchants stood in mud behind flimsy tables piled with precious goods. Often magnificent paintings or carpets lay behind the seller on tattered brown paper or shredding plastic spread over mud, exposed to the elements. The vast ocean of creative splendor contrasted strikingly with the surrounding trampled mud.

The two extremes seemed to symbolize the resplendent but frequently unkempt Russia we so earnestly love. Deep waters of authentic beauty flow from under surface grime and coarseness. We can rejoice that the Lord disregards appearances and looks on the infinite inner beauty in which Russia is uncommonly rich.

The Russian Religious Association arranged for Joan and me to obtain multiple-entry visas to Russia, permitting us to visit and leave Russia repeatedly without applying each time for a tourist visa and prepaying for a Russian hotel. This allowed us to rent a small apartment in Moscow. One month in the apartment cost the same as two nights in any tourist hotel. Sisters Carrie Madsen and Jodi Jorgenson moved from their apartment near the Belorusskaia subway station to another apartment located more centrally in

Display of art work at Izmailovskii Park in Moscow

their proselyting area, allowing us to acquire their well-above-average two-room apartment.

The landlords had moved to their summer home to protect it from robbers and vandals. They had left the apartment completely furnished and emptied a closet and a few shelves for the sisters and then for us to use. This was to be our Moscow apartment until the mission home was ready in June. But within a few weeks the landlady accepted a better offer from a businessman and asked us to vacate the apartment by 1 April. Fortunately, Eric Knapp, an LDS American administrator at the new Moscow Slavianskaia Hotel in the Radisson group, let us use a two-room apartment in a building adjacent to his hotel. He had rented the apartment for family members and other guests who would be visiting late in June and after. Joan and I gratefully moved our belongings to this apartment where we could stay until mid-June. The apartment was lighter and more comfortable than our previous one, and it was located in a better building in which families of the renowned Beriozka [Birch Tree] Dance and Choral Ensemble lived. Brother Knapp's landlord was abroad and happily rented his apartment for western currency. As is common, every inch of the apartment was utilized, in this case, to accommodate the owner's accumulation of books, clothing, housewares, sports equipment, and souvenirs from travel in the Soviet Union and abroad. His skis and poles were skillfully arranged behind the toilet. Along the base of walls were multiple strands of extension cords leading in all directions to strips of electrical outlets. Portions of one closet, one cabinet, and a small refrigerator had been emptied for renters' use.

While looking for a mission office, Joan and I met a man who made an incalculable difference in our mission. We had emerged from the university subway station, needing to reach an address in the area as quickly as possible. A man was waiting to show us a potential office, so we hailed a taxi. Formerly, taxis were licensed by the city, but now, many Muscovites accepted passengers to augment their dwindling incomes.

Nikolai Zavalishin, a resident in a nearby apartment complex, was returning home, but he stopped to offer us a ride for a fee in his clean Volga. Nikolai did not smoke and he drove carefully, was a pleasant conversationalist, and was very thoughtful and accommodating. We exchanged telephone numbers, and over the weeks we continued to work together, soon discovering a deep mutual affinity. Nikolai and his wife, Tatiana, both accomplished vocalists, had been members of the famed Piatnitskii Dance and Choral Ensemble, which had performed throughout the USSR and the world. New economic realities had compelled them to seek additional sources of income.

Moscow has heavy traffic, poorly marked streets, unpainted driving lanes, and very aggressive, unpredictable, and, increasingly, inadequately trained drivers. The new rich may choose simply to bribe officials and receive driver's licenses without any instruction. Combining all these factors with my progressive myopia led to a decision to have a mission driver for our car. In time Nikolai became our driver and dear friend. On long trips to and from airports, markets, and around town with Church leaders and guests from Frankfurt and Salt Lake City, he provided reliability, humor, and warmth, which everybody appreciated.

Extraordinarily quick of mind, he occasionally startled and even embarrassed us when we were with General Authorities by his imaginative and always successful exchanges with traffic police. For example, he regularly persuaded police to let us through areas temporarily blocked off:

"These men are from America and need to return to their hotel for an important meeting. They have just pledged one million dollars to municipal orphanage seven [with street number and name of director]," he would say, or,

"Our guests are Americans, and we're returning from a meeting at the Supreme Soviet."

"But this area is closed to *all* traffic by order of the mayor," the traffic policeman would protest.

"I know the mayor's assistant [full name] well. If there's any problem, he'll take care of it for us in a blink!" And Nikolai would proceed.

How delightful it was to return from several strenuous days of travel to see Nikolai waiting for me with engaging conversation about recent news of the country, city, and our families. Listening to his colorful Russian and good-natured accounts of an endless array of interesting happenings was as refreshing as a canyon breeze in August. We often talked of missionary work in Russia, Church teachings, and his questions about Church literature that I gave him to read. Nikolai towers among the many who enriched my mission.

Joan described an important Russian holiday in which the missionaries participated:

> March 8th was a big holiday in Russia—Women's Day, not just Mother's Day. It is customary to bring flowers when you visit anyone on that day, so three people who were coming for interviews with Gary brought me tulips and carnations—always in odd numbers. Even numbers are for funerals.[1]

This year, some missionaries took part by distributing flowers to elderly ladies trudging the Moscow streets.

While attending a Moscow group meeting not far from the university, Joan and I had the opportunity to be present at the Sunday School class of a gifted teacher. Svetlana (Lana) Zhuzhleva had been contacted by Elders Adam West and Mark Bjork late at night on a subway station escalator as they were returning to their apartment. Her husband, Aleksandr, later also became interested and joined the Church, and their two small, lively daughters, Nadia and Daria, attended with their parents. Sister Zhuzhleva masterfully engaged those present in a discussion of the Holy Spirit. His influence, she explained, was more like summer rain that refreshes and cleanses, not as a river flowing uninterruptedly. She described the Spirit's voice as though calling to us from a room crowded with other voices, all competing for attention. One voice beckons us to riches, another to power, a third to the cheap thrills of violence and pornography, and others to many more areas of self-indulgence and degradation. The voice of the Spirit calls quietly and barely perceptibly, but when we come closer and are more attentive, moving away from the other voices, his clear message can be heard. In every decision we make and action we perform, we choose which voice we will follow.

The alert Elder Chad Daugherty introduced us to an investigator who helped us locate a mission home facility, and our most senior missionary, Elder Joseph Pace, led us to what would become the new mission office. He diligently studied the English-language *Moscow Times* newspaper and found an advertisement for a recently renovated office directly across a two-lane street from the Chistye Prudy ("Clean Ponds") subway station on the central "boulevard ring," a mile north of the Kremlin.

The office was on the fourth floor of a nineteenth-century building adjoining a central post office. The entrance was through one of the worst passageways in downtown Moscow, past a basement public toilet around which, when the toilet was locked, any area served as an outdoor comfort station. The stairway was also decrepit and offensive. The office itself, however, was nicely remodeled to a high Russian standard.

The office consisted of four rather large rooms, a kitchen (to become a duplicating and work room), a toilet and bath (in and above the bathtub we stored boxes containing Russian copies of the Book of Mormon and supplies), a twelve-by-twelve-foot foyer onto which the four rooms and kitchen opened, and an entryway off the foyer large enough to seat eight guests and accommodate magazine and coat racks. The facility was nearly ready for occupancy. Everyone to whom Elder Pace showed the rooms eagerly approved, and arrangements were quickly made to move the mission office from Helsinki to Moscow within a month.

Joan detailed the move to Russia and the first group of missionaries to arrive directly in Moscow:

> Arrangements have been made for a Finnish moving company to start packing the office in Helsinki on April 6th. They will leave on April 7th and hope to unload in Moscow on April 10th. The Deweys are busy buying a six-month store of office supplies and hoping to foresee what might be difficult to purchase there. Moscow has quite a few foreign stores, with more opening all of the time, so hopefully we will be able to buy what we need there. If the Deweys determine there are some things that can't be purchased in Moscow, we can arrange to bring them in when they move our household in June. . . .
>
> The arrival of our ten March missionaries [in Moscow] was quite a change from the normal routine. A small bus was rented by the APs which transported the new missionaries and their baggage from the airport to a building [the science and mathematics school] that the Church rents for Sunday services. There the new missionaries met their assigned companions and took taxis to their apartments, where they left their luggage and freshened up. We met three hours later back at the "meeting house" for a dinner of pizza from Pizza Hut and an ice cream cake from Baskin-Robbins. The most common comment from the new missionaries was about the hair-raising taxi rides to their apartments.
>
> We had a testimony meeting following dinner, and these missionaries were equally tired as those in Helsinki. The next morning the missionaries came to our apartment for interviews and then a general orientation meeting. We will make a few changes in the routine in May when new missionaries arrive, and by July, when we receive our next missionaries, we will have our mission apartment in which to eat a home-cooked meal. Starting in August we will be getting new missionaries every month instead of every other month.[2]

The month's most significant and demanding activity was preparing to divide the Moscow branch and three groups into five branches, one each in the north, south, east, west, and central areas of the city. Generally we combined three subway line "spokes" into a branch. I had hoped to call five Russian brethren to serve as branch presidents and interviewed twice that number whom I knew or who were recommended to me by Andrei Petrov and the missionaries. My purpose was to learn of their individual circumstances and spiritual maturity.

I discovered that many desired to serve, but several felt unable to do so now for reasons of employment. They were working at two and even three jobs in order to survive. Another fine brother was moving to a rural agricultural collective to raise food for his family, and a few seemed to be too inexperienced in the Church or too youthful. One brother's wife had been severely beaten by robbers posing as policemen. Her needs precluded his serving for a time. Some of these brethren served as branch presidents when additional branches were created.

When the division occurred on 29 March, all Moscow members met at the Donskaia Street branch facility. Andrei Petrov was sustained as counselor in the mission presidency, because my request to create a member district with Andrei as president had not been approved. The Petrovs, the five new branch presidents— Russians Boris Mokhov, Mikhail Avtaikin, and Sergei Martynov and American missionaries Elder Cameron Poole and Elder David Robbins—all bore their testimonies and spoke briefly, as did Joan and I.

I set apart the new Russian branch presidents, and Andrei Petrov set apart the American branch presidents. Each received printed instructions regarding what required their most urgent attention during the first week, the second week, the first month, and early in their administrations as branch presidents. The now thirty-eight Moscow missionaries accepted and filled the assignment to visit all 219 members during the next week. They distributed color pictures of the Savior and made certain that all knew when their branches would meet the next Sunday and how important each member was to the success of the Church in that area.

During this March, Andrei Petrov and I attended an invigorating two-day conference of Russian parliamentarians and religious leaders at the Russian legislature building (White House). The conference was organized by Viacheslav Polosin, the chairman of the Supreme Soviet's Committee on Freedom of Conscience, Religion, and Charity, who was an ordained Russian Orthodox priest and an influential legislator. Including the LDS Church, forty religious groups were represented, most prominently the Russian Orthodox delegation.[3]

During the conference we learned of the great difficulty the four thousand registered religious congregations (among them, 2,500 Russian Orthodox, 250 Baptist, 72 Adventist) were having recovering their property confiscated during the Soviet era. Over the years, church holdings had fallen under control of the ministries of defense, culture, education, health, and agriculture and had been used to serve their purposes for decades. On the second day of the conference the floor was open for suggestions on legislation to promote the interests of religion in Russia. Andrei Petrov made several astute comments in relation to the wording of draft legislation and established himself and the Church as credible contributors.

This month Elena Chebotaeva was baptized. Her struggles to accept baptism and remain faithful have been experienced by many:

> I found out about the Mormon Church from my friend Tatiana Pashkina, who invited me to visit church with her. At first I decided to go out of curiosity. I had grown accustomed to seeing in Russian churches stern old men and women, and sad younger people. But in this church, I was astonished to see the happy faces of the missionaries, the vivacity and warmth of the members, and the camaraderie among everyone. I liked seeing many young people there.
>
> I enjoyed certain lessons very much, and others I found quite boring. But new acquaintances helped me to keep coming back, again and again. I began wanting to meet with the missionaries. At one of the sacrament meetings, I went up to Sister [Tressa] Harmon and asked if she would meet with me.
>
> I am a shy person, so this was a very difficult step for me. I was disappointed when Sister Harmon explained that she would be unable to give the lessons to me because she lived in a different area. She said that the Elders lived in my area and would visit with me. She apologized and walked away. I was very upset. I had wanted to meet only with the sisters. I decided for myself that I wouldn't approach any one else and that with this, my attempt to meet with the missionaries would end. All this passed through my head for one to two minutes following my talk with Sister Harmon. I said a couple of words to my friend and set off toward the exit.
>
> It was there that Sister Harmon caught up with me and said

Elena Chebotaeva

that she and her companion Sister McLennan [had received] permission to meet with me. I was very touched by the attention given to my request, and I gladly set up an appointment with them. This was my first step into The Church of Jesus Christ of Latter-day Saints.

It was very difficult for me to make the decision to be baptized. My parents had baptized me as a young child into the Russian Orthodox Church. A question tormented me as it torments all Russians: "If I were to be baptized again, would I be betraying my Russian Orthodox heritage?" I was especially concerned about this heritage, because I didn't know much about the church itself. I hadn't even known what the Bible was. I had thought the Bible was those incomprehensible words that the priest says during a church service. The creation of the world, life on the earth before the birth of Christ, the birth of Christ, his life and death—all this was simply folklore to me. As it turned out, I knew a lot about the Bible without even suspecting that those things had come out of the Bible.

My family did not object to my joining the Mormon Church, although my mother was surprised at me. She considered this simply a passing fancy that had suddenly appeared in Moscow's intellectual circles. My friends were more harsh. They felt as though I had betrayed the Russian Church. I tried to explain to them why I liked this new church, but they didn't want to understand me. That is why I kept putting off my baptism. Finally I made the decision to be baptized. It was the biggest event of my life. . . . I now attend the Timiriazevskii Branch. I was a teacher, but now I am the second counselor to the Relief Society president. I feel as though I have become a better person and that I am kinder to others. My relationships with my husband and my son have also improved.

Sometimes I catch myself thinking that I don't want to read the Bible or Book of Mormon. Before I go to bed, I'll just read a novel or watch TV. But sometimes there are days when my hands seem to reach out for these books, and I open the scriptures to the very pages where there are verses corresponding to my mood. These become great revelations for me. I find the very words for which I have the greatest need. I know that I must do much more in order to become a better person. I must pray and ask Heavenly Father to assist me to do this. I trust in his help and this faith enables me to overcome life's trials.[4]

30

APRIL 1992

Elder Douglas and Sister Lois Dewey carefully itemized office items, accurately completed a mountain of paperwork, and, in general, supervised our relocation from Helsinki to Moscow. A Finnish moving company did the packing. While the truck drove to Moscow, the Deweys took the train, arriving on the morning of April 9. None of us expected that the truck would be able to clear customs and be at our office on 10 April, as the moving company projected. On April 9 additional documentation was urgently requested and immediately provided, and at 7:00 A.M. on April 10 the truck arrived at the office entrance. Hearty missionaries carried everything up the four flights of stairs to the office—the modest elevator, as often, was inoperable. With the help of many the office began to operate in a limited way almost immediately.

While I held a training meeting with the new Moscow branch presidents in the Merzliakovskii facility—the smaller apartment we had thought might become our mission office—Joan and several missionaries arranged my office furniture. When I returned later in the evening, I learned of several problems. The electrical power had failed when Joan plugged in a vacuum cleaner. The same thing happened when Sister Dewey attempted to use the photocopy machine. The toilet was clogged—again. Elder Dewey would work time and again in putrid waters and waste with his plumber's helper. The landlord sent a very resourceful Russian electrician named Oleg who, over time, upgraded the power supply to the office, adding many outlets and providing devices to protect our expensive equipment from power surges and brown-outs. Oleg also performed a range of handyman tasks.

Between April and June, I lived and worked mainly in Moscow, and Joan spent most of her time with the children in Helsinki. Typically I stayed from ten days to two weeks in Moscow, followed by three days in Helsinki. On one of my visits to the family after the office had moved to Moscow, we used most of our three days together on a trip to Lapland in northern Finland.

Late in April, Elder Albert Choules of the Europe Area presidency and I visited Nizhnii Novgorod, Kazan, and Perm; Elders Hans B. Ringger and Dennis B. Neuenschwander traveled in late June and early July to Volgograd, Donetsk, Samara, and Saratov— all cities of approximately one million or more inhabitants— gathering information, contacts, and impressions about areas in which missionaries might commence their labors. Eventually the Area presidency decided our mission would begin in Nizhnii Novgorod and then move in stages to Samara and Saratov.

In Nizhnii Novgorod, Russia's third largest city, Elder Choules and I met with our one local member, Grigorii Fomin, who had been taught and baptized in Moscow in November 1991. Now Brother Fomin arranged for meetings with his family members, city officials, and a colleague at the Water Transport Institute in which he had taught. Despite his physical difficulties, Brother Fomin accompanied us to our meetings all day.

His apartment was modest but pleasant. All water had to be carried because city pipes had broken in his neighborhood weeks ago and had not yet been replaced. With him in his apartment were his daughter Anna and her son. Elder Choules and I explained Church teachings and the differences between our church and the "Christian Church" (Russian Orthodox). We held a sacrament meeting, principally for the blessing of Brother Fomin, and bestowed on him the Aaronic Priesthood. Anna, apparently prepared by her father, requested a blessing of health for her ailing ten-month-old son, Dmitrii, which we felt honored to provide. Anna then wondered whether the blessing made Dmitrii a member of our Church, and we explained how one may prepare to join the Church.

We met with the city councilor responsible for religious organizations and learned that the LDS Church and its missionaries would be welcome in the city. When we had sufficient members we should be registered, as were 230 other congregations at that time, including 156 Russian Orthodox, 36 Muslim, 13 Baptist, 4 Pentecostal, 2 Adventist, 2 Jewish, and 1 Hare Krishna. We visited a large, new, Adventist facility and spoke with their leaders. We learned that the Adventists had two thousand members in the Volga-Ural region and projected five thousand by the fall.

In all the cities we visited, we attempted to locate those who had written to our office asking for information about the Church. In Nizhnii Novgorod we found the Zubrilin family. The father was a retired circus performer, an equestrian acrobat. The family had a video player and showed us clips of the father and his horses. We spoke of the Church and provided literature.

In Kazan the Zhirnov family had expressed interest in the Church. We spoke briefly with Mrs. Zhirnov at her door, but Mr. Zhirnov was not home. Late that evening he and his family visited the hotel to discuss the Church further.

In Kazan we were greatly assisted by Natalia Konstantinova, a colleague and close friend of an American Latter-day Saint by the name of Hugh Stengler. Brother Stengler had contacted me several times to report his enthusiasm for many he had met in Kazan, especially Natalia. Following a discussion of the Church we went with her to the city official responsible for religious organizations and received his assurances that our Church would be welcome in Kazan. Natalia also took us to several important cultural and religious monuments in the city, including the attractive Lenin Memorial building in which, she had already been informed, we could obtain permission to hold our Sunday services.

Perm, on the Kama River, is further northeast beyond the Volga and in the industrial and mining Ural Mountain region. In contrast to the charming downtown village feeling of Kazan, Perm is built on the massive scale of modern Moscow: wide boulevards, tall buildings set back from the streets, and considerable distances between immense structures.

We were unable to visit city offices because our trip coincided with May First holiday activities, but we met and were greatly impressed by the Roman family in Perm. The father was a young engineer. He and his wife radiated a genuine interest and spiritual receptivity. While their two children played outside of the apartment, we discussed many Church teachings and bore our testimonies. Later that evening they also unexpectedly arrived at the hotel to continue discussing the Church.

31

MAY 1992

At a conference in Moscow in early May, Elder Albert B. Choules struck a responsive chord among the Russian Latter-day Saints when he affirmed that the gospel of Jesus Christ "allows us to feel peace when all around us is in chaos." Members nodded their assent and later referred to this point in relation to their own lives. A day after Elder Albert and Sister Marilyn Choules met with the missionaries, Elder Dennis Neuenschwander and four additional guests arrived: Frankfurt Temporal Affairs director Peter Berkhahn, Physical Facilities manager Konrad Nagele, Ronald Knighton of Church Curriculum, and Thomas Peterson of the Church's International Magazines.

Natalia Myshkova, a friend of the Church from the former Soviet Union Ministry of Culture, had arranged a meeting with influential city officials in the beautiful eighteenth-century building of the Moscow City Soviet. The officials present included Valerii Borshchov, city councilor responsible for religious organizations in Moscow; Aleksandr Muzykantskii, "prefect," or mayor, within the Moscow city center; and Galina Bodrenkova, city councilor and director of Moscow Charity House, a reliable and experienced organization through which the Church could distribute charitable contributions to the city's needy.

Elder Neuenschwander introduced the group and the Church in Russia, I spoke on the origin of our Church and of its distinguishing teachings, Brother Berkhahn spoke of possible humanitarian assistance for the city, and Brother Nagele described our Church's physical facilities needs. The meeting was formal and restrained, with the Russian city leaders emphasizing that if they were to cooperate with us, we must register our congregations locally. In effect they said that when we had completed our registrations, we could continue the discussion. Church policy was to try convincing city

237

and prefecture officials that Russian national registration was adequate, as the law clearly stated.

At a missionary meeting, Elder Neuenschwander urged the missionaries to rise to the expectations they had as they began their missions, not to be content with their current performance or goals. He also effectively used Acts 2 to teach the missionaries about conversion. At the evening branch presidents' meeting, the five mission visitors discussed their areas of responsibility, set forth plans for supporting the mission, and answered questions.

On Sunday the guests went with missionaries to all the Moscow branches, including the international branch. Ronald Knighton from Church Curriculum went with me to the north and central branches.

During one sacrament meeting I noticed an attractive vase of tulips on one end of a table used as a podium and a modest bouquet of eight or so dandelions in a glass of water on the other end. The bright yellow blooms brought a cheery, unpretentious beauty into the meeting that paralleled the humble but sunny members and missionaries in the Church in Russia.

In Primary I was amazed as a nine-year-old recent convert raised his hand in response to his teacher's query, "Can anyone tell us something about Joseph Smith?" His answer was an extended recitation of much from the *Joseph Smith Testimony* pamphlet. He spoke with moving conviction about Joseph's prayer and the heavenly appearances.

During this month several mission initiatives began to bear fruit. We distributed to missionaries copies of a leaflet formed from one piece of paper folded in thirds, allowing six "sides" or columns. The leaflet contained information on the Church's origin, basic teachings and values, and development in Russia, as well as addresses and meeting times of Church services. It was intended to create a positive image (countering the only thing most seemed to recall when they heard of the Church—polygamy), heighten interest, and serve as a business card. I wrote a draft of the leaflet and then solicited and received comments and improvements from many helpful people, Americans and Russians, before revising it and printing it in quantity.

Also this month we organized a mission training council to

provide leadership training and coordination among the six branch leaders (five in Moscow and one in Zelenograd). Branch presidents, clerks, elders quorum presidents, branch mission leaders, auxiliary leaders, and other branch leaders and teachers generally gathered monthly for this training. In most cases, an experienced missionary couple or expatriate prepared a monthly training topic for each group's members and, as a rule working at first through an interpreter, taught basic principles. For instance, Andrei Petrov and I taught the branch presidents, Elder Douglas Dewey instructed the clerks, and Sister Lois Dewey taught the Relief Society presidents. Within six months we identified a Russian in most groups whom we prepared to teach. The Americans then served as consultants and lower-profile leaders.

Sister Dewey described her experience at one of these sessions:

> I must tell you about the last leadership meeting I held for Relief Society presidencies on August 27. Irina Liudogovskaia is a Relief Society president and also acts as my interpreter for these meetings. The meeting was being held at a building the Church has rented for such purposes. That facility has been under renovation ever since we came to Moscow, but was finally finished. Previously we had held leadership meetings here at the mission office.
>
> Anyway, 7 P.M. came and there were ten ladies present, but no Irina. I was so totally helpless. Two of the women knew a few words of English and I know a few words of Russian, but certainly not enough to teach anybody anything. We had some refreshments that I had brought, and I handed out what material I had prepared. At 7:30 I told them they were free to go or could stay and discuss common Relief Society interests, if they wished. They chose to stay, thank goodness, because Irina and another sister came soon after. They had thought the meeting was at the mission office and had been waiting there.
>
> Needless to say, the meeting was shortened a lot, but we made some good progress. The main thing I want to tell you about is the love and support I felt from these wonderful women. Instead of being upset that they had come so far for a meeting that probably couldn't be held, they felt such empathy for me and were so sympathetic to my situation. After the meeting every one expressed thanks for what they had learned. They are anxious for the next meeting, and for me to visit their Relief Society meetings so I can help them to improve. I think the

interaction I have with the Russian Church members is probably the most rewarding part of this mission to me. The Church is attracting the "cream of the crop" here in Moscow.[1]

At our branch presidents' training meeting in May we discussed a one-page synopsis of the Church's leadership handbook entitled "Providing in the Lord's Way," on principles of welfare assistance. Throughout my mission I remained astonished at how little welfare assistance was requested by the Russians. Part of my purpose this month was to help leaders understand that funds exist to provide short-term aid and to teach the leaders when such help is entirely appropriate. Nevertheless, requests for aid remained few. Everyone was in such difficult straits that few felt their needs to be more severe than others'.

We also discussed the possibility of a two-hour meeting block rather than three hours. Our materials were so few and our teachers so inexperienced, frequently rotating either to new callings or into less activity. Our Primary leaders were especially burdened by the obligation to engage restless children for two hours each Sunday. A shortened schedule seemed appropriate. A sample two-hour schedule was distributed, and about half the branch presidents expressed an interest in trying it.

Late in the month we received our gift computer, laser printer, photocopier, and scanner provided by the Tabernacle Choir supporters mentioned earlier (see p. 163). With this equipment we could begin to translate full-time in one room of our mission office. Brother Johannes Gutjahr from Frankfurt and I interviewed more than twenty candidates applying to translate for the Church. We intended to have four translators working at the computer in four-hour shifts, sixteen hours a day, five days a week. We first selected eight—then nine when an additional exceptional candidate appeared—and invited them to work one week in two-hour shifts each day translating Sunday School Gospel Doctrine lesson materials. They were paid one dollar per hour in convertible currency, a fair wage at the time. At the end of the week, their translations were printed without the translators' names and evaluated by a committee of four well-read Russian Church members and I.

From the nine we chose the skilled translators Irina Liudogovskaia, Elena Eliseeva, Saule Zhoshina, and Anna Saveleva, who immediately began translating teaching materials under the coordination of a fifth translator, Andrei Lokshin. Using this system and equipment, we produced a considerable volume of material in a relatively short time. Yet despite our best efforts, the translations were uneven. Russian LDS terminology was still evolving, and some concepts or terms were rendered variously. We did not allow time for careful stylistic and content reviews, and our desktop publishing was not as attractive as Church publications.

The pressure we felt in Russian-speaking areas was to have some kind of informative and inspiring Church material every Sunday. On the other hand, Church Translation had to protect against our inadvertently teaching false doctrine. Soon the Frankfurt translation operation assumed its normal supervisory function. A substantial portion of translation time shifted to such items as ward and stake financial records books, although wards, stakes, and a sophisticated banking system did not yet exist in Russia. After translation, each work was submitted to time-consuming reviews, initially in other Russian cities. The finished products, however, more nearly reflected the polished Church content and quality standards appreciated internationally.

Joan commented on the logistics of working without a mission home in Moscow and on the preparations for our family's move:

> Last week I traveled to Moscow on Tuesday, May 19, and arrived just in time to get a simple supper of taco salad ready while Gary interviewed Elder [Matthew] Malovich before his departure from the mission. . . . On May 21 four elders and one sister arrived from the MTC. Three of them are from southeastern Idaho, so we are beginning to have quite an Idaho contingent in our mission. Another of the elders is from Oulu, Finland, so we now have an international force of one Finn, one Swede, one Russian, and forty-five Americans.
>
> Though the new missionaries had no experience with the Russian language before the MTC, they were full of enthusiasm and a willingness to use what they had learned. . . . We served them dinner in our office.
>
> While in Moscow, Gary and I went to see how close our new apartment is to completion. One of the apartments is coming along well and looks like it will soon be completed, but the other one where the bedrooms and laundry room are located is

far from finished. . . . The contractor, being optimistic and in our opinion unrealistic, still maintains that the apartment should be completed by June 12th. We have tentatively changed our moving date to the following week, hoping that by then it really will be ready. I will fly to Moscow for a meeting with a man from Frankfurt for what is supposed to be the "final inspection" on June 1st. By then we should have a more realistic estimate of the completion date.[2]

At our meeting with Elder Choules early this month, he had requested that I arrange for a group of missionaries, including those I would consider sending to begin work in Nizhnii Novgorod, to bear their testimonies in zone conference. On May 19 Elder Hans B. Ringger telephoned to inform me that two of these missionaries would be transferred to the Russia St. Petersburg Mission in June. They would become two of the four missionaries to initiate missionary activity in the city of Riga, Latvia. In one year, July 1993, a new mission would be established in that city and encompass the three Baltic states. I was grateful our mission was able to contribute to the worthy cause of inaugurating missionary work in Latvia.

Among those baptized in May was Aleksei Goncharov, another of the Goncharovs' extended family, a nephew of Moscow's first locally baptized member. This is the story of the changes his conversion brought:

About three years ago, I was a rough guy who walked the streets and behaved like a hooligan. I never thought about how I would live in the future. I should say that for a while, I had a wonderful life. This lasted until I grew to a more mature age. For some reason, my father began drinking, and each time he drank, he would drink more and more. I had never expected that everything could end in the way that it did. My father and mother later took to arguing, which started to repeat itself more and more often until the day of their divorce.

And only one single person supported me through the hard times—my grandmother. Since that time, she has raised me. Sometimes we disagree, but I can say that she tries to do all that she can to help me become a good person.

Once my Aunt Galia [affectionate form of Galina] invited me to church. I went without really taking it seriously. But I saw the people who attended this meeting and sensed a spirit of reverence there. The elders who later conducted the discussions with me spoke about the gospel of Jesus with love towards him as an elder brother. Afterwards, I decided to learn as much about the gospel as I could.

I have also tried to do all that I can to help them. I now know that the devil will not be able to take me from this path because the gospel teaches me the right way to live, how to avoid foolish behavior, and how to be united in all things. I openly and sincerely say that this Church is the true path to God. And I am sure that my spirit will be strengthened by the teachings of Christ and that he will help me share the divine love and warmth which we have in the Church.

There is much that I still must learn, but I am now trying to help people have joy and happiness in this world where we must come to understand God's love. . . . And I would like once again to confirm that this Church is true and I love it with all my heart and with all my soul. Soon it will be my turn to serve a mission, and I will strive to be worthy of this.[3]

32

June 1992

Two months after we moved into the mission office in Moscow, our telephone system was installed. For the first time I now could telephone from my desk and talk in private. Until then, to use the telephone I had walked through the Deweys' office to the open foyer and then spoke on the telephone at the reception counter in the presence of whoever was visiting. What a convenience the new system was! At the same time we also were connected to a satellite line that bypassed the Moscow city system and allowed us to send and receive telephone and fax messages from abroad with ease. Earlier in 1992 I had attempted with very little success to telephone Helsinki and Frankfurt from various Moscow telephones. Parts of the city provided services unavailable in other sections, and calling abroad from our office was difficult. Frankfurt had also discovered that its offices could rarely reach us and so authorized us to contract with a western telephone firm in Moscow for satellite communication services.

Also, our mail from abroad was only sporadically delivered to our mission postal box in an old wing of the next-door post office. Missionaries received mail from parents and friends after long delays. We found that letters from Moscow to the United States tended, with some variation, to take two to three weeks, but from the United States to Moscow, the time was much longer and delivery unreliable. Only one of my parents' first seven letters to Moscow ever arrived. The problem with mail persisted, and in June the Church Missionary Department authorized use of a pouch system (weekly express mail) from the United States, decreasing the time for delivery to two weeks, generally.

Although many small things remained to be done in the mission apartment, our family moved to Moscow, leaving Helsinki on 17 June and arriving the next day. We had made plans, including hotel reservations, to drive to Moscow in two ten-hour days, but when the moving company loaded our belongings, the driver said he would be arriving in Moscow on the eighteenth rather than on the earlier-agreed-upon nineteenth. He wanted to return to Helsinki in time for the very important summer solstice holiday, on which the Finns enjoy more than twenty hours of sunlight.

So we left Helsinki in our Volkswagen van at 6:00 A.M. on the seventeenth and arrived at our Moscow apartment just over eighteen hours later in the very early morning of the eighteenth. I drove from Helsinki to Vyborg, as I had often done. There we met our driver Nikolai Zavalishin, who had arrived that morning by train. He drove the remainder of the trip—and throughout the rest of our mission. Several times I offered to drive on the open highway, but he demurred, insisting that driving the German van was for him an indescribable pleasure. Joan had prepared plenty of good food for the trip, so along the way we stopped very little.

The road to Moscow generally was two lanes, but in quite good condition. We went through dozens of small villages—two rows of wooden cottages in poor repair lining the highway. Many of the structures featured attractive wooden carvings along the roof line and around the windows and doors but needed paint. A few were beautifully painted with trim in bright blue, green, yellow, or red. Often we saw women carrying buckets of water. Each village had a meager general store. Very rarely the village church remained, typically in a state of advanced dilapidation.

Fuel stations were conveniently located along the highway, but none had fuel for sale to travelers who were not truckers or farmers. Nikolai, with his impressive powers of persuasion and affability, regularly convinced reluctant attendants to sell us fuel. At Nikolai's urging, we had carried from Helsinki forty liters of diesel fuel, but thanks to his efforts, we did not need to use it.

When we arrived at our apartment after midnight, workmen were still rushing to complete several projects. They left when we spread our sleeping bags and blankets on the floor. The next morning missionaries arrived early to unload the truck and carry furniture and personal belongings up the two and one-half flights of stairs and to assemble and arrange furniture and appliances. In one apartment were three large bedrooms, bath, toilet, and laundry

Mission apartment is behind the tree on the far right
at the level of the first arched balcony

(formerly a kitchen), with a TV and couch in the foyer. In the other was a guest room, living room, dining room, small study, kitchen, bath, toilet, and entrance foyer. Although, according to Joan's list, more than twenty small projects remained uncompleted, the apartment looked wonderful with its clean white walls, glistening wooden floors, and completely remodeled bathrooms and kitchen, all done to Scandinavian standard. The missionaries who helped us move in were impressed and referred to our apartment as "the palace."

Joan depicted our move to Russia and early days in Moscow:

During the last part of May and early June we were busy preparing for the move, but also knew that our time to enjoy the loveliness of Finland was coming to an end, so tried to spend as much time as possible savoring the natural beauty there. . . . The children hated to leave Finland after having become very much at home there and did not want to leave friends. . . .

Missionaries unloaded the truck bringing the furniture and boxes up 2 1/2 flights of stairs. They felt like we must have brought half of Helsinki with us. Once everything was inside we could hardly move around because of all of the boxes. There was not any place to put them out of the way. The first few days were horrendous, trying to sort out pieces of the white furniture which had been dismantled, trying to find basic things like tools, vacuum cleaner, bolts for beds, etc. We had no lights in the kitchen and laundry, no plugs for the drains in the tubs, and the shower doors allowed water to go all over the floor, no hot water, no water at all in the dishwasher, no electrical outlets in the kitchen and a malfunctioning clothes dryer. Every day of the first week had a crisis of some kind. . . .

Life here in Moscow is quite comfortable now that we are able to find things in our apartment. Most of the unpacking is done but I still have many small projects to take care of. Nikolai drives me to do my grocery shopping every few days.

We have been visiting the different branches with Gary on Sunday, where we all bear our testimonies in Russian. Today we attended the west branch, where fifteen members and forty-five investigators were in attendance. Some of the investigators came as the result of hearing the missionaries sing in the metro. The missionaries were thrilled, especially since they have to work harder in the summer to find people to teach. The Russian branch president was in China on business, so the meetings were conducted by one of the missionaries.[1]

Less than a week after we moved to Moscow, Betsy, Katie, and Jon began studying Russian with Lana (Svetlana) Zhuzhleva, a graduate from Moscow State University in psychology and the remarkable Sunday School teacher whose lesson on the Holy Ghost I wrote about earlier (see p. 227). Each day she worked with our children for at least four hours, typically taking them to some place she felt they would enjoy—museum, Gorky Park, horse riding stable, picnic area in the woods—all the while speaking Russian slowly and encouraging the children's participation. Her assignment was to prepare the children to survive in their nearby school, a fifteen-minute walk or five-minute ride by crowded early-morning city bus. We paid her $1.50 per hour, a generous wage at that time.

Betsy's enthusiastic example helped the younger children remain motivated and positive through difficult times, and Lana's patience, persistence, discipline, and imagination engaged the children's interest. One day while they were walking together, Lana noticed a small child playing along a busy street. She inquired about the child's parents, and the little boy led them to a public toilet. His mother, intoxicated, lay behind a dingy curtain. Lana talked with the lad about the danger of being too close to traffic, handed him a chocolate bar we had given her for her children, and matter-of-factly introduced our children to a side of life they had never experienced. On another occasion Lana's dollars were stolen right before the children's eyes as they stood at an amusement booth in a tourist area. Betsy, Katie, and Jon learned far more than just the Russian language from their excursions with Lana.

Late in the month, our forty-four missionaries and the family participated in an invigorating three-day missionary conference in Suzdal, a small, eleventh-century town one hundred miles northeast of Moscow. At the time it cost very little to travel by chartered bus, stay in Russian-standard hotels, and eat group meals in modest local restaurants. We trained in and practiced referral dialogues, sign-boarding techniques, subway contacting, and telephone skills when following up on contacts or appointments. We watched a Church training video and discussed its application to our mission. I reviewed mission policies and our mission vision. Later the assistants to the president and Joan and I spoke, and each missionary bore testimony. Interspersed among training and drill sessions, we had a bus tour past the many old Russian Orthodox churches and monasteries, a culture evening, district skits, a singalong of Church hymns, and a sports evening.

When we returned Saturday afternoon, we learned that two members of the Europe Area presidency had arrived unannounced in Moscow and were surprised to find us all away. From their cordial but unambiguous reprimand, I was reminded of the importance of seeking Area presidency approval for nonroutine decisions.

Far more perturbing, a hot water connection had come loose in our apartment's laundry room, flooding the laundry room and adjacent TV area and ruining the ceiling of an apartment below us. Building engineers, unable to open the unfamiliar Danish locks, had shut off the water on Thursday to the twenty-six apartments in our wing. I immediately turned off the water supply to the laundry room and telephoned the building maintenance department, but the maintenance duty officer insisted that the water could not be restored to the building until Monday because his experts "were normal people and took the weekend off."

Distasteful as I found it, with adequate monetary incentives he relented and rotated the valve. Despite such complications, our family's adjustment to Moscow went well.

During the month a handsome, intelligent, young man in his mid-twenties, Igor Sorsov from Novomoskovsk (three hours' train ride south of Moscow), visited me in the mission office. He and I had corresponded over several months. During that time, Igor had read Church materials and asked penetrating but friendly questions about the Book of Mormon and *Gospel Principles*. Previously he had investigated several churches and joined with the Baptists while continuing his search. Igor shared his enthusiasm for the spirit and message of the Book of Mormon with his friends and fellow Baptist Church members, but their early interest and approbation were followed by suspicion and anger.

On this trip I presented him with a Doctrine and Covenants and Pearl of Great Price in English. A few months later he sent me an unsolicited but impressive translation of the Pearl of Great Price into Russian. He and his wife eagerly awaited the missionaries and urged me to send them to Novomoskovsk. I explained that my authority extended only to specific cities, and we agreed to continue our contact. Two of Igor's letters to me show his search for and devotion to the truth:

> I am very thankful to you for not leaving my homeland of Russia, which has suffered much, without a knowledge of the truth. In seventy years, it has withered to such a point that it needs generous watering. I read about Joseph Smith and the Book of Mormon a long time ago—five years. This interested me and my brother greatly. We searched in the Bible for a description of the Lamanite and Nephite tribes. But at this time, we had read about that in only a few lines from anti-religious literature, and therefore, we were unable to find anything about this in the Bible. We didn't know that they had left Jerusalem six hundred years before the birth of Christ.
>
> At that point we knew that the Latter-day Saints (although we still only knew you as "Mormons") lived in the state of Utah and that the capital of Utah was Salt Lake City. We sent off a letter, but the address was rather simple: USA, Utah, Salt Lake City, Church of Jesus Christ of Latter-day Saints (all this was written in our broken English). There was no answer. This was probably a result of our "era of stagnation" [under Brezhnev]. At

*Igor Sorsov holds a gift copy of
the Doctrine and Covenants
and the Pearl of Great Price*

this point in time, the censors were still raging. In whatever church we asked, or whatever encyclopedia we checked, everywhere we looked, the information was either meager or lacking altogether. No one knew about Mormons, so I began writing to religious organizations, asking them for your address. But none of them responded.

I didn't lose hope, though. I sought, prayed, and asked God to help me find the church. Christ promised us that if we will seek, then we shall find, and if we will knock, then it will be opened to us. And once, the Lord "opened" the door of a bookstore and I found what I had sought for many years. On the shelf stood a Book of Mormon. Someone had sold it to the bookstore to make a little money. There is nothing valuable or sacred for such people—their godhead is money and commerce. But on the other hand, as Judas Iscariot played a very important role in the fulfillment of the Plan of Salvation through his betrayal, so it is with my personal salvation. God put it into the heart of this man to sell his Book of Mormon in our city.

Without giving it a second thought, I bought the book for 30 rubles. There was another copy in the bookstore, so I advised a friend of mine, who was also interested in such things, to buy it.

And so he did. In it there was the address of Duane and Thelma Leany. I wrote them and thanked them for their thoughtfulness. But most of all, of course, I am thankful to God.[2]

After additional letters, I received this communication:

> I greet you with the love of our Lord Jesus Christ. Forgive me that I promised to visit you and have not come. As we say, "man proposes but God disposes." Not long ago my wife gave birth and contracted mastitis. She is still in the hospital. My mother-in-law and I are taking care of the child. That's how I've spent my entire vacation. Now I just go to work, return, and visit my wife in the hospital. I am racing like a squirrel on a wheel.
>
> You know, brother, things are going badly. Just recently they [the Baptists] summoned me to a meeting where my church membership has been and informed me that I had been excommunicated. They also excommunicated several others, but for unchristian-like behavior. Me they excommunicated because I married a non-member without their permission, although her (my wife's) faith is a hundred times deeper than theirs, and because I have engaged in heresy. So all those who had been interested in Christ's true teaching immediately thereafter turned from me. And those who had been enthralled with the Book of Mormon and were dissatisfied with their standing in their own church now told me they didn't understand much of the book and that it wasn't what they needed! I only replied that time will show who is right and who is wrong.[3]

33

July 1992

In early July, Sergei Martynov and I spent an entire day searching all over Moscow for office furnishings for the Merzliakovskii facility. We visited six large furniture outlets and found very little that was acceptable. With encouragement from the physical facilities people in Frankfurt, Brother Martynov continued to search and located a factory that produced custom office furniture. Joan found some reasonably attractive light wood folding tables and chairs. By opening six tables and placing them together end-to-end in two rows, we were able to approximate a conference table around which leaders could sit and take notes during leadership meetings. The price for such furniture was high, but still much less than furniture purchased in Frankfurt and shipped to Russia.

I had the enjoyable experience on Tuesday evenings of meeting with groups of investigators who had completed the early missionary discussions. The purpose was to provide an additional witness of the message the missionaries had been sharing and to review our divine origins and purpose on this earth and the role of scripture, prophets, and individual inspiration in our search for eternal meaning. We also discussed how to discern a personal spiritual witness. The investigators were impressive and, unexpectedly, they helped one another immeasurably, frequently answering each other's questions and testifying of how God helped them to resolve doubts and problems now troubling others.

Beginning in July the Moscow mission expanded to the first of four additional cities far from Moscow, occasioning, once again, increased travel. The first new city to be opened for missionary work was Nizhnii Novgorod, 230 miles east of Moscow. With more than one-and-a-half million inhabitants, Nizhnii Novgorod is Russia's third largest city.

After a pleasant overnight train ride, Elders Russell Nelson Jr.,

Weldon Dodd, Tommi Sankala, and Robert Couch arrived in Nizhnii with Joan and me on Tuesday, 21 July. We visited with Brother Grigorii Fomin, who had arranged for missionary apartments and meetings with local officials, and then we went to a relatively quiet, wooded area within the city's magnificent sixteenth-century kremlin overlooking the Volga and Oka Rivers. There we offered prayers of thanksgiving and dedication of ourselves to our finest effort in this grand city. Prayers were offered by Brother Fomin, Elder Nelson (the Nizhnii Novgorod missionary leader), and me. Brother Fomin and Evgeniia Dubovnika, his vigorous and supportive colleague at the Water Transport Institute, went with us to meet city and regional officials responsible for religious affairs.

After cordial, largely ceremonial discussions, these officials took us to meet with Boris Dukhan, a deputy city mayor who attempted to explain to us how our labors would be complicated by several factors. First, because of military industry here, the city had been closed to foreign tourists until approximately one year ago, more than half a decade into perestroika. Citizens, he felt, were conditioned to be suspicious of foreigners, especially Americans. Second, the Russian Orthodox Church was strong in Nizhnii Novgorod and inhospitable to competing religious organizations. Both concerns were real but not insurmountable.

Then, as if to demonstrate the concern Russian Orthodox adherents have for the preservation of their position, our meeting with Deputy Mayor Dukhan was abruptly ended by twenty or so irate women of all ages who had come to protest the mayor's pledge to give a formerly Orthodox Church building, now freed from government use, to the Free Orthodox group, which had broken from the Orthodox Church.

The day after our family arrived in Moscow from Helsinki, our driver Nikolai began to fill out paperwork, visit myriad offices for signatures and official seals, and pay the fees to register the van under the aegis of the Russian Religious Association, to be used primarily for the mission. On occasion, Andrei Petrov of the Association had to accompany Nikolai. Working steadily each weekday, Nikolai needed close to three weeks to complete the registration procedures and secure license plates for the car. On 8 July he brought a representative from the most reliable Russian automobile insurance company to our office, and we arranged for car insurance and a power of attorney for Nikolai to drive the van. Finally the vehicle was officially registered.

Sherman Krump, the managing director of the Missionary Department, and his wife, Ardeth, visited us briefly in Moscow. His purpose was to gauge the effectiveness of Missionary Training Center preparation, gain a feel for the missionary work in Russia, and learn of missionaries' successes and challenges. While in Moscow he spoke at a 24 July commemoration for all members. The meeting was intended to help our Russian members feel closer to their adopted Mormon ancestors through learning of struggles and triumphs not unlike their own. The Krumps also visited and addressed the Zelenograd branch.

I was pleased to receive from the Church Translation Department in Salt Lake City a copy of hymn translations and a letter stating that "the production of the Russian hymnbook has entered its final stages." I was startled to discover that these translations were the same ones we had studied carefully the year before. What had happened to the improved translations Brother Vadim Viazmin completed? I had copies of his initial translations, but the later ones I had never seen because he worked on them while living in New York City, and I thought he had sent them directly to Salt Lake.

One evening I invited our five member translators to gather at the mission home around the piano to sing the Salt Lake City-translated hymns. All came, and Andrei Lokshin brought his sister Natalia, a pianist. We observed that most phrases seemed fine, but in each hymn there were pockets of infelicitous expression and disjunctions between musical meter and Russian stress patterns, rendering the hymns at times imprecise and awkward. I asked Andrei to report the Moscow translators' evaluation and concerns. We later found ourselves on a carousel with experts from Salt Lake, Frankfurt, and Moscow all trying their best to fulfill their assignments well in order to strengthen the Church in Russia. The result was a handsome edition of the hymnbook that became available in 1994.

In July painters erected a large wooden scaffold along the back wall of the building in which the mission office was located, including along windows into the offices. Because a thief could easily mount the scaffolding, enter our offices, and steal equipment or materials, we were compelled to engage a night watchman to guard our property. The scaffolding remained until September, long after most of the painting had been completed, except for a strip from roof to ground that included both sides of my window and a new ground-level entrance. In the end the scaffolding was removed without the final strip being painted.

34

AUGUST 1992

July and August are challenging months for Moscow missionaries. Muscovites spend as much summer time as possible at their garden plots, especially those who have cottages, which range from quite comfortable to ultraspartan. Communing with nature and providing food for the winter are urgent priorities. Often leaders on whom missionaries depended to conduct meetings and teach classes were unable to attend Sunday meetings for weeks. Investigators who seemed radiantly golden during the first two discussions suddenly left the city for a month or more. Missionaries had to be content with forming a deep pool of investigators who had responded well during early discussions and hoping to continue teaching them after 1 September when the school year began. Our slogan during these and other difficult times became, "We're getting along, and we'll make it!" (*Spravliaemsia i spravimsia*).

Joan recorded this glimpse into the economic troubles in Moscow that affected Church members daily:

> Life in Moscow continues at a hectic pace. Inflation is rampant. . . . As foreigners we have no problems whatsoever, but I continually wonder how the Russians can hang on. The sidewalks sprout new kiosk booths daily, offering a wider variety of expensive foreign products. Last week I found some Skittles for the kids, Finesse shampoo with German instructions, and canned beans from Switzerland. Wages are increasing for the Russians, but not nearly as fast as the inflation rate. People seem to be getting by with food from their gardens, but what will happen when winter comes?[1]

This quotation from the English-language *Moscow Times* clearly portrays the situation:

> Imagine if, in the United States, wages in six months rose

from $25,000 to $50,000 per year, while the price of a gallon of milk jumped from $2 to $20, and the price of bread from $1 to $18 per loaf. Imagine that the highest denomination banknote rose from $100 to $5000 and that people actually walked around with them in their pockets! Imagine that suddenly all the best goods were labeled in a language you couldn't read, say, Chinese or Greek. Imagine trying to make up the shortfall in your salary by moving out of your home to rent it to a non-American for more money than you could earn in six months.[2]

Sister Laura McLennan agreed to serve as our first sister leader in Moscow. She coordinated companion exchanges for training our eight single sisters and helped Joan and me become more aware of sisters' concerns and needs. She and those who followed her provided a sterling example, shared their strengths with less-experienced and occasionally discomfited sisters, and helped us learn in a timely manner of ways for Joan and me to better support individual sisters and prevent or address problems.

The month included meetings with two unusual nonmembers. The first of these nonmembers was Viacheslav Shmeliov, an accomplished Russian sculptor who believed in the gospel, the Church, and the Book of Mormon and wanted to be baptized but who struggled against personal barriers. I had appreciated a long discussion with him in the mission office, during which he shared his impressive insights from the Book of Mormon. Later I visited him in his modest basement studio full of striking art created over the decades. One piece particularly impressed me: a bust of two devoted leaders of the Baptist faith, a father and son, I believe, who had died during the Stalinist terror owing to their unswerving fortitude and spiritual integrity. I felt again as I admired this sculpture that so many courageous, devout followers of Christ in Russia deserve our deep respect and sincere tribute.

The second nonmember was Dmitrii Dudko, a saintly Russian Orthodox priest who had resisted decades of Communist pressures to conform and, as a result, suffered years of deprivation in Soviet prisons. A young Russian Latter-day Saint who knew and loved Father Dudko had requested several times that I speak with him about our shared faith and the distinguishing teachings of the Church. Conflicts in schedule had prevented him from visiting my office and me from attending his lectures when he was in Moscow, but finally a semblance of a meeting occurred.

I went to a public library where Father Dudko was presenting a weekly lecture and discussion series on vital gospel topics. I soon realized that Father Dudko had not known of my coming or my position as an LDS mission president. I listened quietly to his thoughtful, sensitive elucidations of Christ's teachings. So many surrounded him to ask questions afterward that I was unable to do more than express admiration for his righteous strength and for the spirit of personal purity that emanated from him as he spoke.

From California, Elder Wayne and Sister Barbara Barker arrived in our mission this month. Neither spoke Russian, but both studied vigorously. Their great contributions came in strengthening members by allowing them to meet a mature married couple and explore questions that had been saved for such senior stalwarts. Sister Barker was a professional psychologist who provided essential counsel relating to missionary concerns. Elder and Sister Barker organized a temple preparation seminar for the first large group of Russian members to attend the temple. They admirably prepared these Saints for an enlightening and spiritually deepening experience.

Also in August, the Moscow and Zelenograd branch presidents convened for their monthly branch presidents' meeting at the mission home. This time the Russian branch presidents brought their wives, and we all enjoyed the delicious meal Joan had prepared. At the meeting that followed, I felt thankful and moved by the increasing spiritual strength all the Russian presidents and their wives displayed.

One of the most frequently heard accusations of any Russian who joined our Church was that he or she was merely opportunistic. The world has known only one perfect person, but these branch presidents and their wives were striving to learn gospel truths, feel the Spirit, and give selflessly to their branch members and others.

During our mission there were setbacks, of course. About a third of our baptized members apparently fell away—but who knows what yet lies deep in their hearts. Many others battled great odds to persevere and endure. Given their backgrounds and current pressures, our Russian leaders and their members were steadily becoming more saintly, and I felt invigorated and humbled to be among them.

During August a future Moscow branch president, Vladimir Krivonogov, was baptized. His conversion story follows:

I was born in a village near Ekaterinburg. My father was a peasant farmer and his family had been nonbelievers for generations. My mother was the daughter of a merchant from the Urals and believed in God. I am a military radio engineer by education. I served in the armed forces for twenty-seven years. Now I am a retired lieutenant-colonel in the reserves.

How did I come to God? In early July of 1992 on a warm and sunny Saturday, my family and I were strolling in the square off Pokrovskii Boulevard. Two very nice young men approached us. They introduced themselves as members of The Church of Jesus Christ of Latter-day Saints: Elder [Mark] Pingree and Elder [Michael] Balle. They created a very favorable impression. I especially remember their faces: big smiles and clear eyes. You could see right away as you looked at them that they knew why they were living on this earth.

At first I was merely curious. I wanted to find out who these Americans were. As a professional soldier I had been taught for many years that America was our Enemy Number One. We invited them home and started talking with them about God. Up to this time I had no desire to know God and I neither had read the Bible nor had any intention of doing so. But I absolutely believed that in the infinite ocean of worlds existing in the universe, without doubt there was an intelligence higher than our own. This was my God. Therefore, it was easy for me to speak with the missionaries. Following our discussion, they invited us to a church service at Sretenko Street. . . .

I had not planned to choose a church for my own. Up to this time, I had already learned something about the rites and services of the Muslim, Catholic, and Russian Orthodox faiths. I could see clearly that if I had to decide which church to join, I would begin by getting to know God's servants, or for those interested in The Church of Jesus Christ of Latter-day Saints, the missionaries. We later realized that all of us, the members of the Church, are God's servants. But at first, it was the elders who won our hearts.

I testify that the ordinances in our Church are more perfect and more wonderful for me than in any other church. During our services we feel neither alone with ourselves or alone with God, but rather, we feel a unity with our brothers and sisters, and with God. I especially love the way we pray. It is not a type of memorized dogma, but rather a creative flight for one's thoughts and soul. Through our prayers, we make our choice between good and evil, between light and darkness, between God and Satan. Through our method of prayer, the believer can become more perfect in his faith.

I love the emphasis that the Church places on the family, health and work. Belief in God and the Word of Wisdom are the connecting links of these principles. I testify that the organization of our Church is perfect. Under such a structure, there is no occasion for greed or jockeying for position or authority. As such, the Church is protected from apostasy.

I am happy that the missionaries, while engaged in their labors, crossed my path. I am happy that together with my family and other believers, we are progressing towards God in our true Church of Jesus Christ of Latter-day Saints.[3]

Also in August the missionaries in Nizhnii Novgorod baptized their first family, Irina Kosheliova and her children, Marina and Zhenia. This is their story:

In July of 1992 I met the missionaries of our Church for the first time. It happened by chance. Before this, I hadn't known about The Church of Jesus Christ of Latter-day Saints, or rather, I knew only that which was written in the encyclopedic dictionary, and even that was scant and not very reliable.

That July, missionaries came to our city for the first time. Elders Dodd and Couch were speaking with people on the street, telling them about the Bible, the Book of Mormon, and the Church. Their discussion interested me, so we became acquainted. The missionaries began coming to our family and conducting discussions. On the 22nd of August, my family was baptized. We were the first family to be baptized in Nizhnii Novgorod.

It's always hard to be first. Therefore, I am very grateful to Elders Dodd and Couch for their attention, kindness, and concern for us. They helped us to overcome all of our doubts. With their help we received Christ with all our hearts. With firm conviction, we became members of The Church of Jesus Christ of Latter-day Saints. Peace and harmony now prevail in our family. All of us— my daughter, Marina; my son, Zhenia; and I, the mom—are very happy. We will always remember the missionaries because, owing to their consideration and kindness, our lives have been saved. Our lives have been filled with new content and meaning.[4]

35

SEPTEMBER 1992

Elder Dennis Neuenschwander and I visited the lower-Volga cities of Saratov and Samara early in September, and on the twenty-second Joan and I went with four missionaries (Elders Benjamin Ritchie, James Nichols, Michael Ferguson, and Matthew Sonntag) to begin missionary work in Samara. Elder Neuenschwander had introduced me to city officials and other contacts he and Elder Hans Ringger had made in July, and I became familiar with the city, its prominent features, meetinghouse possibilities, means of locating apartments, and promising proselyting areas.

I was very impressed by the Samara officials Iurii Shisheliov of the city council and Vladimir Iurin of the mayor's office. Both were excellent hosts. Each time we visited them, they arranged for radio and television coverage of our discussions of what we proposed to bring the people of Samara. With the missionaries, Joan and I participated in a prayer at the Volga River, during which we expressed our gratitude for being able to serve in this prominent city and our commitment to give our best effort in the Lord's service here.

Our members and mission were greatly blessed during September by the visits of two apostles, President Howard W. Hunter of the Quorum of the Twelve Apostles, and a week later, Elder L. Tom Perry. Elder Neuenschwander and others facilitated the visit of President Hunter with skill and sensitivity. He and Sister Inis Hunter were traveling as guests of industrialist Jon Huntsman, who arranged for President Hunter to meet with Church members and leaders in separate, memorable meetings.

Nearly sixty district, branch, and elders quorum presidents from the Kiev, St. Petersburg, and Moscow missions attended a leadership meeting at which Elder Neuenschwander and the three mission presidents (Howard L. Biddulph, Charles Creel, and I) led training sessions on the temple, the law of the fast, home teaching,

261

priesthood executive committee meetings, and related topics. President Hunter met with the group for the final hour, introduced himself amiably, and enjoined the leaders to be worthy and diligent. After the meeting, although he was very tired from the long flight, President Hunter greeted individual leaders before they returned to their missions.

The following day, Sunday, President and Sister Hunter, Elder and Sister LeAnn Neuenschwander, Joan and I, and three Russian members, Taras Gerasimenko, Nadezhda Lashmanova, and Sergei Martynov, spoke to about five hundred people at a Moscow conference. President Hunter discussed the last verses of Luke 9, in which the Savior describes his disciples as those who put their hands to the plow and do not look back.

Joan wrote this account of President Hunter's visit:

> While President Howard W. Hunter spoke at a priesthood leadership meeting for leaders from the three Russian-speaking missions, Katie and I took Sister Hunter on a walking tour of Red Square and GUM department store. Two months ago she had knee replacement surgery and is still recovering. She is doing very well, considering that she had complications following surgery. . . .
>
> On Monday the Hunters were the guests of Jon Huntsman, Utah industrialist and long-time friend of the Hunters. He took them on a VIP tour of the Kremlin and to meet government officials. In the evening we were invited to an elegant banquet hosted by Jon Huntsman at the Metropole Hotel (Moscow's most elegant). Also present were several officials of Huntsman's organization, two of his sons, and [former Soviet ambassador to the USA] Iurii Dubinin, and his wife and daughter. The Dubinins became friends with the Huntsmans when the ambassador visited Utah in the spring of 1990. . . . On Tuesday the Hunters left on the Huntsman jet to visit Kiev and Armenia, where Jon Huntsman is funding a major humanitarian project. . . .
>
> The children are going to school without many complaints even though it is difficult. Lana [Svetlana Zhuzhleva] comes in the afternoon to help them with their homework and they are picking up a little more Russian. Jon says he knows all of the words in order to play tag—the favorite activity between classes. Betsy has been to a few parties—at one they bought watermelon instead of beer in her honor. She is having plenty of opportunities to tell others about her religion. Katie has a devoted

following of girls her age. . . . All in all, I am very proud of how the children are doing and their willingness to try something very difficult and different.[1]

Elder Hans B. and Sister Helen Ringger accompanied Elder L. Tom and Sister Barbara Perry to Moscow for a brief visit and meeting with all fifty-four of our missionaries, followed by a fireside for members and others. At the mission meeting Elder Perry answered a broad range of missionary questions. At the fireside he inspired all with his vigorous talk on sacrifice and on the power to increase our blessings immeasurably through sharing the gospel message and our good lives with families and friends.

On the day after the Perrys' departure, Joan and I accompanied Elder and Sister Ringger to Sergiev Posad (Zagorsk) to visit Russia's most important monastery and theological academy. Sister Ringger had corresponded with a young man named Vasilii who was studying at the academy to become a priest. Being so near the monastery, she hoped to meet him and share additional information. He was pleased to meet Sister Ringger in person and graciously escorted us on a tour of the academy's art treasures.

While he spoke of Orthodox beliefs, Elder and Sister Ringger listened politely and appreciatively, occasionally commenting on similarities and differences with our Church. Vasilii appeared very impressed by the Ringgers and better disposed toward our faith. I have wondered what the seed planted that day might grow into.

Another of the month's highlights was the first Moscow mission youth conference held near Zelenograd in the facilities of a former Pioneer (children's) camp. The conference was planned by youth representatives of the branches, with wise counsel and energetic leadership from youth council coordinator David Neubert and his wife, Lori. All activities and presentations were organized around the theme of "For the Strength of Youth." The illuminating Church pamphlet from which we derived our theme had been translated and duplicated for the event. Nearly all the branch presidents attended and learned to know their young people much better. The three-day conference featured games, seminars, a service project, a dance, and much time for building friendships.

After several months of trial and refinement, at the end of

Group of Moscow youth with branch president Gennadii Ten
(front row, far right)

September the revised two-hour schedule suggested in May was presented to all the branches for adoption. We essentially followed the Church Curriculum Committee suggestions for the Church in new areas with limited materials: Sunday School and Primary followed by priesthood/Relief Society/Young Women/and continued Primary meetings, concluding with sacrament meeting. We continued to rent our facilities for three hours to serve those who wished to visit with Church friends, and many did, although others appreciated the opportunity to spend additional time with their family members who are not LDS.

The following letter is from Arthur Cadjan, a young Zelenograd scientist baptized in September. Subsequently he studied at BYU and married a young woman who had served as a missionary in Moscow:

I began thinking about God long ago. While studying theoretical physics, and more specifically the regeneration of life in living systems, and in the process of observing and researching the wonderful diversity of nature and, at the same time, its amazing harmony, I came to the understanding that all this could not possibly be the result of evolution, much less of something purely coincidental, but that at the bottom of all this must be one organizational beginning—a creator, God. . . .

I understood that for me the true God is a God of love. When I understood and felt that Heavenly Father gave his Beloved Son as a sacrifice in the name of this love, and when I understood just how brilliantly the demands of justice, love, and free agency had been met, I firmly decided that Christianity would be my path. . . .

For me there was still one unresolved question, which church to join? Again and again, I prayed to God and asked him to help me understand where the truth was. Soon thereafter, my words were heard. . . . Last year I "accidentally" met the missionaries, and suddenly I felt as though I wanted to be with them, to be just like them. I saw joy, confidence, and peace in their eyes. They knew the truth and were happy. I yearned for this truth and I wanted to be happy also. An inner voice prompted me to be with them and gain my place in their church.

And with joy I joined the Church. My life changed. Of course, I didn't get more money, I didn't become a millionaire, I still don't have my own home, my own family car, prestigious job, any valuables or the like, but I have so much more than all that. I have the Truth. I know what to live for. I know what is important in life and what is not. I have many brothers and sisters, and I have an inner confidence in the future and a feeling of security. I now have hope that everything in my life will change for the better, and that with God's help, I can be happy here on this earth. I have begun to feel that I also have changed. I now have the remarkable opportunity through the power of the priesthood to serve people. All of this gives me strength and an extraordinary joy for life.

Every day, in my experience, I have become more and more convinced of the truth of these words of scripture: "Inasmuch as ye shall keep my commandments ye shall prosper in the land; but inasmuch as ye will not keep my commandments, ye shall be cut off from my presence." (2 Nephi 1:20). I am endlessly happy to be a member of The Church of Jesus Christ of Latter-day Saints, the true Church of the living God. I thank our Heavenly Father for his Church and that he helped me find it. I'm thankful for his son Jesus Christ, our Savior and Redeemer, and for the Holy Ghost.[2]

36

OCTOBER 1992

During October, two Russians from Voronezh, a town of nearly a million people in Russia's heartland 280 miles south of Moscow, visited me in my office. Both were among those who had come to know fifteen BYU students teaching English since January 1992 to nursery school children in Voronezh.

For months the Russians had regularly attended Sunday services with the students. As their understanding of the gospel and the LDS Church grew, their desire to receive the missionary discussions also increased. I explained that I could not send missionaries to Voronezh, because my authorization did not extend that far. Also I remained concerned about having good people baptized in distant places without permanent Church support to assist and sustain them. They countered that the leaders of the kindergarten program had a long-term commitment to Voronezh and that those most interested in the Church would willingly come to Moscow to be taught the missionary discussions.[1]

Vladimir Kabanov, a young university student, and Nina Bazarskaia, a professor of English at the Voronezh Forestry Institute, each made several trips to Moscow to meet with missionaries, attend Church services, and eventually be baptized. Thus, primarily as a result of the good personal example, friendliness, and testimonies of young Latter-day Saints living in Voronezh, the beginnings were laid there for the Church. The Russians in Voronezh had naturally noticed the good fruits of the students and desired to partake themselves. This proved an effective way to share the gospel.

Joan's letter home described the mission presidents' seminar we attended and the trip to Saratov to begin missionary work:

> Last week Gary and I were in Frankfurt for three days for the Mission Presidents' Seminar. It was wonderful to be with dear

friends again and to learn from each other. More than half of the group came the same time we did, and we have become very close. We were also able to spend time with the Warners [Dale and Rene] (our former office couple and now mission president in Bulgaria) and compare notes with the Creels [Charles and Susan] in St. Petersburg and the Biddulphs [Howard L. and Colleen] in Kiev. This year we did not have any sightseeing excursions, so I can't say that I have seen anything typically German. We attended a session in the temple, which was delightful.

The next Monday afternoon Gary and I and two missionaries left [Moscow] by train for Saratov. It had been raining all day, and every time the train stopped in villages in the night we could hear rain falling on the top of the car. The track was quite uneven and the beds not very comfortable, so we heard a lot of rain. Saratov is a city founded by Germans on the Volga River. It now has about one million inhabitants and was closed to foreigners until earlier this year. We visited the center of the city, which consists of a pedestrian street between old buildings that look more European than Russian.[2]

On 20 October missionaries began laboring in Saratov; Elders Matthew Rose and Cameron Poole were soon joined by newly arrived Elders Matthew Bond and Jeffrey Williams. Unlike Voronezh, here the Church was unknown. A young contact on whom we had depended to make early arrangements had failed. After overcoming problems registering the elders in a hotel, arranging to meet with city officials, and learning about sources for apartments, we began to feel more secure. We visited the centrally located Institute of Agricultural Mechanization and arranged with the rector to begin holding Sunday meetings in an ornate, well-lit, three-hundred-seat auditorium.

Joan's letter for this month provided details concerning life for Russians at this time:

I'm sure you read articles and hear on television about the unstable economy here. In the last ten days the ruble has plunged to as low as 350 rubles to the dollar, but is now back up to about 310 rubles. Prices for foreign goods and souvenirs in the kiosks rise as rapidly as the ruble falls, so it all works out to be pretty much the same for us. But of course for the Russians things are going from bad to worse. . . .

Heating and hot water in Russia are supplied on a district basis rather than by individual buildings. . . . Fortunately our region started supplying heat on the first of October, and the weather turned cold on the second. Most of the missionaries now have heat, but the office still does not. We bought a few heaters in Helsinki before we came, so the office staff has been able to get by with sweaters, thermals, and the heaters. . . . The elevator at the office has not been working for a month now. The motor burned out and a new one or whatever is needed to repair the present one cannot be located.[3]

Upon returning to Moscow we learned that Sister Laura McLennan and Sister Erin Whitelock had been robbed at gun- and knife-point in a taxi and then set free. In addition, one pair of elders had moved in with another because they had been harassed and threatened near their apartment. Missionaries generally felt reasonably safe in Moscow, but crime rates continued to rise and additional security measures became necessary. I prepared another sheet of recommendations, including returning home by 9:30 P.M. (9:00 for sisters) while the streets and sidewalks were still quite busy, speaking only Russian outside of the apartment in order not to project foreignness and vulnerability, and verifying that apartment doors had substantial locks. As in other missions, we had only a few additional robberies, although each represented a painful trauma and financial loss.

Arrangements had been made earlier through Elder Hill, a Humanitarian Services missionary serving with his wife in Frankfurt, to send in care of Galina Bodrenkova's Moscow Charity House two large containers filled with tightly banded bales of used clothing. Similar shipments were sent to St. Petersburg and Kiev. Part of the Moscow clothing was intended to help the city's needy, and part was for our members. Ms. Bodrenkova asked our missionaries and members to help unload and sort the clothing, which did not correspond to the packing slips. The assistance was gladly provided. The Charity House established strict criteria for distributing the clothing to the poorest of the city's population, not intentionally but effectively excluding our members from receiving much of anything.

Months later two more containers were shipped, one for the city and the other specifically for the members. This time, members' clothing was taken to storage facilities and distributed through the district and branch Relief Society presidents. Solomon's wisdom was required to avoid offending members by appearing to give more or better articles to one person or family than another.

This month a team of three Salt Lake City doctors (Brothers Harris, Goodrich, and Taylor) arrived in Moscow to evaluate our mission's medical status. Elder Joseph Pace, our retired physician with excellent Moscow contacts, and his wife, Sister Pauline Pace, hosted the doctors. They examined medical facilities, spoke with United States embassy officials about air and water standards and realities, and met with two chronically ill missionaries.

They confirmed what Elder Pace had taught us: Moscow had adequate medical facilities and doctors, but the air and water conditions were poor. Moscow is a large city with what appeared to us all to be terrible automobile and especially truck exhaust pollution. Water quality was unreliable. It left the reservoirs uncontaminated, but sometimes broken pipes allowed harmful substances to toxify the water. As a result of the doctors' report to the Missionary Department, eventually missionaries received sophisticated water purification systems from Utah that apparently solved the significant problems with drinking water.

Our best source of investigators was referrals from members or other friends of the Church, but in areas where there were few members the missionaries had to use other means of finding people to teach. Standing by a signboard with pictures of the Savior, prophets, temples, or families produced good contacts. Sometimes, however, cantankerous detractors verbally and occasionally physically assaulted the missionaries. It also proved difficult to attract families to displays.

This month we prepared a dialogue that missionaries began using to meet families who were out walking together. The advantage was that missionaries could be prompted by the Spirit to choose with whom to speak. They approached a family and complimented them on their family, mentioned how important their own families were to them back home, and said that they represented a worldwide Christian church. This church, they explained, taught, along with much else, knowledge that could help them become an eternal family. The missionaries then identified themselves more fully and requested an opportunity to meet with the family and continue the discussion. Many missionaries experienced success with this approach, especially on Saturday and Sunday afternoons when Russian families often take long walks together.

A missionary in Moscow, Sister Jodi Jorgenson Nichols, discussed her success with this family approach:

> During the summer months, and even in the winter, we also did a lot of street contacting. In contrast to signboarding, we took a more aggressive approach and simply began talking with people as they were walking along the street. A favorite pastime of many Russian families is to take walks with their children. . . . Not many missionaries had been street contacting families once winter hit, but President Browning felt strongly that we needed to be out contacting families on Saturday and Sunday afternoons, a time when *whole* families were together.
>
> We had a specific dialogue we had memorized for street contacting, so every missionary knew what to say and how to approach a family, whether the missionary had been out in the field one month or twenty-one months. . . . The response was usually quite positive. We typically were able at least to get their phone number if we weren't able to line up an appointment right away. Of course the response wasn't always positive, but for the most part people would politely listen to us and then let us know they "weren't interested in religion." If they were interested, and then again even if they weren't interested in religion, they excitedly invited us to their home as guests. You will not meet a more hospitable people than the Russian people. They were often thrilled at the idea of having two "American guests," or any type of guests for that matter.
>
> These efforts to find and bring families into the Lord's Church have been very successful. Several families who are providing the necessary leadership in new and growing branches have come into the Church as a result of missionaries contacting them on the street.[4]

One experienced missionary endured a Job-like trial this month when he learned of the passing of his mother in Salt Lake City. To be so far away at such a time is among the harshest tribulations I can imagine. Upon speaking with his bereaved but faithful father, and after considerable personal prayer, Elder Pingree decided to continue his mission. This decision and his courage and diligence remains a holy memory of one called upon to bear a heavy cross.

The following paragraphs from Elder Mark Pingree's journal tell the story:

March 13, 1992: Yesterday I found out some bad news. A man from my home stake called to tell me that he had a package from my family that he had brought over for me. In this package was a letter from my mom and one from my dad. My mom's letter had written on the envelope, "read dad's letter first." Not knowing what to expect, I read my dad's letter first. It said that my mom has cancer and that she had a big operation. It explained that she will need to go through chemotherapy for about six months. I really could not believe what I was reading; it didn't seem real. I still do not know what to think. It is just really hard to be here not knowing anything. I am so far away and I have always heard about things like this happening to others, but I never thought it would happen to me. I just hope and pray that my family is O.K.

September 25, 1992: Monday when I was at the office for district meeting, something very interesting happened. President Browning called me into his office. There was a Russian man by the name of Vladislav [Meshcheriakov]. He started to tell me how he and his wife, Natasha, had been in Salt Lake and met with my family. These Russians had been in Salt Lake making a video documentary of the Church. For part of this documentary, they chose to film my family having family home evening at my home in Salt Lake. I was then able to watch my family on TV there in the office. It has been over a year since I have seen them. My mom is skinny, and she had a cloth covering her head. She has lost all of her hair due to her sickness. It was amazing that I was able to see my family like that, half the way around the world. President Browning asked me and my companion to teach Vladislav and Natasha the discussions.

October 28, 1992, 1:45 A.M.: At about 10:30 P.M. I got a call from President Browning. He and his wife were on the phone. He was speaking in English, so I knew it was not just about missionary work. He told me that my dad had called and needed to talk with me about my mom. He said that she had had a big operation, and explained how he wanted me to call home. After I finished talking with him, I tried calling home for about an hour. I could not get through and the operator told me that I had to wait until after 12:00. To keep my mind off things, I went to the kitchen and said a prayer, and then read the scriptures. I read the last section of the Doctrine and Covenants and the two Official Declarations. While I was reading I received a sense of peace and calmness. By the time I was done it was almost 12:00.

It took me about an hour to finally get through. I was finally able to talk with my dad. I could tell that he was shaken up. He was crying as he was talking with me. He explained that they had operated on mom and found more cancer. He said that she only has a 5% chance of living now. It really helped to talk to my dad. This really hurts me and I know this next little while will be very hard. But, I know I will receive help from Heavenly Father. When I left on my mission, there was no sign that something like this would happen. I have a lot of thoughts going through my mind right now. I think I'd better go to bed and get some rest.

October 30, 1992: My dad just called me tonight to inform me that my mom passed away two hours ago. I did not talk to him for very long. He told me that my two little sisters do not even know yet. Life can change so fast. I am very grateful for my mom and everything she has done for me. I don't fully understand why this happened. But, I feel and believe that this was supposed to happen when it did because Heavenly Father would not allow this to happen without a purpose.

November 2, 1992: Today I received the last letter that my mom had written to me. I think she knew that this would be her last letter to me. I cried as I read the letter because she passed away just a few days ago. Although it was very painful and heart-breaking to read the letter, I also received much comfort.

November 8, 1992: Today my companion and I met with Natasha. She felt that by showing my family first, then me serving a mission in Russia, that it would make the story more interesting.

January 15, 1993: Today, the documentary of the Church was broadcast on national television. It was great to see my family again.

On January 23, 1993: Vladislav was baptized and confirmed a member of the Church.

Postscript: A few months later, Vladislav was able to baptize his wife, Natasha. In the fall of 1994, I was able to be present in the Salt Lake Temple as Vladislav and Natasha were sealed to each other. I am very grateful that I had the opportunity to serve a mission in Russia and that I was able to meet and help many people like Vladislav and Natasha.[5]

It was a privilege this month to set apart Muscovite Svetlana

Zhitina as a missionary in the St. Petersburg mission. She brought a large group of friends and family members to the mission office for the occasion, providing me an opportunity to express admiration for her devotion and fortitude and to build a relationship with her nonmember family. Sister Zhitina served honorably and diligently in St. Petersburg.

Among those baptized this month was Oksana Gronskaia, a Russian sister whose conversion story is memorable:

It has been almost a year since I became a member of the Church. I can't believe that only a year ago I didn't even think about God. A year and a half ago, I went to a soup kitchen to help set tables for elderly people. These people were fed for free by an American church [not LDS]. I met two sister missionaries there [providing community service]. They were very considerate and amicable. Sisters [Carrie] Madsen and [Jodi] Jorgenson really wanted to visit with me. I took down their phone number and gave them mine simply out of courtesy.

They called me many times, but I was too busy and concerned with all my own problems. After a little while the sisters stopped calling, and I erased this episode from my memory. I couldn't imagine that I would ever run into them again. In the summer, I went with my school to a festival in North Carolina. I made many new and interesting friends there from all around the world. There were even students participating from BYU. Those who knew that [the BYU students] were Mormons made fun of them, and I wondered why they went to bed early instead of going to a bar or a night club.

The better I got to know them, the more I liked them. They were very honest, clean, and chaste, and had a good spirit about them. I had a wonderful time talking with them about this and that. And I thought to myself, "Could it be at all possible that their faith in God makes them the way that they are?" (I had known people who claimed that they believed in God but were in no way any better than those who considered themselves atheists.) It was all so strange and uniquely new to me. Even still, I was not prepared to believe everything that they said. My atheistic outlook didn't allow thoughts about a living God. My friends from BYU pled with me to find the missionaries. I promised them that I would—because I really wanted to do something nice for them.

I knew that in Moscow there were already many missionaries from many different churches and that it would be hard to find the Mormons. I did recall that I had the phone number of the sisters of some American church. I decided to call simply to check. And lo, a miracle! They turned out to be the very ones I was looking for. This was my first witness. It was a wonderful and important experience for me. The Lord works in mysterious ways, and he, unnoticed, guides our lives, helping us choose the right path.

In the Book of Mormon, there is a verse which was my first favorite verse. It is 1 Nephi 11:22—"the love of God, which sheddeth itself abroad in the hearts of the children of men; wherefore, it is the most desirable above all things." When I obey the commandments, when I act in the way that our Father has commanded, I feel his love—the love that is most joyful and most desirable for the soul. I really do love the gospel. Without its burning in my heart and in my head right now, there's simply no way I could last. There would be no reason to. But Jesus Christ lives, God is our Father, and there is purpose to this crazy world.[6]

37

NOVEMBER 1992

Overshadowing everything this month was the abrupt departure of Elder Douglas and Sister Lois Dewey, our dear friends and extraordinary office couple. Although Elder Dewey had not felt well for many weeks, he continued to work with his typical precision and congeniality. As his health deteriorated, on November 8 he requested a priesthood blessing of health. In the meantime, Elder Joseph and Sister Pauline Pace were preparing to return home because Sister Pace was experiencing heart problems. Before their departure they arranged for Elder Dewey to be carefully examined at Russia's best hospital. These tests indicated severe problems. The liver showed what appeared to be metastasized cancer.

Among the saddest days of our mission was 19 November when we accompanied the Deweys to the airport for their departure to Logan, Utah.[1] We would certainly miss them and their titanic strength, but our sorrow was because Elder Dewey was so ill and weak. For weeks he had declared that he would not leave his mission early and preferred, if necessary, to die serving at his post. In the end he had no choice but to follow his wife's, doctors', and Missionary Department's mandates. Preliminary medical examinations in Utah and a whisper of returning strength gave momentary hope for recovery, but these were followed by a diagnosis of pancreatic cancer and Elder Dewey's death in early February 1993.

Although many gave much, none contributed more to establishing the Church in Russia than did Elder and Sister Dewey. As I recall Elder Dewey, I picture him, a gentle man of refinement and order, standing in the mission office toilet room, a plumber's helper in his hands, working with a wry smile of resignation under conditions far beneath his dignity. On that occasion I commiserated that

Elder Douglas and Sister Lois Dewey at their mission office desks

had I a voice in the matter, I would recommend celestial laurels for him on the basis of this act of humble service.

Excerpts from Sister Dewey's journal portray their first direct proselytizing efforts in Moscow:

May 31, 1992: This afternoon we did our first real proselyting and had considerable success. We made up a "signboard" that said in Russian, "If you speak English, even a little, please talk to us if you would like INFORMATION about The Church of Jesus Christ of Latter-day Saints." We dressed the signboard up with pictures of Christ and other things illustrating the Church. We took the signboard across the street from our office to the boulevard park next to the metro station, so that most people leaving the metro station would see the sign. We spent about two hours there and had many people come and look at the signboard and talk to us as best they could. We gave out considerable literature about the Church and had several very good conversations.

A lady medical doctor stopped and talked at some length and invited us to her apartment next Tuesday evening. Another woman who is the head of a nearby school/library invited us to send our Russian-speaking elders to the school to talk about the Church. We felt very good about our efforts and hope to do it again.

June 13: We had a special experience with the lady doctor we had become acquainted with while "signboarding" in the park. Last Sunday evening we went with two of our young Russian-speaking elders to teach her, Tatiana, the first discussion. She was receptive to all that was taught her, which was rather unusual considering that she was raised an atheist. At the end of the discussion, Elder Pingree asked if she would give the prayer and she agreed. It was very spiritually moving to listen to a former atheist offer a childlike prayer for the first time in her life. We will take her and two of her grandchildren to church with us tomorrow to a Russian-speaking branch.

July 11: Yesterday morning Tatiana Kubatko, our doctor friend, was baptized in a lake at a beautiful park quite a ways from here. She is out of town tending her land most Saturdays, so couldn't join the regular baptism services that are usually held on Saturday mornings. The weather has been really cold for a whole week, so it was questionable whether the baptism would take place or not until the last minute. Yesterday morning was still pretty chilly and mostly cloudy, but she wanted to go ahead with it. We all traveled a good ways on the metro, then took the tram for a long ways, then walked about a mile to get to the lake. Since we were missing work, I was thinking pretty negative thoughts about the elders for scheduling the baptism in such a faraway spot.

When we got to the lake the sun was shining and it was really warm. It was so beautiful and peaceful, and the service was something wonderful. Needless to say, I repented of my negative thoughts in a hurry. Tatiana looked absolutely radiant and said the water didn't even feel cold. Her daughter and two grandsons were there along with some missionaries and a member friend. Elder [Mark] Pingree baptized her and Doug [Dewey] did the confirming. She bore her testimony at the end and thanked God for the gospel and for the beautiful day and her beautiful friends. She is such a happy person that you feel good to be around her. Last night she invited us all to her flat for dinner.[2]

Early in the month, Elder Robert K. Dellenbach of the Europe Area presidency and his wife, Sister Mary-Jayne Dellenbach, arrived for a mission tour of Moscow, Nizhnii Novgorod, and Samara. Meetings of General Authorities with the missionaries and members were always uplifting and invigorating, and those with the Dellenbachs were particularly so. Elder Dellenbach chose to speak with our missionaries about exactly what they needed at this moment of considerable struggle and some discouragement. In very personal and moving "conversations," as with close and trusted friends, he described his first weeks as a young missionary when trials oppressed him and his eventual and firm decision to serve the Lord with all his might. With members and investigators he recounted the First Vision with great sensitivity, warmth, and conviction. He augmented our understanding and faith regarding the Restoration and the need for acceptance of the gospel and Christ's Church through baptism.

About midmonth, Elder Dellenbach and Elder Dennis B. Neuenschwander returned to Moscow with Peter Berkhahn, Konrad Nagele, and attorney Richard Johnson to participate in an auction of a building and land near the Prospect Mira subway station. Andrei Petrov, as president of the Church's Religious Association, was prepared to serve as voice at the auction, but the prices bid from the beginning were far above those within our authorization. Competing for properties in the commercial market would be prohibitively costly. Apparently, our best hope still lay in working through city and prefect governments. That would require registering the Church within the cities and prefects in addition to nationally.

At the invitation of Professor Igor Iablokov, I spoke on 17 November to thirty professors of the Moscow University College of Humanities' Department of Philosophy and Religion. Later, on 19 December, Aleksandr Krasnikov, one of the professors present this month, hosted me for a talk before two hundred Moscow University humanities students in their senior (fifth) year of studies. Subsequently, on 1 April 1993, a professor of philosophy arranged for me to speak before philosophy professors and graduate students who had not been present at my first lecture. In each case I briefly presented the history of the Church generally and in Russia, the Church's place in Christianity, and some of its distinguishing teachings, particularly the stages and purposes of life within the eternal family and eternal progression. I enjoyed being in a university auditorium again and speaking to people for whom objective inquiry is a chosen way of life. Although I provided addresses and times of our Church services in Moscow and the mission office address, to my knowledge none of those to whom I spoke at the university joined the Church. Still, I hope they will be more balanced in their scholarly treatment of the Church.

Late in the month I was authorized to call the first two Moscow district presidents: Andrei Petrov for the south, southeast, east, and central branches; and Albert Walling for the north, west, and Zelenograd branches. They were sustained and set apart on 6 December. At the time we had few priesthood brethren who could serve in district callings. Over the months a counselor and two clerks were added to the organization. Now that I again had no counselors in the mission presidency, I especially appreciated the weekly meetings with Presidents Petrov and Walling, in which we discussed mission, district, and branch concerns in a mutually beneficial training setting. At our monthly leadership meeting for all branch presidents, Andrei Petrov masterfully presented training material and other information.

Also this November Sergei, Irina, and eleven-year-old Marina Leliukhin were baptized in Saratov. They were especially well prepared by the Spirit to accept the gospel and bear responsibility for establishing the Church in their area. They learned quickly, led naturally, and fellowshipped other families and individuals joyfully.

I recall speaking with Sergei in April 1993 after he became the first branch president in Saratov—the first city on the Volga River to have an organized branch of the Church. We discussed concerns, needs, and accomplishments of branch members and of his family. He mentioned that recently he had been able to work with a BYU performing group for a few days and had been paid a stipend in dollars. The family could have used this windfall to address a number of urgent needs, but Sergei and Irina concluded that they would apply this money toward Marina's mission account. The ruble was devaluating too quickly to save, but dollars were stable and could be safely kept to achieve a later goal. I think of Marina and her parents and of the opportunities she and others will have, thanks to the devotion and selflessness of families whose missionary sons and daughters will help liberate spirits and ennoble hearts around the world.

Brother Leliukhin described his family's conversion:

*The Leliukhin family—Sergei, Irina, and daughter Marina—
with missionary Sister Susan Metcalf*

Our little Mormon family consists of me, Sergei, my wife, Irina, and our daughter, Marina. We were all baptized together into The Church of Jesus Christ of Latter-day Saints November 22, 1992. Immediately after my baptism I received the Aaronic Priesthood, and then I baptized my beloved wife and daughter.

I was raised in an atheistic family, and I myself was an atheist. When I had occasion to visit an Orthodox Church and would see the many elderly women there, the thought would occur to me that these women would soon die and then the church would be closed. That would be the end of religion.

Even though before our marriage my wife Irina lived in a Muslim family in one of the republics of the former USSR, she is Russian and was baptized into the Orthodox Church while staying with her grandmother briefly in Russia. From her grandmother, she learned her first lessons about faith and Jesus Christ.

When our daughter Marina started school, she began asking

us to baptize her. Apparently she wanted to wear a cross around her neck, just like her best friends. At that time I had not been baptized, although I was beginning to understand that baptism was probably necessary for an individual. That was in 1990 when the Orthodox Church experienced tremendous growth. . . . I began to read many religious books, primarily by Orthodox writers. The central point I started to understand was that for a believer, the church was the foundation of his life. When I knew that I could find the strength within myself to lead a religious life, I decided to be baptized and become a member of the Orthodox faith.

I was baptized along with my daughter on November 1, 1990. I am very grateful to the Orthodox Church for helping me to accept the gospel, although it was difficult for us to grow within the Orthodox Church, for we were left to ourselves. This led to the summer of 1992, when we almost stopped attending church. We were ashamed of this, but we didn't have the strength to change anything.

In June I was on business in Ukraine, in Donetsk. It was here in this city that I first met the Mormon missionaries. They invited me to their Sunday worship service, but I was already due back in Saratov on Sunday. I told my wife about the encounter, but soon forgot about it.

On the 25th of October I observed my thirty-third birthday. On the 26th, as I returned home from work, I was walking along the main street of the city. Ahead of me I saw two young men wearing backpacks. Walking quickly, I passed them and approached the green traffic light. I could have quietly crossed the street, but an unfamiliar power would not allow me to continue on my way. I still remember that feeling well.

These two young men caught up with me and asked me how to get to one of the streets in the city. I said that I could show them to this street. While we walked together for about ten minutes, these Mormon missionaries told me about their church. At the end of our conversation, we agreed to meet at my place the next morning.

Now we remember with a smile how I did not want to accept a Book of Mormon from the missionaries because I considered ourselves Orthodox, like our ancestors, and we didn't need anything else. It turned out that we became disciplined students. Having received our assignment on Tuesday, we finished everything that they asked us to do by Saturday. On Saturday we had the first complete missionary discussion, at the end of which, having learned that on Sunday would be the first worship service in the city, we asked for permission to come. We really liked the atmosphere. After the service I had a desire to pray, which I did when the missionaries came over for the second discussion.

At the beginning of the discussion we did not yet know that we would be confronted with the question that would change our entire lives: Will you be baptized into the Church? We had not discussed this as a family beforehand, but we answered in the affirmative. Oh, how many times we have had to respond to the question, "Why were you baptized?" Having learned about the true Church, the restored gospel, and the plan of salvation, we sensed within ourselves tremendous changes, both internal and external.

Internally, we felt confidence and elation. Externally, our relationships within our family and with other people changed. We knew that we needed somehow to preserve this. The only thing that could help us do this was baptism. We were the first to be baptized in our city [Saratov]. Before our baptism, we didn't have any doubts that we were taking the right step.

After our baptism we encountered misunderstandings and even some aggressiveness from our relatives. But a year and a half has now passed. Of course during this time there have been some unpleasant conflicts. But we were confident that we would endure.

Even though a total understanding is still far away, relations towards us have become more tolerant. And my cousin, who is an avowed atheist, has begun, bit by bit, to show some interest in the Church. I'm not rushing things, but I am trying to help her understand that we should all come into this Church.

Immediately after our baptism, all of us—my wife, daughter and I—received callings in the Church. The opportunity to serve the Lord in his Church has helped us in our spiritual development. We feel our own growth so much as we try to help other Saints to grow through our callings. In a week, it will be one year since I was called to be president of our branch, the first branch in our city. My wife is president of the Relief Society. Our daughter helps out in the Primary.

When the missionaries experience difficulties with investigators, they invite members of the Church to the discussions. Thus we have often received the opportunity to be missionaries.

For us it has been very satisfying to realize that after our help, people have made the decision to be baptized.

There is still one more amazing fact—there is a very clear difference between our lives before and after our baptism. The Church teaches us that in order to be worthy of the Holy Ghost and of our Father in Heaven's help, we should work hard to improve ourselves. We must never stop along the way. We have a clear understanding and a bright testimony of this. We do not intend to lose the wonderful fruits of our labor in the Church, which we have received from our Father in Heaven. We trust in his help.

Quite recently, on the 12th and 13th of March [1994], I had the opportunity to listen to an Apostle of God, Elder Dallin Oaks, at a conference in Moscow. Perhaps this will be difficult to understand, but the Spirit told me that I was listening to and learning specifically through an Apostle's life in the Church. I have no doubts about this.

At the conference I saw the familiar faces of many members of the Church from Moscow, whom I had not seen for more than a year. How joyful was our reunion! Then the thought came to me that before our meeting in the Celestial Kingdom, many, many years would pass. How great will be our joy at that reunion![3]

The following brief letter is from the exuberant Olga Sumina, who is typical of the fine youth who have joined the Church:

I'm fifteen years old. . . . My life has changed dramatically since being baptized. Everything is wonderful now! It is so incredible. I never thought that I would live such an interesting life.

I have believed in God for a long time and I have prayed to him. Now I know the truth, and it is wonderful. I want to live righteously, and I want to do good. I feel the help and support of the Holy Ghost, and the endless, universal love of our Heavenly Father.

I have a mother and a father and a younger brother. He is also a member of the Church. I didn't understand before just how much I love and adore my family—and just how important they are to me. I believe that my family will come into the Church and that we will be a happy family in the kingdom of

Olga Sumina

our Heavenly Father. I know that this Church is true and that God is with us. . . .

Excuse me now, it's just that I am in a hurry. Another girl and I are going to Nizhnii Novgorod to stay with some members of the Church. It's too bad that we will not be at the [Moscow] picnic this Saturday.[4]

38

DECEMBER 1992

In December I received a call from Konstantin Blazhenov, the former USSR Council on Religious Affairs official who had helped register the Church in Leningrad, now serving in the Moscow Bureau of Religious Affairs. He invited me to his office to discuss several items. When we met, Mr. Blazhenov inquired about the growth of the Church in Moscow, the current number of congregations, the kinds and amounts of charitable assistance given to the city, and whether we had acquired buildings or land on which to construct chapels for the Church. He spoke of the ten prefects (districts) in Moscow and suggested that good possibilities existed for developing relations with prefects in the north and south of the city. On a map he pointed out where Baptists, Seventh Day Adventists, and Pentecostals had received land in other prefectures on which to construct church buildings. He emphasized that prefects can grant land with city approval, but some benefit to the community (recreation area, medical equipment, or other compensation) would lessen the force of opposition from competitors for the land or from opposing churches.

Then Mr. Blazhenov gave me, as he had leaders of other denominations, a copy of proposed Russian Republic legislation that would revise the liberal freedom of conscience act from 1990 in many ways, including several changes that would disadvantage religious organizations having world headquarters in a foreign land. Severe restrictions would be placed on proselytizing, publishing, and fund-gathering activities. Further, several current legal protections would be considerably diluted. Mr. Blazhenov had recalled the high quality legal research and analysis previously provided by David Farnsworth and recommended that the Church marshal its resources to represent concerns shared by other non-Russian faiths.

Little time remained before the revised bill would be considered in the Russian legislature and, most likely, approved. Many Russians had been offended by the avalanche of foreign churches entering Russia, each aspiring, he said, "to free the benighted natives from their atheism and ignorance." Many groups from abroad had behaved irresponsibly in Russia, raising unreasonable expectations at mass rallies, baptizing hundreds, and then leaving the newly "saved" without ongoing church support or organization.

After the meeting, I contacted the Europe Area legal office in Frankfurt and reported my conversation with Mr. Blazhenov. Richard Johnson now served as legal counsel for the Area. Soon a team including Brother Johnson, William Atkin (an international LDS lawyer serving in Moscow), and Cole Durham (a BYU law professor with expertise in international freedom of conscience issues), and the Area presidency prepared a most thorough and persuasive response, invoking legal precedent and current enlightened freedom of conscience policy from around the world. My first meeting with Mr. Blazhenov occurred on 8 December; I delivered the Church's considered response on 16 December. Mr. Blazhenov was impressed by the care and swiftness with which the materials were prepared.

In the following months the Church, owing especially to Professor Durham's tireless efforts to gather reliable information and organize international seminars, contributed much to an enlightened debate on this issue. I believe that thanks in significant measure to the labors of Professor Durham and others cooperating with him, the drastic changes proposed in the 1990 law were not implemented in 1993.

When in March of this year donated funds were absorbed from mission accounts into general Church funds, we no longer had the means to purchase the third computer we needed for the office. Our second computer was being used day and night by Russian member translators. For months office missionaries and member leaders were hindered from coping with an ever-increasing volume of work by our having available only one office computer. When I explained our needs to one authority, he suggested that because a second mission computer was not authorized out of normal

Church funds and because our needs were legitimate, I should try to find someone to donate money for the computer and purchase it myself. At this same time the family of Elder Mark Pingree sent to the mission a considerable amount of money contributed at the funeral for Sister Pingree in lieu of flowers. Combining this gift with a gift earmarked specifically for a third computer by Elder Douglas and Sister Lois Dewey upon their departure, we purchased a good quality computer and printer.

During this month I traveled to Samara, where part of my assignment was to contact Efim Vyshkin, a university professor assisting Gary Packer from Frankfurt in finding property for a new mission home and office to be ready by June 1993. Although the decisions on these matters were made in Frankfurt, I was invited to provide counsel when possible. I visited three sites, all of them improbable. But Mr. Vyshkin had located apartment space in a building under construction that Brother Packer felt could be used if a more desirable mission home and office were not ready in six months. This apartment became the mission home for the new Russia Samara Mission. An office was then located in the same block.

At the monthly branch presidents' meetings we began distributing photocopied sheets with four hymns on each sheet, two to a side, principally those translated by Vadim Viazmin. It was clear that the new Russian hymnbook would not appear soon, and the small selection of hymns in use since the registering of the Church in Russia was wearing thin. Other Russian-speaking missions used many additional hymns, some borrowed from the Baptist hymnal and others selected from the Salt Lake–translated hymns our translators and members considered deficient. I noticed over the months that our new hymns were sung infrequently. This may have been because of their unfamiliarity or the inconvenience of additional sheets folded and placed loosely in the current twelve-page booklets. We also dispensed copies of audiocassettes sent to us by the Tabernacle Choir. We urged branch presidents to play this beautiful music as prelude and postlude when a pianist was not available, as quite often was the case.

At this same meeting we addressed a considerable problem in our mission: all too often new members of the Church were not given an opportunity to serve. The branch presidents were concerned about overwhelming new members and hesitant to delegate to them responsibilities that might not be met. We discussed a considerable list of appropriate callings (hymnbook distribution, chair and microphone arrangement, greeter at the door, second counselor in an auxiliary). Too many of our new converts found it difficult to feel a part of the Church and desired a calling they could perform well.

For two days during Christmas week we gathered with our now seventy-four missionaries in Moscow for a mission Christmas conference. The first day focused on language instruction, which the assistants to the president and I provided, and on a missionary training video prepared in Salt Lake City. In the evening we relaxed with skits and a modest gift exchange and watched *It's a Wonderful Life*. The film's powerful message of the force for good of one principled and determined person was heartening for our missionaries. The second day we discussed ways to find and teach more families who would anchor our branches. Joan spoke of the meaning of Christmas and gave to each district leader money provided by a friend in Boston. She asked that each district purchase food items to pass out on Christmas Day to the needy elderly as missionaries encountered them on the streets.

I emphasized how the effects of our deeds radiate far beyond our expectations and reviewed four mission goals that had evolved over the months and become mission anchors. These were, first, to present the Lord with our "more excellent sacrifice" (Hebrews 11:4). This occurs as we develop missionary skills and the attributes of the Savior and address missionary priorities, saving other concerns until we return home. Second, to strive to harvest and not merely to glean. To do this we would try to teach ten missionary discussions per week (our average was less than one-half that), and use a referral dialogue in each discussion or meeting with members and investigators. Third, to establish the kingdom and not just baptize. This meant we would baptize the well prepared and sincere, including families and potential priesthood holders; aim to build strong branches; and only speak well of members and branch leaders. And fourth, to love Russia, Russians, and Russian. We would speak Russian as much as possible in order to become and remain prepared to teach capably individuals from all levels of society and learn to admire and respect Russian culture. After a testimony meeting, always the highlight of a missionary gathering, the missionaries returned to their areas.

Sister Galina Goncharova, assisted by Sister Jodi Jorgenson and many other Moscow Saints, organized a Christmas program for all the branches. The scriptural account of the birth of Christ was interspersed with choral singing of translated Christmas hymns. Members portrayed scenes from the Bible, complete with children holding large cut-outs of animals and angels with little wings on their caps. In conclusion, a member read a translation of President Gordon B. Hinckley's booklet entitled *The True Meaning of Christmas.* The 250 members who attended seemed to enjoy the program, although some apparently expected a far more formal and polished performance. We all agreed next year to have branch or district commemorations at which "amateur" participation would be better understood.

Parts of the Christmas letter I wrote in late November 1992 summarize some of my feelings about the year's events.

> Soon after our family moved from Helsinki to Moscow late in June, I was awakened around 2:30 A.M. by a booming, mournful, repeated cry in Russian: "Heeelp meeee!" Concerned about what might happen were I to go to [the distressed man] in the dark, I waited to learn whether neighbors also sleeping behind open windows would respond. One did. But to every question came the same answer, just "Help me!" Finally his cries ceased. Apparently he walked on.

> Again in the morning as I jogged from our apartment to the Moscow State University and panoramic observation point overlooking Moscow, I heard his gruff groans. It was early in the morning, and I was alone in the heavily wooded park. At first I ran by without looking in his direction. But after a few seconds I decided to return and inquire about his need. When I arrived, I could find no one. He was gone, as it now appears, forever. This surely was a real man suffering real pain, but today I think of him as an emblem of Russia, crying for help from under a towering mountain of affliction. While here, our mission's challenge is to respond in an appropriate manner and time to cries for help. From us missionaries, the assistance will be primarily spiritual,

which also is very urgently needed, and finally most consequential. . . .

Let me close with a wonderful memory. In September Elder and Sister Howard W. Hunter visited Moscow and spoke to five hundred gathered at a Sunday service. The meeting went well and was fulfilling as spiritual nourishment. But what I will recall occurred after the meeting when hundreds quietly filed past Elder Hunter and shook his hand. No one took much of his time, but all wished him good health and joy. I stood next to Elder Hunter, translating for him, and had the unforgettable experience of looking into our members' eyes as they spoke to him. I wish I could convey the nonverbal expressions of faith, purity, and human warmth that flowed from their smiles and gaze. To think that a few months ago most of them were just learning of the gospel and Church, and that a few years ago they would have had great difficulty professing any religious conviction. Now they radiated gratitude and love for an apostle and prophet that was both inspiring and confirming.

During December one of the first members from Voronezh was baptized in Moscow. Her husband was baptized about a year later and has served as president of a branch in Voronezh. Her rich conversion story follows:

My name is Nina Bazarskaia. I live in Voronezh and am an instructor of English at an institute. I was born in Voronezh and have lived here for forty-five years. I was an only child, as my mother had a serious heart disease, and the doctors forbade her from having children. She could not imagine her family without a child, though, and so despite all the prohibitions in the world, I was born. My parents were then students and lived with my mother's family.

My childhood was spent in the home of my grandmother, my mother's mother. She came from a family of teachers, graduated from two institutes, and taught English and German in the same institute where I now head the department. She was very energetic and completely devoted to her family. As it turned out, she and my grandfather separated when my mother was only eighteen; therefore I rarely saw my grandpa and knew only that he was a scientist, a professor, and a very unhappy man.

As a child, I often wondered how it was that my mother had parents—for I knew about them—but my father did not have them, and it seemed as if he had never had them. There was

The Bazarskii family with an American friend on the left.
Left to right: Oleg, Nina, and Aleksandr

never any talk about them. Only when I grew older did I understand the reason. My father's parents came from a family of
Orthodox clergy. My great-grandfather was a deacon, and
Grandpa was a priest in the Orthodox Church. But in 1937, most
of my uncles, aunts, and cousins from this large family were
shot. My great-grandfather (who was ninety), my uncles and my
grandfather were arrested and sent to a concentration camp in
the north where they perished. My grandfather sent his last letter from the camp in 1943, four months before his death at only
fifty-seven years of age. My grandmother died when my dad was
eighteen years old, and my mother's family became, in essence,
his own family. This entire family history was shrouded in
secrecy because it was dangerous to talk about such things out
loud right up until 1989.

Thanks to the heritage of my parents, I knew about God
very early on. I don't remember exactly who told me about
him—my mom, dad, or grandmother. In our family the most
precious relic was a small gold cross, with which my mom,
myself, and later my son were baptized. My mom taught me my
first prayer when I was seven years old. She even trained me to
turn to God in prayer during difficult moments of life, and also
to pray before going to sleep. I knew from my childhood that it
was essential for me to live honestly, according to the Ten

Commandments. Otherwise my soul would end up in hell after I died.

So I grew up with God, but never went to church, and I didn't read the Bible until I was forty. Once I became an adult, I tried to attend church in other cities when I went on professional trips. Prayers before the icons of Jesus Christ and the Virgin Mary, and repentant tears always brought my soul a quiet peace and comfort. At nineteen I married. My husband, a physicist by education, was a thorough atheist and at the beginning laughed at my "faith" and prayers. He later began to take my faith more seriously, maintaining that a woman definitely should believe in God in order to be a good wife.

The year 1985 brought great changes into my spiritual life—I was able to openly go to church, fearing neither the KGB nor any unpleasantness at work. In 1989 I defended my [Ph.D.] dissertation and became the head of my department of foreign languages. And then came September 1991 and my first-ever international linguistics conference in Zvenigorod near Moscow. There occurred what was for me a momentous meeting with some professors from Utah. In our lives there are many coincidences. And so it turned out that by sheer coincidence I was drawn into a discussion about contemporary Russia. I sat in the corner and silently listened to the others, shy because of my English (not once in forty years had I needed to speak English with a native speaker). Suddenly I heard a question: "And how has the status of the church changed?" and I felt that the question was addressed as if to me personally.

In four or five phrases I tried to explain how much the church meant to me and my family, and how happy I was that now I could speak of my faith openly, and I didn't have to fear being a believer. This sincere but awkward answer, as it turned out, touched many people in the room, especially the gray-haired professor who had asked the question. It was Dr. [Robert] Blair from Brigham Young University. We became acquainted, and I invited him to Voronezh.

In the winter of 1992, while on assignment in Moscow, he came to Voronezh. This is how I first heard about the Church. . . . Two more months passed, and in the spring of 1992 Dr. Blair came again with his family to see us for the celebration of the Orthodox Easter. I invited them to a church Easter service. I myself had been eagerly awaiting this event: that spring I was fasting, and for the first time in my life attended confession, and I thought I was beginning a new life without any mistakes or deceit.

While on my way to church that day, I hoped to experience

there the feelings of Tolstoy's heroes, so well described by him in *Resurrection*. But it turned out otherwise. The Holy Ghost did not descend upon me; and though the ceremony and the brilliance of the golden clothing were dazzling, the service itself did not touch me at all. It was as if I were in attendance at some theatrical act in which there was not a trace of holiness.

I returned home discouraged, convinced that my personal sins had not allowed me to experience any feelings of redemption at the service. . . . I requested a Book of Mormon and began to read it, but my first attempt cleared up little. During the summer of 1992, however, students from Brigham Young University arrived in Voronezh to teach English in nursery schools. I came to their Sunday meeting and was struck by the atmosphere of love and warmth that prevailed there. I wanted to become like them, and I wanted my son to be with them. These were unusual Americans, people unlike others I knew.

At first I wasn't going to change anything in my life. "Would it really be impossible to be a member of the Orthodox Church and at the same time follow the principles of the Mormons?" I would ask myself. But soon after that I felt it would not be possible to continue that way for long. Sooner or later I would have to decide for myself which side I would be on: with the Orthodox Church or with these new, unfamiliar people, whom I wanted to be like.

This choice tortured me and would not allow me a moment's peace. All the while it seemed to me that by choosing the Mormons, I would betray the faith of my fathers and that God would not forgive me for this apostasy. I prayed and asked God for an answer, and it came. One day during the summer while I was sitting on the bank of a river gazing into the water and persistently thinking about the choice I had to make, I heard a distinct voice, which said: "You will not betray anyone, you'll simply progress farther and believe more deeply. And Christ will remain the same."

It's difficult to describe the feelings that I experienced, having heard this voice: surprise, joy, relief, happiness. I continued to attend the students' meetings, and then I took the discussions from the missionaries, frequently going to Moscow on business, and it was there I was baptized on December 15, 1992, on the eve of the students' flight back to America. My son and my friends, who had shown me the path to God, were with me.

Many events have transpired in my life since that memorable day. On January 16, 1993, the first missionaries arrived in Voronezh. The Voronezh group, in which there were three members of the Church, was born. On February 18, my son was baptized. In our family there were now two members. The group grew and we all hoped for our numbers to increase, so that our Church family would grow. My life changed. I became more tranquil, tolerant, and patient. Problems in our family life gradually diminished. For the first time in my life I understood the meaning of the words "quiet happiness," that is to say, harmony with one's self—peace of mind. During that year I became convinced that faith is capable of growing, and much that I had doubted a year ago now seemed true and right.

During the summer I received a calling to be the Relief Society president in our branch. The Church is my life: I believe and know that no matter what trials may come my way, to deprive me of the Church would be to deprive me of my life.

I don't know what exactly it was that first influenced my husband: whether it was the example of my son and me, or his interaction with the students, the mission president, or the missionaries; but in September 1993 he began to regularly attend church. At first, he did this to please me, but gradually he began understanding all the more sensibly. His path to God was his own, and on January 15, 1994, he was baptized into The Church of Jesus Christ of Latter-day Saints. Now we are all together. This summer our son is planning to go on a mission, and we are all preparing for this event. [Elder Bazarskii served in the Latvia Riga Mission.]

The first time I saw the student members of the Church I said to myself, "This cannot be a bad church with such good people." Now I can testify that this Church is true, and that it leads people to light. This Church gives people hope, and with hope it is easier to overcome those trials which are sent to us. I know I am not alone. My family, friends, and brothers and sisters are with me, as is our Heavenly Father, who wants me to be happy.[1]

Finally, in December Joan described our Moscow holiday season:

It has been interesting to see first-hand the holiday season in Russia. December 25th is a normal working day for the country. Santa, or Grandfather Frost, as he is known here, is part of the New Year's celebration, as is the tradition of decorating an evergreen tree or branch. When a member of the Church who knows English very well [Irina Liudogovskaia] was asked to speak to a group of Americans about Russian Christmas traditions, she had to research the subject to find out what was done before the Revolution, because the traditions disappeared during the years of

Communism. The Russian Orthodox Church continued to have Christmas as a church holiday, but it was celebrated on January 7th because the church did not change to the Gregorian calendar when the rest of the country did after the Revolution. . . .

The New Year holiday is comparable to Christmas, in the tradition of a big feast. The children and I went to the market on December 31st and it was terribly crowded as people bought fruit, vegetables, nuts and meat . . . . Nikolai [Zavalishin] tells us that traditionally the holiday begins at midnight and includes an all-night party with plenty of food and alcohol. I saw more than the usual number of drunks on December 30th and 31st, indicating that some start celebrating earlier. Some families open their presents just after midnight, but those with small children wait until morning so that Grandfather Frost can deliver his bag of presents. . . .

I had made arrangements for all of the missionaries serving in Moscow to have Christmas dinner at the homes of American families living here, so we did our part by having twelve missionaries at the mission home for a turkey dinner. After dinner they sang Christmas carols and hymns, and played with some of Jon's presents before resuming their missionary activities that evening.[2]

39

January 1993

Voronezh, a city of about one million people, is located in the lush Black Earth region of Russia nearly 280 miles south of Moscow on the Voronezh River. Early in January, I traveled there to make arrangements for missionaries to arrive later in the month. Nina Bazarskaia met me at the train station and accompanied me to see city officials, potential proselytizing areas, apartments, meetinghouse facilities, and city markets. The Voronezh market was better supplied than ours in Moscow, although at this time of year little remains but potatoes, cabbage, dried (and usually smoked) fruit, and honey.

Three Voronezh citizens had already been baptized: Vladimir Kobanov (who later served as a missionary in Arizona) in October, Nadezhda Senchakova in November, and Nina Bazarskaia in December. And others were growing in interest and faith. When missionary elders Russell Nelson Jr., David Wilsted, Chad Benson, and Neil Mahoney arrived on 16 January, they found a comparatively solid foundation. At Church services the next day, approximately thirty attended, including now nineteen students from BYU and the University of Utah (a new group of nursery school teachers for another semester), the three Voronezh members, and several friends of the Church who had attended the private meetings of the initial group of teachers.

Elder Wilsted provided a clear window into the difficulties our missionaries faced:

> I remember one of the greatest challenges of our mission to be the pace at which the Lord called missionaries to great levels of responsibility. The challenge to learn the language, teach discussions, serve in leadership positions at both the missionary and branch levels, and prepare Russian members for the same, provided great opportunities to come closer to the Lord and to

his Spirit. Among many goals centered around blessing the Russian people, one of my greatest was to learn to recognize the promptings of the Spirit, and to obey them. The Lord must have heard my prayers, because his blessings and the opportunities to do so came in abundance.

After three months in Russia, I was called to be a senior companion. I clearly remember the fright and insecurity of such a responsibility, but this experience only brought me closer to the Lord. Being almost completely inexperienced in the field, I began to learn to rely on the Spirit in my actions, speech, and decisions. The next two months of being a district leader and new missionary trainer also brought experiences that necessitated a complete reliance on the Spirit. In January 1993, I was called to be one of the first four missionaries in Voronezh and leader of the Voronezh group of the Church.

I remember feeling humbled and unworthy of such a task. When I was set apart, however, the thoughts of doubt fled and the comfort of the Savior filled me with a pioneering spirit and confidence that the Lord would help me succeed in watching over the present and future Voronezh members, and in establishing a branch in that part of his vineyard. This period of my mission provided new experiences and opportunities I had previously not known. On 14 March 1993, I ordained Sasha Bazarskii [Nina's son] a priest in the Aaronic Priesthood. He was our first priesthood holder in Voronezh. Both his father and his mother were present. I could see the feelings of gratitude for her son in Sister Bazarskaia, a devout member of the group, and the questioning but accepting look of his father, Oleg, as the ordination was completed. . . .

I remember one Sunday in particular. After conducting the meeting, I interviewed one person, instructed another in Sunday School responsibilities, set apart two people in their new callings, and gave a blessing of comfort to another member. Upon returning home I began to pray with little success about whom the Lord wanted called as the group's Relief Society president. After several minutes, a frightening realization which had previously not occurred to me suddenly encompassed my thoughts: "I've never done this before!" It was sobering. I reflected back on the past months and realized how the Lord had blessed and guided us all in establishing his Church. Not even five months had passed, and already the Voronezh group had grown from a small congregation of three members to a branch that held family home evenings and had a Sunday School presidency and instructors, a Primary president, priesthood holders and leaders, a chorister, Relief Society leaders, and a branch activities committee.

I reflected upon the great work of the Savior, and how, indeed, he does establish his kingdom and preach his gospel by the weak things of the earth. I felt greatly blessed to be in his service and saddened to leave the branch in June 1993, although the next twelve months would bring still more abundant blessings. I had never met such wonderful people as I did in Voronezh. I was amazed at the members' willingness to serve, and their trust in the Lord to help them fulfill their callings. Often they were content with my simple but wanting answer to their comment, "Well, I'm not quite sure what to do in this calling." Occasionally I would reply, "Well, I'm not quite sure either. May the Lord bless you!" And he truly did.[1]

For weeks, preparations had been underway to create eight additional Moscow branches. Originally the plan was to make new groups, but with ten or more members in each new area, we decided to apply immediately for branch status. That would allow for a branch of the Church to be in operation along each subway line radiating from the center and one within the circle line in the city's center. In all, Moscow would have fifteen Russian-speaking branches, including Zelenograd. Finally, with branches or groups in Nizhnii Novgorod, Samara, Saratov, and Voronezh, our mission would have twenty-five Church units.

The mission engaged Brother Gennadii Ten to search for the large number of new missionary apartments (sixteen new missionaries would arrive in February) and meetinghouse facilities required by the latter part of February when the branches would be formed and six missionaries assigned to each branch. Brother Ten undertook the task with relentless determination. With district and missionary leaders I defined branch boundaries and identified as many Russian branch presidents as possible for the new branches.

This month I learned that two of our missionaries had been robbed in Samara. A thief or thieves went through their second-floor apartment, stealing approximately two thousand dollars worth of electronic equipment, money, books, clothing, and food. Although the crime was promptly reported, nothing was ever recovered. This was the most any of our missionaries had lost.

Early in May 1993 two Moscow missionaries suffered a similar loss. Later in January a young American Latter-day Saint came to the mission office, distraught and in need of a blessing. His computer and five years of research had just been stolen from the Ukraine Hotel. Apparently an accomplice distracted him as he placed his luggage in the elevator. The doors closed, and the elevator disappeared with his valuables.

In Samara, I began a practice that seemed to fill a need for our members in cities outside of Moscow. Shortly after the two-hour block of three meetings, I met with members only. Almost all present stayed. I encouraged them to ask whatever questions they wished. Their response was surprising. I was certain they already knew the answers to many or all of their questions. Perhaps they wanted to verify their understanding and gain additional support. Some may have wondered whether I might give different answers. Among the questions: "May baptized members drink tea, as do all Russians?" "May divorced women participate in Church activities?" "Do the apostles and prophets receive revelation today?" "Why is baptism necessary for one already baptized in the Russian Orthodox Church?" "What are the main differences between our Church and the 'Christian Church'?" Members also frequently expressed a yearning for more information about the history of our Church, the words of the living prophet, and developments within the Church worldwide.

This month a scholarly young Russian in his twenties visited me in my Moscow office and announced that he wanted to have his name taken from the Church records. He had been reading through the *Encyclopedia of Mormonism* and was disappointed that Mormon divorce rates for marriages outside the temple were not much less than American averages, that the Mormon average per capita income was not as high as he had expected, and that Mormons did not perceive their families as much happier than those of other Americans. I had not anticipated these concerns because normally the *Encyclopedia* had been a most valuable and inspiring source of information on a broad spectrum of topics. We spoke in depth about the issues concerning him, discussing the broader contexts and possible reasons for the statistics that were troubling him. Through the help of many, this fine member regained his spiritual bearings and continued to grow in faith.

On the All-Russia TV channel two forty-five minute programs were shown about the LDS Church in Utah. These were the programs done by Vladislav and Natalia Meshcheriakov. The first featured interviews with prominent Utah Church members and leaders. The second program showed Elder Mark Pingree's family, among others. The family was filmed during a family home evening that included mention of and prayers for their son and brother Mark, who was serving a mission in Moscow, Russia. The Meshcheriakovs also showed Elder Pingree as a Moscow missionary, grateful for the teachings and support of his family. Life among the Utah Mormons was portrayed as the embodiment of a shimmering ideal of personal, family, and community perfection.

With my full endorsement, a few Moscow missionaries had provided technical assistance to the Meshcheriakovs prior to the telecast, transcribing from videotape hours of Utah interviews in order to assist translators. What none of us had expected was that the final frames on both nights would give our mission address as a source for additional information and a free copy of the Book of Mormon. We received thousands of requests for information and books. The overwhelming majority came from Russians living in towns far beyond our mission boundaries.

Over the next several weeks, volunteer members assisted our office missionaries, duplicating a letter of response, wrapping copies of the Book of Mormon, stamping and addressing the parcels, and carrying mounds of them to the nearby post office. The telecasts created good-will for the Church, buttressed our members, and dispelled prejudice. Viacheslav and Natalia Meshcheriakov were baptized and later aided Frankfurt Public Communications officer Michael Obst.

During January Sister Elena Goliaeva was baptized. In a letter she described the changes the gospel made in her life and the events surrounding her baptism:

> I attend the Severo-zamoskvoretskii branch in Moscow. The Lord God brought me to the Church through the missionaries— Elders Price and Benson. Someone had given the missionaries our address. When they first came, my son was at a swimming

Elena Goliaeva

pool and I was home alone. It was September 1992. The sun was setting early. There was a ring at the door. I opened the door. In the poorly lit stairwell stood two smiling young men who appeared to be very clean. They introduced themselves in Russian, but with a foreign accent.

They asked me about my family, about my son. We chatted for a bit. As we parted, Elder Price handed me an invitation to church. He asked that I invite my son also, and added that they were looking forward to seeing him at church. At that time, I knew nothing about Mormons, The Church of Jesus Christ of Latter-day Saints, or missionary work. I went to church out of curiosity.

I had never been to church in my childhood. I didn't know the Bible or the gospel. . . . Of late, it had seemed as though something was missing in my life. I began to think rather often about the meaning of life. I longed to go to church. I went to the Orthodox Church on several occasions. I admired the icons and the beauty of the Orthodox cathedrals. I listened to an Orthodox Church service, but I was unable to pray in their way, and I was unable to find comfort there. . . . And this is when The Church of Jesus Christ of Latter-day Saints came into my life. Do you know what struck me? The happy, joyful, and friendly smiles. The joy of associating with one another.

The first person to meet me at church was Oleg Rumiantsev. He greeted me, introduced himself, was friendly,

polite, and showed me to the meeting room. And next I saw
Elder Benson, with his pure, childlike eyes and a charming, wide
smile. He sat by me. Oh, how much better I felt. I was finally in
good spirits. I wanted to live. I wanted to attend this church. I
wanted to be with these friendly, happy people, and become a
part of this church family. I firmly decided that this church was
the only church for me, for only in this church was my life
important and needed. . . .

And my elders, the missionaries, those dear young men—
when they came to my home, it seemed everything became
brighter. The more they came to visit with me, and the more in
depth I studied the Book of Mormon and Bible, and the more I
met with the members of the Church, the stronger became my
resolve to receive the ordinances of baptism and confirmation,
that I might become a full-fledged member of the Church.

They arranged for my baptism twice, but both times it had
to be postponed due to my being sick. The baptism was set (on
the third time) for the 16th of January. Two days before the baptism, I once again began to feel unwell. I firmly decided, however, that I would be baptized anyway. On the morning of the
16th, I felt terrible. A high temperature, high blood pressure, and
mental anxiety further aggravated my general condition. I tested
the water with my hand. It was cold and I thought to myself,
"What will happen to me after this ordinance? What are the consequences? What complications await?" It was too late to turn
back. I went into the pool.

The cold water enveloped me like a diving suit made of ice.
The thought that God wouldn't let me die here and that all
would be fine flashed through my head. . . . Elder Price baptized
me . . . . and Elder Balle blessed and confirmed me. I am very
thankful to them. And this is how I became a member of The
Church of Jesus Christ of Latter-day Saints. . . .

The next day, I wasn't feeling so well. My temperature had
gone down, my blood pressure was normal, but something hurt
in my chest. I called Elder [Michael] Balle and explained how I
was feeling. He promised that he and his companion and Oleg
Rumiantsev (our president) would stop by. As soon as they came
into the apartment, my mood vastly improved. First they
anointed my head with consecrated oil, and then, laying their
hands on my head, gave me a blessing. Throughout the duration
of the whole blessing, I felt as though strength was flowing into
me. It felt as though the pain in my chest was starting to leave
me, and that it was replaced with gratitude for Heavenly Father,
Jesus Christ, and all people.

The very next day, I felt perfectly healthy and was in a wonderful mood. I understood that God had given me a trial and that he didn't allow me to suffer to the point of a terrible consequence. I am very thankful to Heavenly Father, and I am also thankful to the elders and President Oleg Rumiantsev.[2]

Brother Sergei Vasilev, also baptized in January, testified of his joy and gratitude for the gospel:

My name is Sergei. I am twenty-five years old. I work at the Physics Institute of the Russian Academy of Sciences as a computer programmer. I live with my parents and my brother, who is twenty-one years old. I love my family very much.

I was baptized on the second of January, 1993. I am now preparing to receive the Melchizedek Priesthood. I want to go on a mission in six months. I know that our Church is true and that the priesthood has been restored to the earth through the prophet Joseph Smith.

My path to the Church began about three or four years ago. I grew up in a good family. My father is a biologist and my mother an architect. My parents are good people, and they have raised me well. I knew that there was "good," and I have always had a desire to do good. But I was a bad person and did many wrong things that now I am ashamed of.

At the age of fifteen, I became very concerned with questions regarding the purpose of life. I thought a lot about this question and discussed it with my friends. All their answers were very similar—you should live without giving too much thought to it, be happy, live while you are still alive. Several people said that happiness is found in friendship, love, art, and creativity. I agreed with that, but was puzzled when I thought, "Why are all these people who know what is good in life unhappy? Why do I do bad things even though I want to do what is right?" . . .

I began to read the Bible and tried to live according to the commandments of the Lord. I didn't always have the strength to do so, but I knew that I had found the truth. I began to see changes taking place inside me. I began to find true happiness in my life, and in such a manner two years of my life went by. I read the Bible in its entirety, and I read the New Testament several times. . . . I knew that I would serve the Lord all my life, so I began my search for a church which would teach the truth. . . .

When I went to one of our sacrament meetings for the first time (this was in November, 1992), I felt love, I saw love, I heard love. There was a quiet voice which was snuffed out from time to time by the doubts which arose from hearing things that did not agree with my preconceived notions. I met some wonderful people—these were the most wonderful people I had ever met. I felt the influence of the Holy Ghost and I felt as though I was coming home.

My baptism was beautiful. I felt as though I had been born again. The Holy Ghost witnessed this very powerfully to me. After my baptism, I suffered through two nights of great temptation. I had no idea how long it would last, but it was all very hard for me. Elders [Ryan] Ruchti and [Richard] Aland gave me a blessing of comfort. My faith was greatly strengthened by this experience.

I am very thankful to my Heavenly Father for bringing me into the true Church. I grow with every day. My testimony is getting stronger and stronger. That which had seemed impossible to me before my conversion is now possible. I love people. I want to serve them. That which has transpired with me in my life is a miracle, and is much more powerful than anything I could have ever dreamed of. I sing praises to our Heavenly Father, who can do all things, who can love everyone, even one such as me! I sing praises to Jesus Christ, who has made the path to Eternal Life available to all of us! I sing praises to the Holy Ghost, the Comforter and Testator of Truth![3]

40

February 1993

This month Brothers Peter Berkhahn and Wolfgang Paul from Frankfurt selected Andrei Lokshin and Irina Liudogovskaia to be full-time Church translators. They also chose a facility near the Sokolniki subway station, fifteen minutes from our mission office, for a separate translation office. I was sorry to see translation move from our building, but I understood the translators' need for more space and the Area's need for more direct supervision of Russian translations. We were glad to receive the extra room in our office.

I was pleasantly surprised when two program directors from Russian Television Channel 1 came to my office with videotapes of the BYU performing group programs, which they had telecast since 1978. Now they sought permission to tape the May 1993 Young Ambassador tour and urged us to provide more video material about the history and teachings of the Church for their audience, which extended throughout Russia and the other former Soviet republics.

In a letter, Joan spoke of mission travel and economic ordeals facing our members:

> I made my first visit to Voronezh last weekend. Gary and I took the train on Friday night and had missionary meetings on Saturday. That evening we had dinner with Nina Bazarskaia, one of the three members in the city. . . . The BYU students had invited the families they live with to church, so we had about twenty-five Russians in attendance. . . . The four missionaries assigned to the city are contacting people in parks and on the streets, trying to set up appointments for missionary discussions. Their first two weeks were not overly successful, so hopefully some of the people at church will want to meet with them.
>
> We left for the airport immediately after church and flew back to Moscow in time for Gary to fly on to Saratov. It would be much closer for Gary to fly directly to Saratov from

Voronezh, but there are not any winter flights between the two cities. This is a little hard to believe, considering that each city has over a million residents. . . .

Last week the *Moscow Times* ran a three-part series on inflation that I found quite interesting. Prices increased about 50% during the month of January, which has put Russia on the brink of hyperinflation. . . . Just for fun I did the calculations to see how much something that cost 1 ruble in January would cost by December if inflation was 50 percent a month. The answer was a surprising 86 rubles. . . .

If inflation isn't enough of a problem, add to it the problem of unemployment. Many have lost their jobs as inefficient factories close. I talked to my friend Lucy, who was a guide for Intourist. She has not worked for several months because Intourist, the Soviet monopoly on tourism, has not been able to compete with joint-ventures offering better services at lower prices. She said that they may call her back if business is better in the summer. Her husband, who is employed at a research institute, is also without work, since support for research is almost nonexistent. They have two daughters who are around twenty who they hope will be able to carry the load for a while. The Russians have lived through difficult times in the past and so far are hanging in there in spite of the current problems. Lucy said that even though times are difficult, she still thinks that the future will be better, and that she is glad Communism is gone— although it offered more financial security.[1]

The week of the creation of new Moscow branches, we received our sixteen new missionaries. The missionary force grew very rapidly during our final six months in Moscow—seventy-four new missionaries in six months. During that time only ten missionaries completed their missions and returned home. On 1 January 1993, our mission had seventy-four missionaries; on 30 June 1993, one hundred and thirty-eight. This rapid growth meant I had to ask missionaries to change companions often, move frequently, and become senior companions after little experience. It was difficult, but the missionaries responded with willingness.

The following letter illustrates the conditions our missionaries endured. These comments are from an anonymous missionary letter printed in the March 1993 mission newsletter:

Well, I'm moved in now and we have started working hard. Last week was kind of difficult for me because I was put in a brand-new proselyting area as a brand-new senior companion, and as a brand-new district leader of missionaries starting a brand-new LDS group. I felt a lot of pressure the past few days and, especially the first day, homesickness. Not homesickness for home, but for my last area where my old investigators and companions were.

I knew if I sat around and felt sorry for myself, things would get worse, so we decided to start working really hard. We've been out street contacting a lot and have set up some discussions with good families, and gotten phone numbers from other families. This Sunday we found an *excellent* park, which is really big and really peaceful. We found lots of families walking around. My spirits are really starting to be lifted, and the Lord is blessing us.

One of Joan's letters explained some other effects of such quick growth:

The rapid growth in the number of missionaries has necessitated quite a few changes and has not been easy. Rapid growth in the Church membership has resulted in many new members needing to be fellowshipped and not enough experienced members to fill the role. Missionaries in each branch will be trying to locate and visit the inactive members and invite them to Church meetings. Since we do not have any buildings rented on a permanent basis and have to move frequently, if people do not attend regularly they lose contact with the Church very easily. Our new branch is led by Elder Scott Tobias from Idaho Falls. Of the twenty-five members, fewer than ten were present today. It will take some work to get an active branch going, but Elder Tobias is determined and I'm sure he will succeed with the help of the other three missionaries and the active members.[2]

Elder Robert Couch tells how the fast growth influenced his mission:

Once in Russia, I learned by experience that there were many more trials than there was glory in being a "pioneer." . . . Although any missionary required to learn a foreign language has probably encountered this struggle, I felt particularly overwhelmed. I am not a very attentive listener and it was incredibly difficult for me to try and pay attention to an uninterrupted flow of unfamiliar sounds. The complexity of the grammar seemed infinite. When I would begin to understand Russian phrases, my companion told me, I would be clueless again when the native would use these same phrases. In short, I was sure that when my four-month period allotted me to be weaned from my senior companions was over, I would be packing up my bags for an English-speaking mission.

I recognized my next major obstacle two months after my arrival in Russia. Four of us had been sent to open the first major city outside of Moscow: Nizhnii Novgorod. I had begun to understand the language enough to start picking up on some of our investigators' major concerns. Frequently, the polite Russian people would explain that they were raised as atheists and it was just too hard to "teach an old dog new tricks." Another common concern was that they just didn't have time to study religion because they had to work at part-time jobs in order to supplement their income from regular employment. Their normal salaries weren't remotely keeping up with inflation.

However, I found the most difficult concern in Nizhnii Novgorod to be Russians' feeling of loyalty to the Russian Orthodox Church. Today, loyalty to the prerevolutionary Russian Orthodox Church is a way of showing national pride. Often, very choice spirits would be torn between feelings of patriotism and a desire to accept the restored truth.

When it came time for me to serve without a senior companion, I was panic stricken. Although I was respectful of the progress that my "co-companion" had made in the Russian language, I had much less confidence in him or me than in my previous senior companions. Additionally, I was supposed to be a missionary district leader. I remember vividly the first night my new Finnish companion and I went "signboarding." We grabbed a card table and a newly made signboard covered with a lovely array of Church pictures and scriptures. Although it was already getting dark, we courageously went near the Sports Palace and talked to people exiting the evening's event.

With my favorite smell of autumn in the air, I tried to enjoy the fearsome task we had undertaken. Speaking more in English to Russians who knew some English than in broken Russian, we were ecstatic to receive our first independently obtained phone number. This ecstasy was just enough to keep me from being overly upset that my Russian Bible had been stolen while we were engrossed in conversation (not that the conversation was necessarily engrossing, we were just engrossed battling with the language barrier!).

The next month I received a "golden" missionary. We were admonished not to call them "greenies," so we called them "golden"—probably originating from Robert Frost's poem

"Nature's first green is gold, her hardest hue to hold." No more relying on Elder Sankala's fearless spirit to carry me through discussions. After a month of suffering through intense feelings of inadequacy, I finally started to notice the first signs of significant progress in my ability to understand Russian. But then I was suddenly made a group leader (the equivalent of a branch president). This terrified me even more. I would have been scared to death to conduct a meeting in *English*; after all, I was only an inexperienced nineteen-year-old boy. To conduct a meeting in Russian was simply horrifying.

The next new trial I faced was serving in the mission office. With the unexpected departure of a very competent missionary office couple, young elders had to try to fill their shoes. Not only were we not as qualified as they in these office capacities, but we had a stricter schedule of hours we were allowed to work in the office. When I got in the office, we were anxiously preparing for the arrival of two new mission presidents, two visiting members of the Quorum of the Twelve, and the Young Ambassadors from BYU. These months provided me a very different, yet no less intense challenge. In addition, my companion and I were both zone leaders at the time, while trying to fulfill our responsibilities in the office. I learned significantly more patience and endured more pressure and stress. I also learned more than I had ever hoped about my own weaknesses and need to rely on the grace of Christ to accomplish anything worthwhile.[3]

Elder Scott Tobias gave this perspective on the difficulties experienced by young missionaries and the Lord's reassurances:

The experiences I had while serving as a missionary taught me valuable lessons that forever changed my life and strengthened my testimony. I remember well the day the mission president pulled me into his office and asked me to be a branch president. Despite being very young in the mission and still struggling with the language, I accepted, knowing only the Lord could help me do the job I was asked to perform.

It was only a few weeks after this that an overwhelming feeling of doubt and confusion filled my mind and soul as I considered the responsibilities of the branch, especially the need to teach all the new members how to be good members with firm testimonies. I also struggled with other mission leadership duties and an assignment to train a new missionary. It all seemed to weigh me down into the ground, and I wondered if all this work was worth the pain and misunderstanding. With this

on my mind, my second counselor and I were to go to a leadership training meeting for all of the branch presidents in Moscow.

While on the tram, I decided to pray and let the Lord feel my
heart. As I prayed, I felt his arm on my shoulder and heard him
say, "Fear not, my son, this is my work and I will not let you
fail. I love you and am pleased with your efforts." With that
message, I went forward always knowing that God does know us
and is at the reins and is leading his Church.[4]

Elder Adam West recounted a touching story of conversion and
forgiveness:

A significant part of my mission experience was the interviewing of candidates for baptism. What I found particularly
noteworthy was the experience which many of us had of interviewing women who had had abortions. It was rather daunting
. . . to think of myself, a nineteen-year-old, counseling someone
on an issue of which I had so little understanding. I wrote in my
journal on Friday, May 17, 1991:

Today has not been the most relaxing day. Earlier this morning I had three baptismal interviews. . . . They were all great
interviews, but one of them was especially spiritually draining
and painful. One sister talked with me about an abortion she
had earlier in her life. I cannot tell you how much pain I saw in
her eyes. I have now had two interviews in which abortion was
an issue. Both times I could see scars that had never healed.

One of the hardest things for me about doing that type of an
interview is that the interviewees look to me as one who can
forgive sins. A most beautiful truth of the only true and restored
gospel is that man cannot grant God's forgiveness. Repentance
is between the sinner and God. It is utter hypocrisy to believe
otherwise. . . .

Perhaps the most memorable part of this experience
occurred several days later. I remember that this woman was
probably in her late fifties when we had the interview. She was
such a wonderful woman and was always very thoughtful
around others. The best way to describe her is "angelic." She
told me during the interview that she had the abortion when she
was very young and that ever since she had been plagued with
nightmares. This experience had haunted her all of her life.

She also told me that because of the discussions with the
missionaries and her attendance at church, she had come to realize the importance of the Spirit. She said that she had felt as
though having an abortion was wrong, but the government and
everyone around her had always said that it was proper. As a

result, she decided to ignore her conscience and have an abortion. She then said that those dreams were evidence to her that even when everyone says that something sinful is not sin, it still doesn't take away the consequences or pain of that sin. Further, the gift of the Holy Ghost is our greatest gift, because by it we can know for ourselves what is right and wrong.

About a month after this valiant sister's baptism, she came up to me after a family home evening at the church meeting place and quietly told me that following her baptism the terrible dreams which had haunted her from her youth had ceased. She expressed her gratitude to the Lord for this great blessing of comfort and peace.[5]

Dedicated Church members and those who strengthened them paved the way for a highlight of our tenure in the Moscow mission. On 21 February approximately five hundred members and friends met in the Izvestiia Building in downtown Moscow. Ten of the fifteen Moscow branches were formed or reorganized and their branch presidents sustained. The new branch presidents bore brief testimonies. When the eighth or ninth president began speaking, I started to review in my mind the main points of my talk, which would conclude the conference.

I was prepared to speak on the blessings of attending a large, established ward of the Church. I planned to recall our full Church program and attractive meetinghouse facilities, such as our Pocatello chapel with the Minerva K. Teichert mural entitled *Not Alone* on the wall behind the podium. The mural depicted pioneers struggling across the plains, attended always on the journey by unseen angels. Every week we saw them plainly beside the pioneers, and I learned that a loving Heavenly Father is aware of our burdens and strengthens us enough to bear them. I intended to draw a parallel to the Moscow pioneers crossing to their eagerly anticipated spiritual Zion.

Then I wanted to emphasize how much I had learned and benefited in other ways from living during my junior and senior high school years in the small northern Idaho town of St. Maries, where our fledgling branch of the Church met in a two-room grange hall.

Suddenly and unexpectedly an intimation filled my consciousness and instantly encompassed my whole being. I no longer reviewed my talk or listened to the speaker. I had a distinct and powerful impression that the spirit of the Prophet Joseph Smith was rejoicing with us in this historic meeting. I believe for a moment my spirit felt his spirit of youthful buoyancy, joyful enthusiasm, and expansive vision.

As I reflected on this, I realized that 150 years had passed since the 1843 appointment of the first missionaries to Russia and that this day of fulfillment must be an occasion for heavenly rejoicing and grateful recognition of the efforts of so many over those fifteen decades.

Late that afternoon as I exited the subway station and began the walk to our apartment, I had the distinct feeling that, in one sense, my mission had been fulfilled that day. The next four and a half months were the most demanding of my mission—but a central purpose had come to fruition. Branches of the Church, some with only a dozen members but others with fifty and more, now spread throughout the city. An organization was in place that could sustain the growth of the Church in the capital of Russia.

The organizational meeting uplifted others also, as is shown by this letter I received from Elder Michael Price in February 1993:

> The last couple of days have been like a roller coaster. Yesterday I was informed of the passing of my grandmother, which dropped my spirits for a time. But then today at the combined meeting I saw three men who I baptized become branch presidents over newly formed branches, which gave me a great sense of satisfaction, knowing that my presence here has indeed had an influence on the growth of the Church. It's the best, seeing the fruit of your labor as those fruits ripen into strong members of the faith.[6]

Ten days later, district presidents Andrei Petrov and Sergei Martynov and I met with the fifteen branch presidents in a training session. To be with these nine Russian branch presidents, four missionaries and two American expatriate presidents of Russian-speaking branches, was exhilarating.

During February several joined the Church in the city of Saratov. Two Saratov Saints shared their conversion experiences. Svetlana Nuzhdova related the following testimony:

> Jesus Christ is our Savior, teacher, and elder brother. All of his life's experiences are true. He lives and will return to the

earth. I know that the prophet Joseph Smith truly received a commandment from our Heavenly Father concerning the Book of Mormon and the establishment of the Church on the earth. And I believe that today's living prophet and apostles are also blessed of the Lord that they might fulfill their holy calling.

All this I now know without doubt. True, it didn't come to me right away. I wavered for a long time before being baptized in the Church. But I saw the steadfast faith of our missionaries and thought it could not be by chance that their faith was so great. I heard many testimonies from the members of our Church about its truthfulness, and I followed their example. That is, I constantly pled with my Eternal Father that he might let me know "the truth of all things." I read the Book of Mormon and attended my Sunday meetings. And suddenly the time came when I realized I could no longer live outside of The Church of Jesus Christ of Latter-day Saints; only as a member of this Church could I be happy.

I was baptized on February 21, 1993. Since that day, there have been genuine miracles in my life. I receive many blessings, and the Holy Ghost accompanies me wherever I go. I now know what the purpose of life is, and I am trying to live in such a way that I might not stray from that strait and narrow path leading to eternal life. . . .

I have a calling in the Church—I am a Sunday school teacher. I am happy that my involvement in the Church helps the newer members to find out more about our Church. I am also very happy that my mother made the decision to be baptized. God has heard my prayers![7]

Aleksandr Pigasov shared this account of his family's finding the truth:

There comes a day in the life of every man when he begins to think about the meaning of life, about good and evil, about right and wrong. Then he comes to God. It is then that several questions arise of their own volition, as it were: Where is truth? Which faith is the one true faith? And where might one search for this single, unfeigned faith? The most correct and sure way is to ask God himself. For only he, the creator of all that exists, can give a true and sure answer.

God blessed our family by sending the missionaries into our lives. My wife and I were amazed when coming home from a discussion to hear our four-year-old daughter say, "These nice men have the truth [*istina*]." After my wife and I glanced at each other, we asked Katiusha to repeat what she had said. Once again we heard, "They have the truth." You will understand our astonishment and puzzlement when you learn that we had never even heard that word from her. She didn't even know its meaning prior to that day.

Later, we had more experiences which further convinced us that God had truly revealed the truth to us and given us the free agency to follow or reject him. We are sure of the correctness of our decision, and we have the opportunity to be constantly convinced of this as we receive God's blessings. Often we hear, "Why are you members of a foreign religion—brought over from across the ocean?" But is it not true that God is the creator of all that exists on the earth? And is there really a difference to him where you live—in Siberia, along the Volga, in Russia or in America? No, there is one God, and it doesn't matter to him where you are, but rather with whom you are.

We always read the Book of Mormon. The truthfulness of this book is inarguable, for the words written in it have either been confirmed already, or are being fulfilled in our day.[8]

Elder Michael Ferguson wrote a letter to me in October 1995, explaining how he met the Pigasov family:

Every Tuesday and Thursday morning Elder Nye Nelson and I gave service hours, so we usually took an hour during the day for personal study time lost those mornings. Well, it was around one o'clock on a snowy, cold day, and we decided to just extend our lunch time and use from one to two o'clock for that hour we missed in the morning.

I started reading my scriptures and had a strong impulse to go contacting. But, I told myself, "NO, NO, it's freezing, you left early this morning, so you're entitled to this time to study." The feeling kept getting stronger until I finally looked at Elder Nelson and said, "Let's go contacting for a little while before our two o'clock discussion."

It was amazing. Not one minute had passed from the time we left our apartment to the time we ran into Aleksandr and his family walking down our street. The conversation went well and we set up a discussion. I only taught two of the discussions because the Pigasovs lived in another area, but I knew in my heart that we met by the will of God.

I will forever remember the baptismal interview that I attended with this wonderful family. As I sat across from Aleksandr he said, "Elder Ferguson, do you remember the day we met on Naberezhnaia?" I said, "Yes, of course." He said, "My family and I never walk that way, but Katia [his four-year-old daughter] that day cried and cried and cried, and begged to go on that particular street. We didn't understand then why, but we do now." The room was filled with the Spirit. That family was touched by the gospel of Jesus Christ, and I in turn was touched by them.[9]

41

MARCH 1993

Elder Dennis B. and Sister LeAnn Neuenschwander toured the Moscow mission once more with us before our release. We visited missionaries and members in Nizhnii Novgorod, Samara, Saratov, and Moscow. Elder Neuenschwander taught the missionaries about the Beatitudes, emphasizing their spiritual dimensions. Thus, "blessed are the poor in spirit" suggests freedom from pride. With the members and other guests, he movingly recalled his family's four-generation heritage in the Church and expressed appreciation for those early ancestors who had the meekness and courage to accept unfamiliar truths and to provide a good example and foundation for later generations. Now these new Russian members were making the same difficult commitments and laying the same firm foundations of faith for generations to follow. Someday the posterity of early Russian members will bless their forebears' names, as Elder Neuenschwander does his.

In a letter home Joan spoke of the beautiful Russian Easter celebration and mission events:

> The Russian Orthodox Easter service begins with a procession outside of the darkened church, representing the fruitless search for Christ's body. Then the joyful announcement "Christ is risen" brings the procession back into the cathedral, where hundreds of candles have been lit, brightening the opulent interior as a symbol of the glory of Christ's resurrection. Often the letters XB decorate anything having to do with Easter. The X is the first letter of the word "Christ" and the B stands for the word meaning "is risen." What a shame that the American experience is often limited to Easter bunnies, new clothes, and candy! Seventy-four years of communism did not ruin the holiday, but will capitalism?
>
> Elder and Sister Neuenschwander spent a week with us in mid-March for a mission tour with member and missionary meetings in Nizhnii Novgorod, Samara, and Saratov, and a

district conference and missionary meeting in Moscow. Sister Neuenschwander and I returned to Moscow a couple of days earlier than our husbands and participated in a leadership meeting for the women working in Primary, Young Women, and Relief Society. This was the first time that we had a joint meeting rather than separate ones for the various organizations, and it worked out well. The women enjoyed coming together with others from the branch, and they were able to visit with many friends from other branches. We even had some women who attended who didn't have any callings—they just wanted to come. The Sunday morning session of the district conference had 574 people in attendance.

This past week we had four missionaries finish their missions and go home, and fifteen new ones arrive, so we now have 110 missionaries. I managed to come down with strep throat during the week, but I had some penicillin at home and started taking it immediately. I was feeling much better by Thursday when the missionaries arrived, and I cooked dinner for twenty-three people.[1]

While in Saratov we learned that the elders had just baptized their sixth full family—husband, wife, and child or children. All the missionaries wanted to teach families, as well as single individuals, but in this branch the missionaries and early members had transformed the dream into a reality.

Before Elder Neuenschwander returned to Frankfurt he attended a two-day conference with members of the Russian parliament and foreign experts on freedom of religion legislation. Brigham Young University law professor Cole Durham played a leading role in organizing this conference. Their object was to acquaint Russian legislators and religious leaders with international practices regarding religious liberty and freedom of conscience. The hope was that this would help the Russian parliament as it considered revisions of the law on religious organizations. The Europe Area presidency and the Church rendered a service to Russia and religions of the world by arranging this conference.

Our mission had not requested but received from Frankfurt eight hundred more parcels of food for our members. Church generosity in providing the food, as before, was much appreciated. Yet, the Russian priesthood leaders now felt that additional food would be less necessary. They did not want members to expect regular shipments. The amount of assistance provided could only help briefly, and we risked unintentionally offending Russian dignity. Our district leaders, determined to allow members to give as well as receive, invited all to contribute Russian books for Russian-speaking Alaskan school children. Many boxes of handsome new books were collected and mailed to Alaska, blessing Russians on both continents.

42

APRIL 1993

My lifelong progressive myopia was worsening on my mission and especially in Moscow. In March I had gone to a Moscow contact lens specialist, who referred me to the highly regarded Fiodorov Eye Institute of Microsurgery. Their medical consensus was that the elongation of my eyeballs had stretched the blood vessels and was hindering them from delivering nutrients and oxygen to my retinas, causing macular degeneration and, hence, worsening eyesight.

The doctors recommended a procedure called *scleroplasty*, performed in Moscow and a few other Eastern European countries but not in the West. The procedure involves rotating the eyeballs downward to reveal the back of the eye, onto which are placed small oblong strips of human donor sclera (that tough, white part of the eyeball), the purpose being to strengthen the weakened posterior. The reinforcing tissue is intended to stabilize the eyeball, stimulate the growth of additional blood vessels, and thereby prevent further worsening of the eyesight.

Elder Dennis B. Neuenschwander and Garth Wakefield of the Missionary Department encouraged me to consult ophthalmologists and retinologists in the West for additional opinions before having an operation in Moscow. Specialists in Vienna and Utah provided thorough but conflicting counsel. After studying as much of the professional literature as the Institute could provide, my wife and I prayed earnestly to know whether I should have this operation. We prayed with all our hearts to know the Lord's will.

In my life I have found that after prayer, it is best for me to remain on my knees with my eyes closed and my mind and heart as open to inspiration as I can make them and to wait on the Lord. During these moments as we sought answers regarding my eyes, I felt only the tiniest kernel of tender confidence that I should have the operation. We continued to pray, and I continued to feel only barely assured.

Finally, I decided to act on this faint confirmation and scheduled the operation. From that time my confidence grew quickly and held firm. I asked my wife how she was feeling and learned that her experience closely paralleled mine. We did not receive the specific assurance that the operation would end my eye problems, but we felt confident that it was in accordance with the Lord's purposes for me now to proceed.

Before the surgery, I desired a priesthood blessing. I would have been honored to have any two of dozens bless me. As I continued my work in the mission, I felt I would recognize the opportunity to invite someone to provide the blessing as a complement to the moving and effectual prayers of my faithful wife.

At a meeting with two members of the Moscow district presidencies I felt I could ask these brethren to participate in this blessing. After our meeting I invited President Sergei Martynov from the north and President Andrei Petrov from the south to give me a priesthood blessing. As they laid their hands on my head and spoke with humility and power beautiful words of comfort and blessing, I realized a remarkable truth: in *my* moment of need I had come to two worthy Moscow priesthood holders, neither of whom had been a member of the Church when our mission had begun in 1990. I had been among those who taught them to anoint and bless the sick and disconsolate. And the Russian surgeon and I benefited through their faith and worthiness. The passage now of more than four years has shown the operation to be a success. My eyesight has not deteriorated further.

We were pleased to be in Moscow during the Easter holiday. Within the Church we tried very hard to ensure that the Easter services were carefully prepared and well presented. Newly translated Easter hymns had been distributed weeks earlier for use in these meetings.

In the late Easter afternoon, Joan and I went to the nearby Dmitrii Donskoi monastery graveyard. As all over Russia, the graves were decorated with flowers, Easter eggs, sweet bread, and candy. Though the ancient custom of offering food for departed ancestors arose in the pagan Slavic past, visiting the graves of loved ones on Easter, with its joyous promise of resurrection, appealed to us very much. We also realized the squirrels and birds appreciate the food after a long Russian winter. Russians often break the bread and hard-boiled eggs into small pieces for them.

Presidents Andrei Petrov, Boris Mokhov, and Mikhail Avtaikin came to the mission office one day to express their concern that they were legally responsible for temporal affairs about which they knew too little. Russian attorneys had explained to them that not only the Moscow mission but also the St. Petersburg and the new Saratov missions used the imprimatur of the Russian Religious Association. Further, they were concerned that arrangements for Church employees in Translation and Physical Facilities might compromise the Association. Even if laws were broken inadvertently and in ignorance, they learned that as leaders, they would serve prison terms. They asked to be informed of procedures, decisions, and future plans that concerned the Association. President Neuenschwander and attorney Richard Johnson did their best to comfort and edify these leaders.

Elder Frank and Sister Carol Hirschi, a missionary couple from the Europe Area offices assigned to work with the Church Educational System, had been in close contact with our mission for several months. Plans were well under way to begin seminary and institute classes on the Book of Mormon in September. The instructor and student manuals had been translated and printed, and now Elder and Sister Hirschi visited Moscow to meet with mission, district, and branch leaders to explain the program, generate support, and select teachers for the youth who would meet weekly in groups of adjacent branches. The teachers would be expected to attend two several-hour training sessions before autumn. At the leadership meeting, Elder Hirschi introduced the CES program to a group of receptive leaders.

Joan described the Saratov branch, which was also progressing:

A couple of weeks ago Gary and I traveled to Saratov for the organization of the first branch along the Volga. The first member baptized in the city was called as the branch president. He chose a Russian member as his first counselor and a missionary as his second counselor. He also chose a Russian member as the clerk. . . . The branch is made up almost entirely of husbands, wives, and their small families (usually only one child, rarely, two children). Twenty children attended Primary the day we were there.[1]

During April, third- and fourth-generation members of one family accepted baptism into the LDS Church. Vladimir Iagupev, the father, wrote:

> My atheist parents were nineteen years old when I was born. They were peasant farmers who had grown up in the Urals away from parents and relatives. It was ten years after the [Bolshevik] October Revolution when cathedrals were being destroyed, religious literature was burned, and priests and believers were persecuted. I was not baptized as an infant, and I was unable to develop Christian faith within my family or in such an environment. However, at the age of four or five years and thereafter, I began turning to God and asking him for help, and that help always came.
>
> After the 1941–1945 war, the government became more lenient in relation to the church, and several cathedrals underwent restoration and were even allowed to open. I was living in Moscow at the time and knew of all the cathedrals that were in operation. Questions of faith interested me. I was unable to buy a Bible, so I became acquainted with Christianity through fiction and anti-religious literature. I also spoke with clergymen. I took several guests at their request on tours of the city's churches. We visited churches, a synagogue, a mosque, and the prayer houses of the Baptists, Adventists, and Roman Catholics. I had equal respect for all these confessions, for I was sure that there was one God and that faith was both necessary and useful for everyone. . . .
>
> After perestroika began, American missionaries started coming to Moscow. I attended several of their lectures, obtained a copy of the Bible, and went to a series of lectures at the Adventist church. I decided to join the Adventists, so I was baptized for the remission of sins and received the Holy Ghost.
>
> My daughter, Galina, however, whom, like her children, I had raised in the spirit of true faith in God, said that she preferred The Church of Jesus Christ of Latter-day Saints. She and her children, Sergei and Veronika, became members of this church in 1992. I began to take an interest in this church, and I started attending its meetings. I came to the conclusion that its nature, the content of its meetings, and the manner in which members, missionaries, and leaders treat each other, were easier

to understand and conformed to my view of how the true church should be. . . .

The elders' youth, intellect, conviction, pure intentions, and way of life impressed me. And I admired the lives of the Mormons in America, their approach to life, providing for one's self all that is necessary, having a food supply, helping one's neighbors, paying tithing, and being confident that God and your brothers and sisters in the Church will not abandon you in difficult times. Most important, we must not be passive. We must be active in our community and in our families, continually doing good and always helping others find the true path by the word of God and by example.

In 1993, I, my wife, Nina, and her eighty-six-year-old mother, Mariia (both of whom had been fervent atheists) became members of The Church of Jesus Christ of Latter-day Saints, just like our daughter, Galina, and our grandchildren. I am happy to know that there will no longer be a spiritual void or separation, and that we look at life with the same gospel perspective. It has become easier to live in this difficult time, and we now have greater confidence in the future.[2]

43

MAY 1993

May 1993 was a very full and most joyful month. At various times, all of the members of the Europe Area presidency, Elder Russell M. and Sister Dantzel Nelson, and Elder Neal A. and Sister Colleen Maxwell visited our mission. Most of these visits were in connection with the extensive Young Ambassador tour to Moscow, Nizhnii Novgorod, Samara, and Saratov from 9 May to 26 May. In addition to marvelous Young Ambassador concerts, which again were taped for telecast throughout Russia and the Commonwealth of Independent States, many other related events occurred: meetings with city officials; seminars for invited guests on Latter-day Saint family values, music, the Book of Mormon, and *For the Strength of Youth* standards; and firesides for Latter-day Saints and their guests.

The Young Ambassadors arrived by train from St. Petersburg early on Sunday, 9 May; Elder Robert K. and Sister Mary-Jayne Dellenbach arrived in the afternoon by airplane. In the evening we held a very successful fireside at the Izvestiia Building auditorium, at which two Russian members spoke briefly, the Young Ambassadors sang four songs with spiritual messages, and Elder Dellenbach spoke. The following day I spent a few hours in consultation with artistic director Randy Boothe about the quality of translations of their songs into Russian and about the content of spoken transitions between musical numbers. Translations were shown on a screen above the stage curtains while Young Ambassadors performed their music in English.

Elder Dellenbach, Brigham Young University provost Bruce R. Hafen (accompanying the Young Ambassadors), Michael Obst, four members of the Young Ambassadors, and I made a courtesy call on Mr. Blazhenov and Mr. Merkulov, officials of the Moscow Council on Religious Affairs who had been fair and professional in dealing with our Church. Later, essentially the same group met Mr. Bugaev and Mr. Nokrin at the Moscow City Culture Committee offices. Interspersed with interview sessions for Elder Dellenbach and Randy Boothe by Russian TV, a visit to Red Square and the Tretiakov Art Gallery, the Young Ambassadors performed two spectacular concerts before audiences of approximately one thousand.

On 13 May, Elder and Sister Nelson arrived from Voronezh by train, accompanied by Elder Hans B. Ringger. There they had met with members and missionaries, including their son, Elder Nelson Jr., who was just completing his mission. Later in the day, Joan and I flew with the Nelsons to Saratov for a missionary meeting; a discussion with fifteen city leaders in government, culture, education, and medicine; and a fireside. Elder Nelson shared with the missionaries experiences connected with beginning the work of the Lord in Russia; told of prayers answered regarding missionary work; and discussed principles of self-reliance, courage, and honor. With city leaders, Elder Nelson provided a clear and enlightening introduction to the Church, including distinguishing features, among them Latter-day Saint views on the Godhead, prophets, modern scripture, and restored priesthood authority. At the fireside he emphasized the importance of the family, principles of the Restoration, his call to the apostleship, and the virtue of steady, patient growth toward perfection.

We flew back to Moscow with Elder and Sister Nelson and their son and took an evening train to Nizhnii Novgorod, where we joined again with Elder and Sister Dellenbach and the Young Ambassadors. We all attended Church services in the centrally located Nizhnii Novgorod House of Architects. In sacrament meeting Elder and Sister Dellenbach spoke, as did Elder Nelson Jr., who, with others, had begun missionary work in this city less than a year before. The missionaries had faced many difficulties but persevered. Now the two Nizhnii Novgorod branches had twenty-two and nineteen members, a total of forty-one. Elder Nelson Jr. was overjoyed as he spoke, and, as on several other occasions, he interpreted at the evening fireside for his parents. After a missionary meeting, more interviews, the seminars for city guests, and a Young Ambassador concert, we returned to Moscow.

In Moscow, Elders Nelson and Dellenbach, together with Elder Nelson Jr. and me, presented the director of the fourteen-million-volume Moscow Library with a copy of the *Encyclopedia of Mormonism*, donated by Joan's mother, Laura Wagstaff. The erudite library director, Mr. Fillipov, received the gift with appreciation, especially since the library had been given no acquisition funding for the past three years. We also met with Viacheslav Polosin, the influential member of the Russian parliament's Supreme Soviet and chairman of the Russian Republic's Committee on Freedom of Conscience and Religious Activities.

In response to a comment that the LDS Church currently had eight and one-half million members worldwide, approximately one-tenth the number of Russian Orthodox adherents in Russia, Mr. Polosin stated his opinion that our membership, though smaller, represents a relatively mighty force. Although Orthodox leaders estimate (precise records are not maintained) that they have eighty million adherents, even on a Russian Orthodox holiday only two or three million people attend services. Others may on occasion light candles before an icon but cannot answer simple questions about the life or teachings of Jesus. Mr. Polosin emphasized that much labor remains for his Orthodox Church.

The Moscow segment of the Nelsons' trip concluded with a missionary meeting for our three zones and a renewing of friendship with Ambassador and Mrs. Dubinin, the former Soviet ambassador to the United States who had visited Utah and facilitated Church relief efforts in Armenia and the Tabernacle Choir visit. Ambassador Dubinin now served as the Russian ambassador responsible for addressing the most sensitive areas of Russian-Ukrainian relations, including the Black Sea Fleet and nuclear disarmament. In the evening Elder Nelson presented an inspiring fireside for over five hundred members and guests. He discussed the emergence of the Church in Russia, including the moving story of Brother André Anastasion's translation of the Book of Mormon into Russian.

On 20 May I accompanied the Nelsons and Dellenbachs to the airport, where they boarded a domestic flight for St. Petersburg. I then went directly to the international terminal to greet eleven new missionaries. During the next two days as we welcomed and oriented the new missionaries, Elder Ringger stopped by the mission home after his trip with the Young Ambassadors to Samara, and Elder Dennis B. Neuenschwander joined our district presidents' meeting before leaving to meet the Young Ambassadors in Saratov.

On Monday, 24 May, Elder Neal A. and Sister Colleen Maxwell arrived, accompanied by Elder Ringger. At a missionary meeting in Moscow, Elder Maxwell examined the joys and challenges of missionary work. He spoke of President George Albert Smith's "keep everything you've got that's good and true, and let us add to that the fullness of the gospel" perspective for investigators, and rejoiced in the enriching scriptures of the Restoration.[1] In a fireside he addressed members, missionaries, and guests. His message centered on the Church's distinctive witness of Jesus Christ. The interpreters for this meeting had practiced by translating Elder Maxwell's general conference talks. They were nervous about being able to render adequately his eloquence and profundity, yet they rose to the occasion admirably. The Maxwells and Elder Ringger departed for Frankfurt on 26 May, the same day we bade farewell to the Young Ambassadors as they left for the Baltic states.

The month ended with a farewell trip to Samara, the last time our family visited the missionaries and members there in an official capacity. We checked on the mission home and mission office facilities. Sister Dellory Matthews, whose husband, Kevin, served as financial officer for Huntsman Chemical in Moscow and also as a branch president there, had spent many days in Moscow purchasing furnishings for the remodeled home and office. In the Moscow mission we had begun training the office elders and assistants to the president for the Samara mission.[2]

Following our Saturday zone meeting and final interviews of the now eighteen Samara missionaries, late in a very beautiful evening Joan and I walked along the Volga embankment across the street from our hotel, reminiscing about the missionary and member accomplishments in Samara. At Church services the next day, all three member groups met together in order for our family to share farewell messages with all. Well over one hundred members and investigators attended.

44

JUNE 1993

Weeks before, Anastasiia Maslova from the eastern part of Moscow had received her mission call to the French-speaking Canada Montreal Mission, but the American Embassy refused to issue a visa for her to go to the Provo MTC for language training. Embassy officials appeared convinced that Sister Maslova wanted to emigrate and had no intention of pursuing missionary service. Over days and then weeks, telephone calls and letters were directed to the American Embassy, explaining her call and pleading for reconsideration of her visa application. Attorney William Atkin was particularly active and effective during this saga, and his and others' efforts finally bore fruit. In June Sister Maslova departed for her mission, a month and a half late but victorious, and served well as a missionary.

Two large containers of used clothing from Deseret Industries arrived in Moscow from the Church Humanitarian Services, one container for the city's needy and the other specifically for Church members. I had little idea how fraught with peril the distribution would be. The clothing was not like the food parcels, which were nearly identical—some clothing was very desirable, other less so. Every member needed a particular size and had style and color preferences. From listening to the district and branch leadership talk about the virtual inevitability of envy and accusation, I began to wonder whether it had been such a good idea to request the clothing.

President Sergei Martynov made an important contribution to addressing the problem by renting rooms in a school not in use during the summer. The clothing was divided by unopened bales into piles for each branch. Branch and Relief Society presidents distributed branch clothing according to their understanding of need. Problems remained. Not every branch received an equal share of

JUNE 1993 329

children's clothing, which was particularly valued because children outgrow and wear out clothing and because prices for new children's clothing were becoming prohibitive. There was also no clothing for members in Nizhnii Novgorod, Samara, Saratov, and Voronezh. Regardless of the challenges, many members benefited. And all had an opportunity to develop the patience, tolerance, selflessness, love, and gratitude needed by deserving Saints sharing scant resources.

I spoke this month at the final session of temple preparation class for our first temple-bound Moscow members. This last lesson dealt with the temple experience itself. Elder Wayne and Sister Barbara Barker had organized and directed the eight lessons. The trip had been planned for the end of June by chartered Russian bus to the Freiberg Germany Temple, with nearly four days allotted for travel and three days for the temple. Although in most cases application for Russian passports had been made over two months before, many of the thirty-five members had not received their passports and had been told that passports would not be ready for several weeks. The trip was postponed for a month, and then for another, until finally in September thirty-one members left for the temple. In the meantime arrangements were made for the group to fly to Stockholm, allowing more time in the temple and avoiding the rigors of bus travel.

In Vyborg, branch president Andrei Semionov on his own initiative had translated the *Melchizedek Priesthood Leadership Handbook*. At my request he had sent us a copy which I had our district presidencies review. They considered the translation to be good and discovered much of great value. At our monthly branch presidents' meeting we distributed copies of the handbook, and district presidency members introduced the book, sharing insights and testimony. In addition we read and discussed a translated First Presidency letter of 4 March, which provided clear guidelines regarding the high standards of worthiness required for a young man or woman to serve a mission. Having such translated materials was a great blessing. Over my mission, I observed that a single discussion of a principle or program was rarely enough to lead to implementation; repetition and printed materials were necessary, as were visits to the branches, specific review, encouragement, praise wherever earned, and endurance. As the final branch presidents' meeting in which I would participate drew to a close, I felt joy from having grown with these brethren in the Lord's service.

During June we made our last trips to Saratov, Voronezh, and Nizhnii Novgorod and had our final Moscow city zone meetings. In each city I held zone meetings, interviewed the missionaries, and attended Church services. After our zone meeting in Saratov and interviews with the eighteen missionaries, I met with members and investigators as usual.

Two branch members came for interviews to determine their worthiness to receive the Melchizedek Priesthood. Both appeared worthy, but each had a concern. Aleksandr Pigasov had grown up in a home where he had been taught it was dishonorable to believe in God. He worried that his parents, both of whom had passed away, might now be disappointed in him. I suggested that his atheistic parents, who had not believed in an afterlife, must now feel quite differently than they did while they lived under Communist and other secular influences. Aleksandr, in time, would have the opportunity to bless his parents through holy ordinances, including those of the temple. They, in turn, may well bless his name eternally for that gift to them.

The second prospective Melchizedek Priesthood holder was Anatolii Reshetnikov, a vocational school teacher. I was confident that he would be worthy in every way to receive the priesthood. When I asked if he were a full-tithe payer, he said he had been but had not paid tithing since April. When I asked why, he replied that he had not been paid since then. Many employers delayed salary payments for months while struggling to acquire needed capital. I spoke of the Church Welfare Plan for worthy members in temporary need and of our willingness to assist his family, but he politely declined. By purchasing no new clothing, eating modestly, and using some food from last year's gardens canned by parents and a grandmother, Anatolii was quite confident that his family would survive as well as others. Not all our converts were as utterly guileless as Anatolii, but most were, and the image of their purity shining through a troubled society is deeply moving.

Next I spoke at length with a young university student who sought a personal witness that what the missionaries were

Anatolii and Svetlana Reshetnikov with daughter Sasha (left)
Aleksandr and Galina Pigasov with daughter Katia (right)

teaching him was true but believed he had not been given that witness. As we walked together along the Volga River, we talked of
the whisperings of the Spirit—quiet, delicate, but abiding. I urged
him to listen to the Spirit's gentle assurance to his mind and quiet
affirmation in his heart and to trust those calm, deep feelings in
his soul as he knelt by his bed following prayer and awaited
impressions from the Spirit.

A couple from two of the three member groups in Saratov had
fallen in love and were planning their wedding. They came to see
me to request permission for Elder Weldon Dodd and his companion to attend their reception after the registration of their marriage
in city offices. They wanted him to provide a blessing on their marriage and make a presentation to their family and friends about the

Church's teachings on the eternal meaning of a family. I was impressed that they were not ashamed of the gospel of Jesus Christ. On this happiest of days, they desired to share important truths with those closest to them.

Later Elder Dodd told me that on 19 June, he and Elder Edwin Wells accompanied the Beliakovs to the ZAGS (city registry) for the secular wedding ceremony, then to the nearby landing site of the world's first cosmonaut, Iurii Gagarin, where the couple placed flowers (couples traditionally place flowers at important monuments as a gesture of gratitude for their heritage), and finally to the wedding reception for family and friends. Here Elder Dodd briefly taught the guests and pronounced a blessing on the couple, including an opportunity in time to have their marriage solemnized in a temple. Elder Dodd then blessed the food and drink before the feast and toasts began. As he commented: "I will always remember the couple with their wine glasses of orange soda while others toasted with vodka and champagne."[1] After the elders sang a few hymns, all joined in singing popular Russian songs.

While sitting in priesthood meeting in Saratov, I was impressed by a recent convert to the Church who taught the lesson. He was the young father of a girl and a boy who attended lower classes of grade school. His lesson on the LDS family was, in the main, read from our photocopied manual, but twice he looked up from his printed lesson and deeply moved his listeners as he related episodes from the life of his own family.

One day his son had returned from school with a bad bruise on the side of his face. The father asked his son what had happened. The lad was slow to reply but with urging explained that a school bully had been tormenting one of his classmates. He tried to convince the offender to leave the girl alone. For his trouble, he had received a powerful blow. As the bully walked away, friends of the LDS boy ran up and offered to join him in teaching the ruffian a lesson. But the injured boy explained, "No, I have been reading the Bible and going to a church that teaches that you shouldn't do mean things, even to those who do mean things to you. Let's let him go." The father, who all his life had behaved according to a much more common and harsh ethic, was astonished at the courage and spiritual sensitivity of his little son who not only had heard the Savior's words from the Sermon on the Mount but understood and applied them.

The priesthood teacher later spoke with similar admiration of his daughter. He and his wife had been struggling to hold family prayer. When the missionaries were present, the parents could pray to begin or conclude a discussion, but family prayer without the support of the missionaries remained a hurdle. Finally one evening the father gathered his courage, called the family together, and proposed they hold their first family prayer. At the last moment the father elected to call on his daughter to serve as voice. The little girl readily accepted and offered a sincere prayer, which included thanks for her parents who had welcomed the missionaries into their home and accepted the gospel. The Church had provided her so many blessings, she explained. She concluded with her thanks to her Father for her mom and dad, whom, she said, she loved very much.

As the father related these incidents, tears of admiration and appreciation for his faithful and courageous children trickled down his cheeks.

In the blur of ending our mission, we moved from our mission home to a hotel to prepare the home for President Richard and Sister Suzanne Chapple and their family. Two days before the Chapples arrived, President Arlo R. and Sister Karen Nelson flew into Moscow and checked into a hotel room close to ours. After a day of orientation at the hotel, I flew with them to Samara to meet with assistants to the president and office elders. The Aeroflot flight was particularly crowded and dark, a long plastic light panel overhead in the aisle kept swinging down just over their heads, and we arrived near midnight in a steady rain. But the next day the weather improved, and we met with city officials in a genial get-acquainted session. After a tour of the still uncompleted mission office and home, I said good-bye at their hotel and then walked the city alone for an hour, remembering experiences there for which I was profoundly grateful.

Before traveling with the Nelsons to Samara, I had gone with my family to the Moscow airport to meet the Chapples. Richard Chapple became the Russia Moscow Mission president the moment he arrived, and I had hoped to welcome and congratulate him and his family. But their flight was late, and I had to leave for the Samara flight with the Nelsons. Joan and the children waited to greet the Chapples.

Upon my return to Moscow, Joan and I went to a prearranged reception at the mission home for Church leaders and city dignitaries. All the Church leaders came, and a few of our city friends also paid courtesy visits, including two city councilors, Mr. Valerii Borshchov and Mrs. Galina Bodrenkova.

Late that evening our family left to spend one day in St. Petersburg and one in Tallinn to say farewell to dear friends with whom we had worked closely during the first half of our mission. We met Church members on a Saturday afternoon in the St. Petersburg Summer Garden near where Elder Francis M. Lyman had dedicated and Elder Russell M. Nelson had blessed Russia for receiving the restored gospel. In Tallinn we attended the Sunday meetings of both the Estonian and the Russian branches. We were impressed at how the leadership and members had matured. They were leading, teaching, and bearing testimony with remarkable depth and grace. We returned to Moscow to spend a day in orienting the Chapples and in saying farewell to beloved friends and fellow laborers.

In the days before we left Moscow, three significant events left indelible impressions on us. The first was a memorial service for one of the two first Moscow district presidents, Albert Walling. At the end of June he had passed away in England, where he had stopped briefly for professional meetings on his way back to Moscow after heart surgery in the United States.

Before and after the surgery, he had telephoned me often to report on his progress and inquire about everything concerning the Church in Moscow. Now, his business associate, Kevin Matthews, had arranged a memorial service for President Walling at which several local members, Brother Matthews, and I spoke. President Walling had served with extraordinary diligence, generosity, and love, and all remembered his greatness with thanksgiving and expressed sincere sorrow at his passing. For me, Al perfectly represents so many hundreds of others who wanted with all their hearts for the Russians to enjoy the blessings of the Restoration and who unhesitatingly sacrificed much in order to bring to pass the Prophet Joseph Smith's dream of 150 years ago.

On our last Saturday in Moscow, I experienced a moment of transcendent joy. Early that morning I was privileged to baptize Nikolai and Tatiana Zavalishin. I feel deeply grateful to Nikolai, our mission driver and my cherished friend. He and I often spoke of my faith and Church. His questions were honest and, at times, troubling. He was Russian to his bones and found deep spiritual succor in his Russian Orthodox faith. I shared Church materials, spoke of my understanding of the gospel, and invited him to attend meetings with us when we traveled to Zelenograd together or when General Authorities visited. By degrees Nikolai and Tatiana's interest grew. They were lifted by the spirit they felt in the Church meetings they attended. Nikolai often mentioned how he admired the Church leaders whom he chauffeured through Moscow.

As the end of our mission approached, the Zavalishins asked to have missionaries come to share the discussions with them. Nikolai's driving schedule during our last hectic months prevented them from completing the discussions until near the end of June. On this Saturday, we held a baptismal service for five people in a large, brick public bath facility. A husband and wife being baptized had met Elder Eric Gentry and Nigel Miller while the missionaries were contacting in a park. An older man also being baptized had learned of the Church through the two-part Meshcheriakov TV telecast. And then there were our Nikolai and Tatiana.

I recalled meeting Nikolai the first time when he stopped his car to take Joan and me to see a potential mission office. I thought of his admiring descriptions of an elderly neighbor—a kind of Mother Russia—near their dacha, who each fall assured them that this winter she would die and each spring bounded out of her house to greet them. I recalled being in their apartment with my family, enjoying a sumptuous Russian meal and listening to Nikolai and Tatiana robustly sing traditional Russian songs to Nikolai's skillful accordian accompaniment. I remembered his telling me he had prayed for me in church that morning before I had my eye operations. I thought of his saying to me over and over again how we were the two most fortunate men in the world to have found the wives we did. And I thought of the love I felt for this man, his wife, and his people and of my gratitude that I had the opportunity to serve with so many others in sharing with him

At the baptism of Tatiana and Nikolai Zavalishin with missionaries who taught them the discussions, including (left to right) Elders Robert Hales, Matthew Bateman, Jeffrey Allen, and Tony Stephens

and a precious handful of his compatriots Jesus' promise of a more abundant life.

On this same final Saturday in Moscow, members planned a farewell picnic with our family at Izmailovskii Park. All that day it had rained hard and was cold. We momentarily wondered whether we should even exert the effort to go to the park, considering all else that we still had to do. But Joan and I knew that we must go, even if only a handful of others came. We were surprised to see a group that grew to about two hundred Church members at the park subway station. After waiting in vain for the rain to stop, we all walked under umbrellas along a muddy trail through beautiful green meadows and groves of the white birch trees for which northern Russia is so justly renowned. We stopped in a quiet clearing amid rolling hills. After several minutes of private farewells, we gathered in a large circle and paid tribute to one another. It was moving to hear three young Russian girls recite from memory poetry on love. While we shivered in the wet grass, the rain stopped for a few minutes and the sun shone out from behind dark clouds. Everything appeared radiant, cleansed, and pure, just as I would like always to remember Russia and Russians.

As we flew away from our mission the next day, I thought of

the wonderful people we had just left. I felt assured that the areas in which we had served were now in most capable hands and that the members and missionaries would be blessed in countless ways by their new leaders.

Following are excerpts from the letter of a dear grandmother, Klavdiia Bocharova, who represents the warmth, courage, and spirituality of the extraordinary Russian people:

> I became a member of The Church of Jesus Christ of Latter-day Saints at the age of seventy-nine, the eighth member of the Goncharov family to be baptized. I wavered for quite a long time. I was baptized in the Orthodox Church when I was very young, and I was afraid of betraying my faith. But by reading the Book of Mormon, having discussions with the missionaries, and attending the Sunday meetings, I understood that this is the sure path to our Heavenly Father and to a righteous life. I was baptized by immersion on the 17th of July, 1993, and then received the gift of the Holy Ghost. My oldest son, Aleksandr Goncharov, who has the priesthood of an elder, baptized me.
>
> With the strengthening of my faith, my life has been filled with joy and light. I attend the Severo-zamoskvoretskii branch in Moscow. We have a very respected and worthy branch president, Oleg Rumiantsev. There are also several very considerate, spiritual, and loving sisters: Elena Goliaeva, Olga Petrukhina, Irina Makarova, Tania Akimova and others. Three of my grandsons, Aleksandr, Denis, and Aleksei, have been members of the Church now for a long time. They study the Bible and Book of Mormon diligently, attend discussions with the missionaries, and go to visit new church members with the missionaries. Faith in the Lord Jesus Christ has changed their behavior, and I am so happy for them. They are on life's only sure path.
>
> When I visit with my friends and acquaintances, I tell them about our Church and hope that in the near future we will have many new members of The Church of Jesus Christ of Latter-day Saints. May the Lord God help us Russians![2]

Appendix

GROWTH OF THE FINLAND HELSINKI EAST AND RUSSIA MOSCOW MISSIONS

Number of Missionaries

1990	June	16
	July	16
	August	18
	September	20
	October	28
	November	26
	December	26
1991	January	30
	February	30
	March	32
	April	32
	May	38
	June	38
	July	45
	August	46
	September	56
	October	56
	November	62
	December	64
1992	January	69
	February*	28
	March	37
	April	38
	May	42
	June	40
	July	52
	August	54
	September	60
	October	64
	November	64
	December	74
1993	January	84
	February	99
	March	110
	April	118
	May	120
	June	138

*Russia Moscow Mission created

339

MEMBERSHIP AND MISSIONARY STATISTICS

	City	Members	Missionaries
JUNE 1990	Helsinki, Finland	0	2
	Leningrad, USSR	80	8
	Moscow, USSR	7	0
	Tallinn, USSR	43	4
	Vyborg, USSR	26	2
	Totals	**156**	**16**
DECEMBER 1990	Helsinki, Finland	0	3
	Leningrad, USSR	128	8
	Moscow, USSR	30	6
	Tallinn, USSR	58	6
	Vyborg, USSR	63	4
	Totals	**279**	**26**
JUNE 1991	Helsinki, Finland	0	2
	Moscow and Zelenograd, USSR	85	12
	Leningrad and Vyborg, USSR	279	16
	Tallinn and Tartu, USSR	105	8
	Totals	**469**	**38**
DECEMBER 1991	Helsinki, Finland	0	4
	Moscow and Zelenograd, Russia	160	22
	St. Petersburg and Vyborg, Russia	412	24
	Tallinn and Tartu, Estonia	139	14
	Totals	**711**	**64**
JANUARY 1992	Helsinki, Finland	0	2
	Moscow and Zelenograd, Russia	186	24
	St. Petersburg and Vyborg, Russia	433	27
	Tallinn and Tartu, Estonia	141	16
	Totals	**760**	**69**
JUNE 1992	Moscow and Zelenograd, Russia	283	40
	Totals	**283**	**40**
DECEMBER 1992	Moscow and Zelenograd, Russia	504	48
	Nizhnii Novgorod, Russia	25	10
	Samara, Russia	7	8
	Saratov, Russia	7	8
	Totals	**543**	**74**
JUNE 1993	Moscow and Zelenograd, Russia	624	82
	Nizhnii Novgorod, Russia	48	12
	Samara, Russia	33	20
	Saratov, Russia	53	18
	Voronezh, Russia	13	6
	Totals	**771**	**138**

Much has happened since the end of June 1993. New missions have been created: Russia Samara (July 1993), Ukraine Donetsk (July 1993), and Latvia Riga (July 1993), which became the Lithuania Vilnius Mission in July 1996. These were followed by even more missions: Russia Novosibirsk (July 1994), Russia Rostov-on-the-Don (July 1994), and Russia Yekaterinburg (July 1995). Added to the Russia St. Petersburg and Russia Moscow Missions formed in February 1992 from the Finland Helsinki East Mission (established July 1990) and the Ukraine Kiev Mission formed in February 1992 from the Austria Vienna East Mission (established July 1987), the former Soviet Union now hosts nine missions: six in Russia, two in Ukraine, and one in the Baltic states. The combined Latter-day Saint membership in these nine missions is approximately nine thousand; the largest number of Saints, exceeding two thousand, resides in Kiev, Ukraine.

NOTES

CHAPTER 1
"THAT VAST EMPIRE OF RUSSIA"

1. Myrtle Hyde, letter to Adam West, 8 July 1994; letter in possession of author.

2. *Times and Seasons* 4 (1 June 1843): 218.

3. Reed M. Holmes, "G. J. Adams and the Forerunners," *Maine Historical Quarterly* 21 (Summer 1981): 21, 24.

4. "Letter from Elder George J. Adams" of 21 April 1842 in *Times and Seasons* 3 (1842): 826–28.

5. George J. Adams, letter to Peter Hess, dated 7 July 1843, George J. Adams Letterpress Copybooks, Archives of The Church of Jesus Christ of Latter-day Saints, Salt Lake City, Utah.

6. *Times and Seasons* 4 (1 October 1843): 347.

7. Joseph Smith, *History of The Church of Jesus Christ of Latter-day Saints*, ed. B. H. Roberts, 2d ed. rev., 7 vols. (Salt Lake City: Deseret Book, 1978), 7:158–59.

8. George J. Adams was present at the July 1850 coronation of "King James I," who "was crowned and given a scepter . . . by George J. Adams, an apostate from the Church." B. H. Roberts, *A Comprehensive History of The Church of Jesus Christ of Latter-day Saints*, 6 vols. (Salt Lake City: Deseret News Press, 1930), 2:432.

9. According to the *Deseret News 1995–96 Church Almanac* (Salt Lake City: Deseret News Press, 1994, 306), the British Mission was established 20 July 1837 and the Eastern States Mission 6 May 1839. The next missions were the Society Islands (Tahiti) in 1844 (four missionaries arrived 30 April 1844), Welsh in 1845, California in 1846, and four in Europe in 1850: Scandinavian, French, Italian, and Swiss. Elder Hyde "spent 10 months in Germany in 1841–42, but was unsuccessful in preaching, although he did study German and introduce the language to the Prophet Joseph Smith. He saw translation of a tract into German completed" (*Church Almanac*, 235). The German mission was formally organized on 3 April 1852. In individual articles by country or region, the *Encyclopedia of Mormonism* (ed. Daniel H. Ludlow, 4 vols. [New York: Macmillan, 1992]) states that early missionaries to Jamaica in 1841 were soon recalled because of prejudice. A few British emigrants who went to Australia spoke of their beliefs to friends as early as 1840, but the first missionaries arrived there only in 1851. Other nations frequently mentioned as among the first to receive missionaries are India in 1849 and South America in 1851.

10. "European Intelligence: Russia," *Evangelical Christendom: Its State and Prospects* 5 (1848): 94.

11. A. I. Klibanov, *History of Religious Sectarianism in Russia (1860s–1917)* (Oxford: Pergamon Press, 1982).

12. Smith, *History of the Church*, 6:41.

CHAPTER 2
MISSIONARY EFFORTS BEFORE THE BOLSHEVIK REVOLUTION

1. *Millennial Star* 65 (2 July 1903): 426.

2. *Millennial Star* 65 (20 August 1903): 532.

3. Apparently Elder Lyman's early plan was to arrange for two young men in their twenties to go to Russia for four years. While there they would "in a modest way advocate the gospel and feel their way gently and wisely till they master the situation and can recommend to us the next best step to be taken." (See Francis M. Lyman to Joseph F. Smith, 1 May 1903, Francis M. Lyman Letterpress Copybooks, Archives of The Church of Jesus Christ of Latter-day Saints, Salt Lake City, Utah.)

4. Joseph J. Cannon, "President Lyman's Travels and Ministry," *Millennial Star* 65 (27 August 1903): 548.

5. See "Czar Decrees Reforms," *New York Times*, 12 March 1903, 1; referenced in Kahlile Mehr, "The 1903 Dedication of Russia for Missionary Work," *Journal of Mormon History* 13 (1986–87): 112. The Imperial manifesto declared that Russia's "principles of tolerance" while "recognizing the Orthodox Church as the ruling one, grant to all our subjects of other religions and to all foreign confessions freedom of creed and of worship according to their own rites." ("The Manifesto by the Czar," *Evangelical Alliance Quarterly* 16 [1 April 1903]: 332.)

6. *Millennial Star* 65 (3 September 1903): 565.

7. Mehr, "1903 Dedication of Russia," 117.

8. A. I. Klibanov, *History of Religious Sectarianism in Russia (1860s–1917)* (Oxford: Pergamon Press, 1982), 362–63.

9. Mehr, "1903 Dedication," 120.

10. *Millennial Star* 65 (8 October 1903): 652.

11. *Millennial Star* 57 (27 June 1895): 413–14.

12. Ibid., 414.

13. Ibid., 414–15.

14. Kahlile Mehr, "Johan and Alma Lindelof: Early Saints in Russia," *Ensign* 11 (July 1981): 24.

15. Ibid., 24.

16. *I Found God in Soviet Russia* (New York: St. Martin's Press, 1959), 126, 141; quoted by Marion D. Hanks in Conference Report (October 1959): 24. Rumors of other Latter-day Saints living in Russia prior to the Revolution persist. On 20 July 1992, Arkadii Shubin, a *Pravda* reporter from Kazakhstan, visited me in my Moscow office. During our conversation he asserted that his grandmother had told him she had seen hand-written copies of the Book of Mormon among Mormons living in Samara. When later serving in Samara, missionaries occasionally mentioned that they had heard related claims, but no one was ever able to produce anything definite. A newly baptized Moscow member named Viacheslav Postnov reported in August and October 1991 conversations

that four thousand Mormons still lived in Orenburg in south-central Russia on the Ural river. When I paid his round-trip airfare to Orenburg (at the time, less than the equivalent of ten dollars) for the purpose of gathering more precise information, the results were disappointing. He had difficulty finding any of those four thousand. The few he could locate spoke with him reluctantly and maintained that they were followers of an ascetic Russian Orthodox monk by the name of Mormon (not a common Russian name) and knew nothing of Joseph Smith or of the Book of Mormon. They attended Russian Orthodox Church services but, like the Dukhobors, did not smoke or drink.

CHAPTER 3
PREPARING TO ESTABLISH THE CHURCH IN SOVIET RUSSIA

1. Archives of the Church, André Anastasion file, letter of 18 November 1970, MS 7913, 2 pp.; photocopy of letter in possession of author.

2. *Millennial Star* (4 March 1937): 141.

3. "Truth Will Endure," *Church News*, 4 June 1994, 20.

4. "Visit to Baptist Church in Moscow Was Deeply Moving for LDS Leader," *Deseret News*, 31 May–1 June 1994, 5.

5. "The Uttermost Parts of the Earth," in Spencer W. Kimball, *The Teachings of Spencer W. Kimball*, ed. Edward L. Kimball (Salt Lake City: Bookcraft, 1982), 584, and in *Ensign* 9 (July 1979): 2. See also President Kimball's October 1978 general conference priesthood session address entitled "Fundamental Principles to Ponder and Live," in which President Kimball repeatedly requests that the brethren "pray constantly" for those who are attempting to open doors now closed to missionaries; pray in every family home evening that "doors of the nations might be opened to us and then, secondly, that the missionaries, the young men and women of the Church, may be anxious to fill those missions"; and that the brethren would "never think of praying except we pray for the Lord to establish his program and make it possible that we can carry the gospel to his people as he has commanded. It is my deep interest and great prayer to you that this will be accomplished" (*Ensign* 8 [November 1978]: 45–46).

6. "Fortify Your Homes against Evil," *Ensign* 9 (May 1979): 4.

7. "Go Ye into All the World," address delivered at Salt Lake Institute of Religion, Salt Lake City, Utah, 30 March 1984, 9; photocopy in possession of author.

8. Among important Orthodox beliefs for approximately 130 million adherents are the following. While in Palestine, Christ established his Church and gave the apostles keys to the priesthood. After the Crucifixion, the apostles led the Church, assuring that there was only "one Lord, one faith, and one baptism." When the apostles were killed, authority passed to the bishops, who preserved the apostolic tradition ("lineage is traced through an unbroken chain of ordinations to the Apostles"). Church Fathers (Clement, Ignatius, Polycarp, Justin Martyr, Dionysus, Hypolutus, and others) "canonized the faith and insured that it did not change." Thus, "the Orthodox Church was founded by Christ, fostered by the Apostles, and nourished by the Church Fathers. As such it has not changed its faith." Within Orthodoxy, the Roman Catholic Church (now with approximately 585 million adherents) is officially considered apostate from the date of the formal division of the two faiths in 1054. Orthodox authorities deny a need for a restoration of priesthood authority and ordinances or of a fulness of doctrine.

9. "Drama on the European Stage," *Ensign* 21 (December 1991): 14–15.

10. Liudmila Terebenin, "Manuscript History of the Leningrad LDS Church," n.p.; copy in possession of author.

11. Ibid.

12. Steven Ray Mecham, interview by Matthew K. Heiss, Historical Department, The Church of Jesus Christ of Latter-day Saints, Salt Lake City, Utah, 28 August 1991; copy in possession of author.

13. Early missionaries were Leena Riihimäki, Clarence Dillon, Bruce Bunderson, Richard Wells, Kevin Dexter, David Reagan, Kurt Wood, Heidi Moffet, Stefanie Condie, Bert Dover, Bill McKane, Eric Thorley, Michael Layne, John Webster, and Ivan Stratov.

14. Irina Maksimova, interview by Matthew K. Heiss, 22 May 1995, James Moyle Oral History Program, LDS Church Archives; translation by author. Sister Maksimova was baptized 25 September 1990; she was born 29 January 1955.

CHAPTER 4
TALLIN, ESTONIA

1. Among the earliest were Harri Aho, Wade Ashforth, Kevin Dexter, David Reagan, Eric Lenhardt, Travis Park, Brian Adamson, David Miller, and Alan Johansen.

2. Alan Johansen letter, in Katrin Roop, comp., "Manuscript History of the Church in Tallinn," n.d., n.p.; copy in possession of author.

3. Aivar Lembit, letter, in Roop, "Manuscript History of the Church in Tallinn," n.p.

4. Steven R. Mecham, letter, in Roop, "Manuscript History of the Church in Tallinn," n.p.

5. Ibid.

6. Additional early Church members, among them Kristi Lass, Jana Lass, Alari Allik, Kelli Sekk, Eve Pärimets, and Katrin Roop played centrally important roles in the establishment of the LDS Church in Estonia. Not all have remained consistently active in the Church, but each contributed uniquely and powerfully to the success of missionary efforts.

7. Eve Reisalu, letter, in Roop, "Manuscript History of the Church in Tallinn," n.p.

8. Steven R. Mecham, interview by Matthew K. Heiss, 30 September 1992, James Moyle Oral History Program, Archives of The Church of Jesus Christ of Latter-day Saints, Salt Lake City, Utah; translation by author.

9. Russell M. Nelson, "Dedicatory Prayer for Estonia," 25 April 1990; typescript copy in possession of author.

CHAPTER 5
LENINGRAD, RUSSIA

1. See Finland Helsinki Mission "Historical Events," 3 December 1989; copy in possession of author.

2. Ibid., 7 January 1990.

3. Liudmila Terebenin, "Manuscript History of the LDS Church in Leningrad," n.d., n.p.; copy in possession of author.

4. Russell M. Nelson, "Prayer of Gratitude in the Spirit of Rededication of Russia," 26 April 1990; typescript copy in possession of author.

5. Raija Kemppainen, letter to author; n.d. [1994].

CHAPTER 6
VYBORG, RUSSIA

1. Materials for this chapter come from John Webster, comp., "Manuscript History of the LDS Church in Vyborg," n.d., n.p.; typescript copy in possession of author.

CHAPTER 7
MOSCOW, RUSSIA

1. Dohn Thornton, "Manuscript History of the LDS Church in Moscow," n.d., n.p.; copy in possession of author.

2. Ibid., n.p.

3. Muscovite Igor Mikhailiusenko had been baptized in the United States in mid-1988. As a child he had lost both legs in a trolley-car accident. Brother Mikhailiusenko served the Church's cause by writing articles for the Soviet press about his experiences with and knowledge of the Church. Through him, many became aware of the Church's existence in Moscow and of its central teachings but he was not able to participate often with the LDS community.

4. Thornton, "Manuscript History of the LDS Church in Moscow," n.p.

CHAPTER 9
JULY 1990

1. The Mechams, Kemppainens, Richard Greison (Sweden physical facilities representative), Finnish Espoo Ward members, especially Sister Kirsti Vorimo, and the office missionaries, Elders Harri Aho and Nyles Snyder, had accomplished an immense work.

2. Joan Browning, letter home, 22 July 1990.

3. Andrei Semionov, letter to author, 20 April 1994. Brother Semionov was baptized 25 February 1990; he was born 14 September 1964.

4. Kevin Dexter, Alan Johansen, Ryan Rogers, and Christopher Gooch.

5. Christopher Gooch, letter to author, August 1995.

6. Iurii Terebenin, letter to author, undated. Brother Terebenin was baptized 1 July 1989 in Hungary; he was born 26 July 1948.

7. Vladimir Batianov, interview by Matthew K. Heiss, 22 May 1995, James Moyle Oral History Program, Archives of The Church of Jesus Christ of Latter-day Saints, Salt Lake City, Utah; translation by author. Brother Batianov was baptized 12 April 1990; he was born March 1961.

8. Viacheslav Efimov, letter to author, 9 March 1994. Brother Efimov was baptized 9 June 1990; he was born 27 April 1948.

9. Joan Browning, letter home, 22 July 1990.

CHAPTER 10
AUGUST 1990

1. Galina Goncharova, letter to author, 23 April 1994. Sister Goncharova was baptized 10 June 1990; she was born 14 July 1946.

2. Scott Dyer, letter to author, August 1995.

CHAPTER 11
SEPTEMBER 1990

1. Nadezhda Martaller, letter to author, 18 July 1994. Sister Martaller was baptized 20 May 1990; she was born 11 December 1952.

CHAPTER 12
OCTOBER 1990

1. Andrei Petrov, in John Webster, comp., "Manuscript History of the LDS Church in Vyborg," n.d., n.p.; typescript copy in possession of author. Brother Petrov was baptized 2 September 1990; he was born 6 January 1960.

2. Elders Ivan Stratov and Brian Bradbury left Helsinki on 5 October and on 7 October began what would become an extraordinarily successful mission in Kiev.

3. Sisters Stefanie Condie and Zdzislawa Chudyba (from Poland), and Elders William McKane, Rick Robinson, Heath Thompson, and Adam West.

4. Joan Browning, letter home, 4 November 1990.

5. Karina Oganesian, letter to author, n.d. Sister Oganesian was baptized 19 October 1991; she was born 11 January 1978.

6. Mariia Frolova, letter to author, 3 March 1991. Sister Frolova was baptized 26 January 1991; she was born 30 July 1976.

7. Svetlana Glukhikh, letter to author, n.d. [1994]. Sister Glukhikh was baptized 17 February 1990; she was born 2 March 1963.

8. Natalia Turutina, letter to author, n.d. Sister Turutina was baptized 14 October 1990; she was born 11 March 1974.

CHAPTER 13
NOVEMBER 1990

1. Joan Browning, letter home, 20 November 1990.

2. This cathedral was the largest church in Moscow, completed in 1883 after forty-five years of construction. The magnificent shrine was razed by Stalin in 1931 to build a Palace of the Soviets, which was to be nearly thirty stories taller than the Empire State Building and six times as massive. The palace was to have been topped by a statue of Lenin more than twice the height of the Statue of Liberty. When soil conditions were found to be too poor to suport such an immense structure, other projects were considered but, one by one, rejected. Khrushchev had the swimming pool built in 1960. Today

the massive pool is gone, and a magnificent new cathedral replicating the former edifice is being erected.

3. Adam West, missionary journal, 15 November 1990.

4. Valentin Gavrilov, letter to author, n.d. [1994]. Brother Gavrilov was baptized 24 November 1990; he was born 3 April 1952.

CHAPTER 14
DECEMBER 1990

1. Joan Browning, letter home, 5 December 1990.

2. Amy Barnett, letter to author, 15 August 1995.

3. Especially involved were Donald Jarvis, Thomas Rogers, Alan Keele, and Eugene England.

4. Firestone, letter to author, December 1990.

CHAPTER 15
JANUARY 1991

1. Vladimir Batianov, interview by Matthew K. Weiss, 22 May 1995, James Moyle Oral History Program, Archives of The Church of Jesus Christ of Latter-day Saints, Salt Lake City, Utah; translation by author.

2. Joan Browning, letter home, 9 January 1991.

CHAPTER 16
FEBRUARY 1991

1. The driver of the van was a director of a joint venture with a Swedish company producing a film in Leningrad. He was rushing to the Leningrad Hotel, in which a fire had broken out on the seventh floor, where several of his actors were housed and where equipment and film were stored. The fire resulted in considerable damage and some loss of life.

The fire had started from a defective television set that exploded. Hotels in which we stayed displayed a card atop the TV set asking patrons to unplug TV sets (not just turn them off) when not watching TV in order to lessen the fire hazard.

2. Spencer W. Kimball, "Death: Tragedy or Destiny?" in *Faith Precedes the Miracle* (Salt Lake City: Deseret Book, 1972), 95–106.

3. I pay warm tribute to four fine missionaries, Elders Michael Price, Chad Hutchings, Tony Stevens, and Roy Gunnarsson, who dealt longest with Soviet Customs.

4. "Food Shipment Eases Soviet Hunger," *Church News*, 30 March 1991, 3.

5. Dmitri Mokhov, letter to author, n.d. Brother Mokhov was baptized 3 February 1991; he was born 14 August 1973.

6. Aleksandr Goncharov, letter to author, 15 June 1994. Brother Goncharov was baptized 17 February 1991; he was born 20 March 1974.

CHAPTER 17
MARCH 1991

1. Joan Browning, letter home, 5 March 1991.

2. Vladim Sokolov, *Literaturnaia gazeta* 9, 6 March 1991, 8.

3. For example, see A. A. Kislova, *Religion and Church in the Socio-Political Life of the USA in the First Half of the Nineteenth Century* (Moscow: Nauka, 1989), 83–103; and Ekaterina Barabazh, "Time to Build Bridges," *Moscow Komsomolets*, 7 March 1990.

4. "Mormons," *Great Soviet Encyclopedia*, Trans. of *Bolshaia Sovetskaia entsiklopediia*, 3d ed. (Moscow: Sovetskaiia entsiklopediia, 1974; in English, New York: Macmillan, 1977), 16: 569a.

5. *New Encyclopedic Dictionary* (Petrograd: Brokgauz-Efron, 1911), 27:208–14.

6. Joan Browning, letter home, 30 March 1991.

CHAPTER 18
APRIL 1991

1. Gary Browning, letter home, 7 April 1991.

2. Olga Garasimishina, letter to author, 5 November 1991. Sister Garasimishina was baptized 19 April 1991; she was born 4 April 1971.

CHAPTER 19
MAY 1991

1. Aleksandr Kudrishiov, letter to author, 7 May 1994. Brother Kudrishiov was baptized 13 July 1991; he was born 15 December 1935.

2. Joan Browning, letters home, 14 and 29 May 1991.

3. Joy Saunders Lundberg, "The Strapless Dress," *New Era*, September 1990, 44–46.

4. Anastasia Maslova, interview by Matthew K. Heiss, 14 May 1995, James Moyle Oral History Program, Archives of The Church of Jesus Christ of Latter-day Saints, Salt Lake City, Utah; translation by author. Sister Maslova was baptized 12 May 1991; she was born 19 January 1972.

CHAPTER 20
JUNE 1991

1. Russell M. Nelson, *Ensign* 24 (May 1994): 70.

2. Russell M. Nelson, "Prayer of Gratitude" 25 June 1991; used by permission.

3. Matthew Malovich, in "Russia Moscow Conversion Chronicle," April 1992, 2. Additional details from Natasha's perspective, including her service as a Moscow Primary teacher and Primary president in Moscow and employment as a nanny for a Russian family assigned to the embassy in Washington, D.C., may be found in "More Than a Chance Encounter," *Church News*, 29 July 1995, 11.

4. Valentina Malygina, letter to author, n.d. Sister Malygina was baptized 22 February 1992; she was born 1 February 1951.

5. Olga Borodina, letter to author, 2 May 1994. Sister Borodina was baptized 15 June 1991; she was born 30 May 1954.

Chapter 21
July 1991

1. Elders Christopher Gooch, Matthew Riddle, and Brigham Redd.

2. Joan Browning, letter home, 21 July 1991.

3. Oleg Rumiantsev, letter to author, 26 June 1993. Brother Rumiantsev was baptized 14 July 1991; he was born 1 October 1963. He later became president of the Moscow Severo-zamoskvoretskii Branch.

Chapter 22
August 1991

1. Gary Browning, letter home, 25 August 1991.

2. Ibid.

3. Antonina Reziukova, letter to author, n.d. Sister Reziukova was baptized 3 August 1991; she was born in November 1959.

Chapter 23
September 1991

1. Joseph and Pauline Pace, letter to author, August 1995.

2. Irina Liudogovskaia, letter to author, 20 April 1994. Sister Liudogovskaia was baptized 21 March 1992; she was born 19 June 1948.

3. Joan Browning, letter home, 10 September 1991.

4. Joan Browning, letter home, 24 September 1991.

Chapter 24
October 1991

1. Joan Browning, letter home, 3 November 1991.

2. Oleg Svitnev, letter to author, 27 June 1993. Brother Svitnev was baptized 6 October 1991; he was born 24 November 1932.

3. Viktor Shitulin, letter to author, 23 July 1993. Brother Shitulin was baptized 6 October 1991; he was born 30 June 1947.

Chapter 25
November 1991

1. Grigorii Fomin, letter to author, 27 March 1994. Brother Fomin was baptized 11 November 1991; he was born 11 November 1930.

2. Joan Browning, letter home, 20 November 1991.

3. Oleg Belousov, letter to author, n.d. Brother Belousov was baptized 10 November 1991; he was born 13 December 1975.

CHAPTER 26
DECMEBER 1991

1. Joan Browning, letter home, 6 January 1992.

2. Shirley McMichael, letter to author, n.d.

3. Viacheslav Baltovskii, letter to author, n.d. [June 1993] Brother Baltovoskii was baptized 29 December 1991; he was born 30 May 1967.

4. Anna Malkova, letter to author, 26 June 1993. Sister Malkova was baptized 22 December 1991; she was born 21 May 1966.

5. Anatolii Pushkov, letter to author, n.d. Brother Pushkov was baptized 29 December 1991; he was born 19 April 1947.

CHAPTER 27
JANUARY 1992

1. Joan Browning, letter home, 22 January 1992.

2. Sergei Martynov, interview by Matthew K. Heiss, 16 May 1995, typescript, James Moyle Oral History Program, Archives of The Church of Jesus Christ of Latter-day Saints, Salt Lake City, Utah; translation by author.

CHAPTER 28
FEBRUARY 1992

1. Joan Browning, letter home, 23 February 1992.

2. Iurii Sushilin, interview by Matthew K. Heiss, 15 May 1995, James Moyle Oral History Program, Archives of The Church of Jesus Christ of Latter-day Saints, Salt Lake City, Utah; translation by author.

3. Valerii Kolesnikov, letter to author, 9 May 1994. Brother Kolesnikov was baptized 8 February 1992; he was born 10 June 1949.

4. Andrei Lokshin, letter to author, n.d. [1993]. Brother Lokshin was baptized 1 March 1992; he was born 9 January 1974.

CHAPTER 29
MARCH 1992

1. Joan Browning, letter home, 13 March 1992.

2. Joan Browning, letter home, 28 March 1992.

3. Also in attendance were Muslims, Catholics, Lutherans, Baptists, Tolstoyans, Dukhobors, Molokans, Old Believers, the Free Russian Orthodox Church, Adventists,

Abstainers, Pentecostals, Jehovah's Witnesses, and Mari [autonomous Soviet republic] Nature Worshippers.

4. Elena Chebotaeva, letter to author, n.d. [1993]. Sister Chebotaeva was baptized 28 March 1992; she was born 28 November 1947.

CHAPTER 31
MAY 1992

1. Lois Dewey, letter to author, August 1995.

2. Joan Browning, letter home, 27 May 1992.

3. Aleksei Goncharov, letter to author, n.d. Brother Goncharov was baptized 16 May 1992; he was born 1 March 1978.

CHAPTER 32
JUNE 1992

1. Joan Browning, letter home, 5 July 1992.

2. Igor Sorsov, letter to author, 8 September 1991.

3. Ibid., 4 December 1992.

CHAPTER 34
AUGUST 1992

1. Joan Browning, letter home, 10 August 1992.

2. *Moscow Times*, 10 August 1992.

3. Vladimir Krivonogov, letter to author, 26 June 1993. Brother Krivonogov was baptized 22 August 1992; he was born 30 August 1943.

4. Irina Kosheliova, letter to author, June 1993. Sister Kosheliova was baptized 22 August 1992; she was born 27 September 1956.

CHAPTER 35
SEPTEMBER 1992

1. Joan Browning, letter home, 20 September 1992.

2. Arthur Cadjan, letter to author, 28 July 1993. Brother Cadjan was baptized 27 September 1992; he was born 24 November 1961.

CHAPTER 36
OCTOBER 1992

1. Responding to an inner call to serve in Russia and using Russian professional contacts in Moscow and Voronezh, BYU family sciences professor Trevor McKee and

student leaders Jared Hansen, Tim Simmons, Willie Sproul, and Jon Giullian began work in Voronezh and Moscow. They coordinated the volunteer efforts of teams of students in these two cities (later also in St. Petersburg and Riga) who taught English to Russian nursery school pupils. In an October 1995 letter to me, Professor McKee described the early participants:

> Volunteers of the first group were returned missionaries, honors students, all strong in the Spirit, visionary, motivated, service oriented, dedicated, endowed with leadership capability, representing the best of American and Christian values. We had only a short time to organize and train these students in duolingual education methodology. I simply announced to my classes the opportunity that had come to us. To my astonishment many responded immediately to the invitation to take the training and to go to Russia as English teachers. Many reported they felt the same promptings as they had when they were called to go on a mission.

Students were not called nor did they serve as missionaries, but they went as providers of an appreciated humanitarian service. Nevertheless, inevitably their example of applied Christian values attracted the attention of their host families, Russian nursery school directors and others educators, and additional acquaintances. Those Russians who indicated an interest in the LDS faith were invited to attend Church services and, if desired, to meet with missionaries. By 1995, more than 350 students had participated in this international language program. While I was mission president, several Russians joined the Church through first meeting exemplary international language program participants. Olga Privezentseva, baptized 13 February 1993 and born in 1942, is one example:

> I became acquainted with the Mormon Church through BYU student Clayne Palmer. He stayed with our family from January to June of 1992, teaching English to Russian children. He astonished me with his great love of God, the Book of Mormon, the Bible and his fellowman.
>
> I testify (and have so testified in church) that I have seen the *fruits* of the True Church—the young men and young women from BYU, and of course the missionaries. "By their fruits ye shall know them"—these truly are good fruits.

2. Joan Browning, letter home, 24 October 1992.

3. Ibid., 11 October 1992.

4. Jodi Jorgenson Nichols, letter to author, August 1995.

5. Mark Pingree, letter to author, 18 August 1995.

6. Oksana Gronskaia, letter to author, n.d. Sister Gronskaia was baptized 12 October 1992; she was born 23 October 1972.

CHAPTER 37
NOVEMBER 1992

1. To replace the Deweys on three-day notice was impossible, but many stepped forward and performed the improbable. Elder John Cardon calmly handled complex mission finances, Elder Weldon Dodd became the mission secretary, Elder Roy Gunnarson helped with materials management, and Elder Michael Price worked with referrals and records.

2. Lois Dewey, letter to author, August 1995.

3. Sergei Leliukhin, letter to author, n.d. [1993]. Brother Leliukhin was baptized 22 November 1992; he was born 25 October 1959.

4. Olga Sumina, letter to author, 25 June 1993. Sister Sumina was baptized 7 November 1992; she was born 26 November 1977.

CHAPTER 38
DECEMBER 1992

1. Nina Bazarskaia, letter to author, 21 March 1994. Sister Bazarskaia was baptized 15 December 1992; she was born 19 February 1949.

2. Joan Browning, letter home, 2 January 1993.

CHAPTER 39
JANUARY 1993

1. David Wilsted, letter to author, August 1995.

2. Elena Goliaeva, letter to author, 26 June 1993. Sister Goliaeva was baptized 16 January 1993; she was born 24 December 1920.

3. Sergei Vasilev, letter to author, 27 June 1993. Brother Vasilev was baptized 2 January 1993; he was born 3 February 1968.

CHAPTER 40
FEBRUARY 1993

1. Joan Browning, letter home, 14 February 1993.

2. Ibid., 28 February 1993.

3. Robert Couch, letter to author, October 1995.

4. Scott Tobias, letter to author, August 1995.

5. Adam West, letter to author, October 1995.

6. Michael Price, letter to author, February 1993.

7. Svetlana Nuzhdova, letter to author, n.d. [1993]. Sister Nuzhdova was baptized 21 February 1993; she was born 11 June 1967.

8. Aleksandr Pigasov, letter to author, n.d. [1993]. Brother Pigasov was baptized 14 February 1993; he was born 19 September 1957.

9. Michael Ferguson, letter to author, October 1995.

CHAPTER 41
MARCH 1993

1. Joan Browning, letter home, 28 March 1993.

CHAPTER 42
APRIL 1993

1. Joan Browning, letter home, 19 April 1993.

2. Vladimir Iagupev, letter to author, 23 June 1993. Brother Iagupev was baptized 3 April 1993; he was born 15 September 1928.

CHAPTER 43
MAY 1993

1. George Albert Smith, "Dissemination of the Gospel," *Improvement Era* 49 (November 1946): 687.

2. Elders Jared Damiano, Michael Ferguson, Stephen Godwin, and Michael Balle.

CHAPTER 44
JUNE 1993

1. E-mail message to author, 12 July 1995.

2. Klaudiia Bocharova, letter to author, 17 July 1993. Sister Bocharova was baptized 17 July 1993; she was born in 1914.

INDEX